CHAUCER STUDIES XVII

THE MANUSCRIPTS OF THE CANTERBURY TALES

What do the manuscripts of the Canterbury Tales tell us about the way they came into being, and about the state of the text they transmit? These are the questions Charles Owen's book attempts to answer. His conclusions call into question previous efforts to explain the complexities of the manuscripts, the different orderings of the tales and the extraordinary shifts in textual affiliations within manuscripts. He develops two tests for theories about the manuscripts: one, that they should supply a satisfactory explanation for all the characteristics of Hengwrt; and two, that they should account for how the wide range in the number of independent textual traditions for different parts of the Canterbury Tales came about.

He sees the manuscripts that survive, most of them collections of all or almost all the tales, as derived from the large number of single tales and small collections that circulated after Chaucer's death, and in the case of some of them perhaps before, and that continued to circulate throughout the fifteenth century. This theory takes issue with all modern editions of the Canterbury Tales, which in Owen's view reflect the effort of medieval scribes and supervisors to make a satisfactory book of the collection of fragments Chaucer left behind. It is this collection of fragments, the authentic Tales of Canterbury by Geoffrey Chaucer, which reflects the different stages of the plan that was still evolving at his death.

CHARLES A. OWEN JR is former Professor of English and Chairman of Medieval Studies at the University of Connecticut.

CHAUCER STUDIES

ISSN 0261–9822

THE MANUSCRIPTS
OF THE
CANTERBURY TALES

CHARLES A. OWEN Jr

D. S. BREWER

First published 1991 by D. S. Brewer, Cambridge

D. S. Brewer is an imprint of Boydell & Brewer Ltd
PO Box 9, Woodbridge, Suffolk IP12 3DF
and of Boydell & Brewer Inc.
PO Box 41026, Rochester, NY 14604, USA

ISBN 0 85991 334 1

British Library Cataloguing-in-Publication Data
Owen, Charles A.
 The manuscripts of "The Canterbury Tales".
 – (Chaucer studies)
 I. Title II. Series
 821
 ISBN 0–85991–334–1

Library of Congress Cataloging-in-Publication Data
Owen, Charles A. (Charles Abraham), 1914–
 The manuscripts of the Canterbury tales / Charles A. Owen, Jr.
  p.   cm. – (Chaucer studies, ISSN 0261–9822 ; 17)
 Includes bibliographical references and index.
 ISBN 0–85991–334–1 (alk. paper)
 1. Chaucer, Geoffrey, d. 1400. Canterbury tales – Criticism,
Textual. 2. Chaucer, Geoffrey, d. 1400 – Manuscripts.
3. Manuscripts, English (Middle) I. Title. II. Series.
PR1875.T48094   1991
821'.1–dc20   91–26235

The paper used in this publication meets the minimum requirements
of American National Standard for Information Sciences –
Permanence of Paper for Printed Library Materials, ANSI Z39.48–1984

Printed in Great Britain by
St Edmundsbury Press Ltd, Bury St Edmunds, Suffolk

Contents

Works Cited

Anderson, David. *Sixty Bokes Olde and Newe*, Catalogue of the Exhibition at the Fifth International Congress of the New Chaucer Society, Philadelphia, March 20–23, 1986: The New Chaucer Society, University of Tennessee, Knoxville, 1986.

Benskin, M. and M. Laing. "Translations and *Mischsprachen* in Middle English Manuscripts," pp. 55–106 in Benskin and Samuels eds., *So meny people longages and tonges: philological essays in Scots and mediaeval English presented to Angus McIntosh, MEDP: Edinburgh, 1981.*

Benson, Larry D. "The Order of the *Canterbury Tales*," SAC 3 (1981), pp. 77–120.

Blake, Norman F. "Manuscripts to Print" with four appendices, pp. 403–32, in Griffiths and Pearsall, *Book Production.*

Blake, N. F. *The Textual Tradition of the Canterbury Tales*: Edward Arnold, London, 1985.

Caldwell, Robert. "The Scribe of the Chaucer MS, Cambridge Univ. Library Gg.4.27," *MLQ* 5 (1944), pp. 33–44.

Christianson, C. Paul. "Evidence for the study of London's late medieval manuscript-book trade," pp. 87–108, in Griffiths and Pearsall, *Book Production.*

Crow, Martin. "John of Angouleme and his Chaucer Manuscript," *Speculum* 17 (1942), pp. 86–99.

Dempster, Germaine. "On the Significance of Hengwrt's Change of Ink in the Merchant's Tale," *MLN* 63 (1948), pp. 325–30.

Dempster, Germaine. "Fifteenth Century Editors of the *Canterbury Tales* and the Problem of Tale Order," *PMLA* 64 (1949), pp. 1123–1142.

Dempster, Germaine. "A Chapter of the Manuscript History of the *Canterbury Tales*: The Ancestor of Group d; the Origin of Its Texts, Tale-order, and Spurious Links," *PMLA* 63 (1948), pp. 456–484.

Doyle, A. I., and M. B. Parkes. "Paleographical Introduction," pp. xix–xlix, in *The Canterbury Tales: Geoffrey Chaucer: A Facsimile and Transcription of the Hengwrt Manuscript, with Variations from the Ellesmere Manuscript*, ed. Paul Ruggiers: University of Oklahoma Press, Norman, Ok., 1979.

Doyle, A. I., and M. B. Parkes. The production of copies of the *Canterbury Tales* and the *Confessio Amantis* in the early fifteenth century," from *Medieval Scribes, Manuscripts and Libraries: Essays Presented to N. R. Ker*, ed. M. B. Parkes and Andrew G. Watson: Scolar Press, London, 1978.

Edwards, A. S. G. "Introduction," pp. xvii–xxxii in *Manuscript Pepys 2006: A Facsimile*: Pilgrim Books, Norman, Ok. and Boydell and Brewer, Suffolk, England, 1985.

Edwards, A. S. G. "Lydgate Manuscripts: Some Directions for Future Research," pp. 15–26 in Pearsall, *Manuscripts and Readers in Fifteenth-Century England*.

Edwards A. S. G., and Derek Pearsall. "The manuscripts of major English poetic texts," pp. 257–278, in Griffiths and Pearsall, *Book Production*.

Fisher, John. "Animadversions on the Text of Chaucer, 1988," *Speculum* 63 (1988), pp. 779–93.

Griffiths, Jeremy, and Derek Pearsall, ed. *Book Production and Publishing in Britain 1375–1475*: Cambridge University Press, Cambridge, 1989.

Hanna, Ralph III. "The Hengwrt Manuscript and the Canon of *The Canterbury Tales*, *English Manuscript Studies 1100–1700*, 1 (1989), pp. 64–84.

Harris, Kate. "Patrons, buyers and owners: the evidence for ownership, and the rôle of book owners in book production and the book trade," pp. 163–199, in Griffiths and Pearsall, *Book Production*.

LALME *A Linguistic Atlas of Late Middle English Dialectology*. A. McIntosh, M. L. Samuels and M. Benskin, with the assistance of M. Laing and K. Williamson. Aberdeen University Press: Aberdeen, 1986.

Lovell, Robert Earl. *John Lydgate's "Siege of Thebes" and "Churl and Bird,"* edited from the Cardigan-Brudenell Manuscript. University of Texas Dissertation, 1969.

McIntosh, Angus. "A New Approach to Middle English Dialectology," *English Studies* 44 (1963), pp. 1–11.

Manly, John M. and Edith Rickert. *The Text of "The Canterbury Tales" Studied on the Basis of all Known Manuscripts* 8 volumes: University of Chicago Press, Chicago, 1940.

Moorman, Charles. "Computing Housman's Fleas: A Statistical Analysis of Manly's Landmark Manuscripts in the *General Prologue* to the *Canterbury Tales*," *Association for Literary and Linguistic Computing Journal* 3 (1982), pp. 15–35.

Morse, Charlotte. "The Value of Editing the *Clerk's Tale* for the *Variorum Chaucer*," pp. 122–129 in Pearsall, *Manuscripts and Texts* (1987).

Mosser, Daniel Wayne. *The Alpha Text of the "Canterbury Tales"*, work in progress.

Mosser, Daniel Wayne. *The Cardigan Chaucer manuscript and the Process of Fifteenth-Century Book Production*, Dissertation, University of Texas at Austin, May 1985.

Mosser, Daniel Wayne. "Manly and Rickert's Collation of Huntington Library Chaucer Ms. HM 144 (Hn)," *PBSA* 79 (1985), pp. 235–40.

Mosser, Daniel. "The Scribe of Chaucer Manuscripts Rylands English 113 and Bodleian Digby 181," *Manuscripts* 34 (1990), pp. 129–147.

Owen, Charles A., Jr. "The Alternative Reading of *The Canterbury Tales*: Chaucer's Text and the Early Manuscripts," *PMLA* 97 (1982), pp. 237–50.

Owen, Charles A., Jr. "The *Canterbury Tales*: Early Manuscripts and Relative Popularity," *JEGP* 54 (1955), pp. 104–110.

Owen, Charles A., Jr. "Pre-1450 Manuscripts of the Canterbury Tales," *Chaucer Review* 23 (1988), pp. 1–29, 95–116.

Parkes, M. B. "The Influence of the Concepts of *Ordinatio* and *Compilatio* on the Development of the Book," pp. 115–41 in *Medieval Learning and Literature: Essays Presented to R. W. Hunt*, ed. J. J. G. Alexander and M. T. Gibson: Oxford, 1976.

Parkes, M. B., and Richard Beadle. "Commentary," pp. 1–67 at the end of vol. III, *The Poetical Works of Geoffrey Chaucer: A Facsimile of Cambridge University Library Ms Gg.4.27*: Pilgrim Books, Norman, Ok, in association with D.S. Brewer, Cambridge, 1979–80.

Parkes, M. B. *English Cursive Book Hands: 1250–1500*: Clarendon Press, Oxford, 1969.

Pearsall, Derek (ed). *Manuscripts and Readers in Fifteenth-Century England: The Literary Implications of Manuscript Study*. Essays from the 1981 Conference at the University of York: D.S. Brewer, Cambridge, 1983.

Pearsall, Derek (ed). *Manuscripts and Texts: Editorial Problems in Later Middle English Literature*. Essays from the 1985 Conference at the University of York: D.S. Brewer, Cambridge, 1987.

Ramsey, Roy Vance. "The Hengwrt and Ellesmere Manuscripts of the *Canterbury Tales*: Different Scribes," *SB* 35 (1982), pp. 133–54.

Ramsey, Roy Vance. "Paleography and Scribes of Shared Training," *SAC* 8 (1986), pp. 107–44.

Ransom, Daniel J. "Hengwrt, Ellesmere, and The Variorum Chaucer," *The Chaucer Newsletter*, vol. 8, no. 2 (Fall 1986), pp. 1–2.

Robinson, P. R. " 'The Booklet': A Self-Contained Unit in Composite Manuscripts," *Codicologica* 3 (1980), pp. 46–69.

Samuels, M. L. "Chaucer's Spelling," pp. 17–37 in *Middle English Studies Presented to Norman Davis in Honour of his Seventieth Birthday*, ed. D. Gray and E. G. Stanley: Oxford University Press, Oxford, 1983. Also see pp. 23–37 in Smith, *The English of Chaucer*.

Samuels, M. and J. J. Smith. "The Language of Gower," *NM* 82 (1981), pp. 294–304. Also pp. 13–22 in Smith, *The English of Chaucer*.

Samuels, M. L. "The Scribe of the Hengwrt and Ellesmere Manuscripts of *The Canterbury Tales*," *SAC* 5 (1983), pp. 49–65. Reprinted in Smith, *The English of Chaucer*.

Silvia, Daniel S. "Some Fifteenth-Century Manuscripts of the *Canterbury Tales*," pp. 153–163 in *Chaucer and Middle English Studies in Honour of Rossell Hope Robbins* ed. Beryl Rowland: George Allen and Unwin, London, 1974.

Smith, J. J. ed. *The English of Chaucer and his contemporaries*: Essays by M. L. Samuels and J. J. Smith: Aberdeen University Press, Aberdeen, 1988.

Smith, J. J. "The Trinity Gower D-Scribe and his Work on two Early *Canterbury Tales* Manuscripts," pp. 51–69 in Smith, *The English of Chaucer*.

Smith, J. J. "Linguistic Features of some Fifteenth-Century Middle English Manuscripts," pp. 104–112 in Pearsall (ed.) *The Literary Implications of Manuscript Study*.

Abbreviations

M–R   Manly, John and Edith Rickert, *The Text of the Canterbury Tales* in 8 volumes. Volume numbers are indicated by Roman numerals.

For full identification of the manuscripts, see Index of manuscripts.

Tales

CT	Canterbury Tales	P	Prologue
CY	Canon's Yeoman	Pd	Pardoner
Ck	Cook	Ph	Physician
Cl	Clerk	Pr	Prioress
Fk	Franklin	Ps	Parson
Fr	Friar	Re	Reeve
Gam	Gamelyn	SN	Second Nun
GP	General Prologue	Sh	Shipman
Kn	Knight	Sq	Squire
ML	Man of Law	ST	Siege of Thebes
Mc	Manciple	Su	Summoner
Me	Merchant	T	Tale
Mel	Melibeus	Th	Thopas
Mi	Miller	WB	Wife of Bath
Mk	Monk	WBPT	Wife of Bath's Prologue
NP	Nun's Priest		and Tale

Constant Groups

a	Dd–En^1–Ds, Cn–Ma	Cx^1	Cx^1–Tc^2
b	He, Ne, Cx^1, Tc^2	Dd	Dd–En^1–Ds
c	Cp, La, Sl^2	En^1	En^1–Ds
d	Pw–Ph^3–Mm (–Gl), Sl^1,	En^3	En^3–Ad^1
	Ry^2–Ld^2, Lc–Mg, En^2	Lc	Lc–Mg
	(–Ll^1), Dl, Ha^2	Mc	Mc–Ra^1
c* d*	the constant groups	Ne	Ne–Cx^1–Tc^2
	augmented by MSS	Pw	Pw–Mm(–Gl)–Ph^3
	temporarily affiliated	Ra^2	(Ra^2–Ht)
Ad^3	Ad^3–Ha^5	Ry^2	Ry^2–Ld^2
Bo^1	Bo^1–Ph^2	/a	common ancestor
Cn	Cn–Ma	( )	partial constant group

Acknowledgements

I owe a great deal to the late Rossell Hope Robbins. His request that I read a paper on manuscripts at Chaucer at Albany II initiated this study, first of the early manuscripts, then of the pre-1450 manuscripts, and finally of the later manuscripts. Another important step was the acceptance of the paper, "Pre-1450 Manuscripts," by Robert W. Frank Jr. for publication in *Chaucer Review* and the careful reading with important suggestions for revision by Jeanne Krochalis.

I want also to acknowledge the help generously given me by Daniel Mosser and Jeremy Smith. My debt to an older generation of scholars, especially those who contributed to the eight-volume Manly-Rickert *Text of the Canterbury Tales*, and to those who are currently making manuscript studies such a productive field will become obvious.

Travel to some of the manuscripts examined in preparation for this book was made possible by grants from the Research Foundation of the University of Connecticut and the National Endowment for the Humanities. I want to thank the Librarians at the British Library, the Bodleian, and the Cambridge University Library for their courtesy and help. I also want to thank Mary Robertson, Curator of Manuscripts at the Huntington, for her help during the week I spent with Ellesmere, and Daniel Huws, Assistant Keeper of Manuscripts at the National Library of Wales, for his kindness while I was studying the Hengwrt and Merthyr manuscripts. I am indebted to the Librarian at the Lincoln Cathedral Library, to the Reverend Prebend Hill at Lichfield Cathedral Library, to W.C. Hassell, the Earl of Leicester's Librarian at Holkham, to Glenise Matheson, Keeper of Manuscripts at the John Rylands University Library of Manchester, to R.J. Webb, Administrator for the National Trust at Petworth House in Sussex, to John Chalmers, Cathy Henderson, and Karen Gould at the Humanities Research Center of the University of Texas at Austin, to Leslie Morris at the Rosenbach Museum and Library in Philadelphia, to Jean Preston, Curator of Manuscripts at the Firestone Library in Princeton, to Maggie Fusco of Special Collections at the Joseph Regenstein Library of the University of Chicago, to William Voelkle and Barbara Paulson of the Medieval and Renaissance manuscript Department at the Pierpont Morgan Library in New York City, to Kate Harris, Librarian and Archivist at Longleat House, to David Weston, Assistant Head of Special Collections at the Glasgow University Library, to Colin Shrimpton, Archivist for the Duke of Northumberland at Alnwick Castle, and his assistant, Carol Scott, to Mr. Brown, Librarian at the Bodmer Library, Coligny near Geneva, to Geoffrey Davenport, Librarian at the Royal College of Physicians and his assistant, Julie Allen, and to the Librarians at Christ Church,

Oxford, at Trinity College, Cambridge, at the Pepys Library, Magdalene College, Cambridge, and at the Fitzwilliam Museum.

I want especially to thank the Librarians at the Homer Babbidge Library of the University of Connecticut for the support they have given me. The microfilm reader they have allowed me to use at home, their willingness to purchase books and periodicals in the medieval field, and the efficiency of the interlibrary loan service have been of inestimable help to me.

I should also like finally to thank Raymond Blanchette, for his help with the plates and graphs, and my son-in-law Jerry Cunningham for deciphering and typing the text and formatting it on IBM-compatible discs, my wife, family, and friends for their tolerance of my absorption in manuscripts.

My study of manuscripts had its first public exposure in the 1982 *PMLA* article, "The Alternative Reading of the *Canterbury Tales*." Two other stages on the way to this book were the paper, the very last one to be read at Chaucer at Albany II, Sunday, November 7, 1982, and the article, "Pre-1450 manuscripts of the *Canterbury Tales*," which appeared in *Chaucer Review* in the first two issues of 1988. Papers reflecting different stages of the study have been read at the University of Texas at Austin, at the University of Hawaii at Manoa, at Harvard, at Tel Aviv, and at the NEH sponsored Chaucer Institute, University of Connecticut, Summer, 1987.

Storrs CT
February 1991

I

Introduction

Contributions to our knowledge of the *Canterbury Tales* manuscripts have come to us in recent years from a number of directions. Paleographers with the help afforded by modern systems of exact reproduction have been able to ascribe to single scribes a number of manuscripts.[1] Dialectologists in their creation of *A Linguistic Atlas of Late Mediaeval English* have provided scholars with an invaluable resource and have themselves pioneered in demonstrating its usefulness.[2] Work on the *Variorum Chaucer* has resulted in a reevaluation of the manuscripts for each part of the *Canterbury Tales*.[3] Study of the way

[1] See for the *CT* Doyle and Parkes, "The production." Also their "Paleographical Introduction" to the Variorum Facsimile of the Hengwrt Manuscript. Doyle and Parkes not only ascribe the Hg and El manuscripts to the B scribe of Trinity Cambridge R.3.2 (whose hand they also found in the "Cecil" Fragment of *Troilus and Criseyde*); the Ha[1] and Cp to the D scribe (whose hand they also found in six other *Confessio* manuscripts, a *Trevisa*, and a *Piers Plowman*); they also differentiated the D scribe's hand from a similar hand they labeled ("Delta"), responsible for two *Trevisa's*, a *Confessio*, and two other manuscripts. J.J. Griffiths has since added the Robert H. Taylor manuscript of the *Confessio* at Princeton to the D scribe's list ("*Confessio Amantis*: the poem and its Pictures"). A.S.G. Edwards identifies the writing in Harley 7335 (Ha[5]) and Univ. of Illinois 84 of Lydgate's *The Fall of Princes* as by the same scribe ("Lydgate Manuscripts," p. 19). Daniel Mosser finds the same hand in Manchester English 113 and Bodleian Digby 181. [*Manuscripta* 34 (1990) 129–147].
[2] M.L. Samuels, one of the editors of LALME, is responsible for the most important application of dialectology to the *CT* in "The Scribe." See also J.J. Smith, "The Trinity Gower D-Scribe." For the theoretical background see M. Benskin and M. Laing, "Translations and *Mischsprachen*," A. McIntosh, "A New Approach to Middle English Dialectology," and J.J. Smith, "Linguistic Features."
[3] So far, of the *CT* volumes, six have been published: *The Miller's Tale*, ed. Thomas Ross, 1983; *The Nun's Priest's Tale*, ed. Derek Pearsall, 1984; *The Manciple's Tale*, ed. Donald C. Baker, 1984; *The Physician's Tale*, ed. Helen Corsa, 1987; *The Prioress's Tale*, ed. Beverly Boyd, 1987; *The Squire's Tale*, ed. Donald Baker, 1990. The Variorum editors have confirmed as a whole the textual affiliations outlined in M–R, and have found their evaluation of Hg justified. Ross and Baker express reservations, the latter

manuscripts were produced has led to a revision in our conception of the book trade as it was carried on in fifteenth century England and in the meaning of such words as book, compilation, ordination.[4] Finally the computer has given the comparison of textual data a new range of possibilities.[5]

The time is ripe for a reconsideration of the manuscript tradition of the *Canterbury Tales* as a whole. Indeed a number of reconsiderations have already occurred. But they fall short on at least two counts. They fail to meet what I have come to see as the two crucial tests for theories about *Canterbury Tales* manuscripts. They do not account successfully for the Hengwrt manuscript; they do not explain the wide difference in the number of independent textual traditions for different parts of the *Canterbury Tales*.

Norman Blake in his book, *The Textual Tradition of the Canterbury Tales* (Arnold, London, 1985), has given great emphasis to the Hengwrt manuscript. He sees it as taking precedence over all other manuscripts to the point of denying Chaucerian authorship to passages not contained in it. He goes so far as to deny Chaucerian authorship for the *Canon's Yeoman's Prologue* and *Tale*. Blake proposes that all the manuscripts derive from an unfinished and disorganized copytext left behind at Chaucer's death. The editors and scribes were responsible for arranging and rearranging this single copytext, adding to it links as well as the tale written after Chaucer's death, and giving it the rubrics and marginalia that made it seem a complete work.[6] This preference for Hengwrt does not do justice to certain features of the manuscript itself, to the evident difficulty the people who were responsible for it had in obtaining parts of the text, to the gaps they left in anticipation of finding additional links between tales and endings for the unfinished tales, to the irregularities in quire makeup that resulted (1) from insertion of text, (2) from the need to bring sections of

(justifiably in my view) at the bias in M–R's handling of the textual evidence in the direction of finding the *McT* early, perhaps even pre-Canterbury. For a preliminary report from a Variorum editor, see Charlotte Morse, "The Value of Editing the *Clerk's Tale*." For a comparison of Hg and El, based on data compiled by nine Variorum editors (*MkT*, *ClT*, and *GP*, in addition to the ones already published), see Daniel Ransom, "Hengwrt, Ellesmere, and the Variorum Chaucer."

The Facsimile series includes the Hengwrt manuscript and Pepys 2006. Note also the facsimile of Cambridge University Library Ms Gg.4.27 in 3 volumes, issued by Pilgrim Books, Norman, Ok, in association with D.S. Brewer Cambridge, 1979–80.

4   See M.B. Parkes, *'Ordinatio' and 'Compilatio'*; and a number of the essays in *Book Production and Publishing in Britain, 1375–1475*, ed. Jeremy Griffiths and Derek Pearsall. See also P.R. Robinson, "The Booklet." Daniel S. Silvia, "Some Fifteenth Century Manuscripts of the *CT*," presents some useful statistics on numbers of *CT* manuscripts of each type, especially on those which include works by other poets, whether relatively complete or anthologies.

5   See the work being done by Charles Moorman and Roy Vance Ramsey on the "landmark" manuscripts of the *Canterbury Tales* and by Dan Mosser on the alpha manuscripts of the *CT*. Moorman, "Computing Housman's Fleas" deals with the *General Prologue* only; but his work in progress will include all the *CT*.

6   This is the position arrived at in chapter 3, "Problems and Proposals about the Manuscript Tradition," pp. 44–57, in *The Textual Tradition*.

text to an end with the end of the tale.[7] The exemplars used by Hengwrt were clearly not all in the scribe's possession when he started his copying. The order he evolved reflected to some extent the time when exemplars came into his possession. The theory of a single copytext as source for all manuscripts does not do justice as well to the textual differences in the early manuscripts, and especially to the great differences in the number of independent textual traditions for different parts of the *Canterbury Tales*, from two for the *Monk's* and *Parson's Tales* to twelve for the *Franklin's*.

A second theory about the manuscript tradition of the *Canterbury Tales* was advanced by Larry D. Benson in "The Order of the *Canterbury Tales*", *SAC* 3 (1981) 77–120. He attempts to show that all the manuscript orderings derive from two made by Chaucer himself. These two he labels "the Type a" (p. 82) and "the non-Type a" (pp. 98 ff). The first is the Ellesmere-a ordering. The second is the one preserved for us in Harley 7334 (Ha⁴) with the *Gamelyn* omitted. Benson assumes that a number of complete manuscripts circulated before Hengwrt, perhaps even during Chaucer's lifetime (pp. 108 ff), and that the disarrangement of tales resulted from the breaking up of the copytext for convenience in copying (p. 77). But the earliest manuscripts of the *Canterbury Tales* are without exception by single scribes. In the production of these early manuscripts the breaking up of a collected text would have been an inconvenience. Furthermore three of the six in the first twenty years after Chaucer's death, Hengwrt, Harley 7334, and Cambridge Dd.4.24, have gaps for connecting links and completions of tales that are not filled at all or are filled by passages that don't fit. They show the kind of uncertainty one would expect from early efforts to arrange the material, rather than the careless misplacing of large sections of text already in their "correct" places in other manuscripts. Perhaps most important, Benson would derive Hengwrt from the non-type a through three intermediaries, a c, a d, and a distortion of d, "all in existence before Hg was written" (p. 108). He thus ignores the evidence developed by Manly-Rickert and Germaine Dempster that the d arrangement evolved from c and used many of the same exemplars; it could not have come into existence until long after Hengwrt was written.[8] His "distortion of d" is an even later development, the earliest manuscript to incorporate it having the estimated date in Manly-Rickert 1430–1450.[9] That the manuscript

---

[7]   Space was left in quire 22, a double quire of sixteen leaves, for the *SNT*, in a different ink from the tales that precede and follow. The quire that brings section IV to an end with *Mel* has ten leaves to permit the already completed section III beginning with the *MkP* to follow. Section III itself was completed in the same ink used on the inserted and altered links connecting the *SqT* with the *MeT* and the *MeT* with the *FkT* in the early part of section IV. Section II, consisting of Fragment D (*WBPT*, *FrPT*, and *SuPT*), comes to an end with a quire of six leaves and betrays by the color of its ink late insertion in the only gap permitted by continuity. For the "sections" in this note, see Doyle and Parkes, "Paleographical Introduction," xxiv and xxv in the *Hengwrt Facsimile*.

[8]   See M–R I: 96, II: 482f; Germaine Dempster, *PMLA* 63 (1948) 456–484, especially 462–464.

[9]   The manuscripts named by Benson as having the distortion of d used as "model" by the Hg scribe are Fi–Ii–Ra²–Ht. Ii, the earliest, is dated by M–R 1430–50. The others are all post-1450.

with the best text for most of the tales would have no access to the manuscripts ordered by Chaucer or to any derived from them except for one with links and a tale missing and with the ordering badly deranged involves an unreasonable set of assumptions. Finally one would expect from the procedure outlined by Benson an almost even number of textual traditions for each section of the *Canterbury Tales* instead of the wide range in number already noted.

John Fisher in his presidential address to the Medieval Academy, "Animadversions on the Text of Chaucer, 1988" [*Speculum* 63 (1988) 779–93], supported the single copytext theory for the production of the early manuscripts and suggested that the differences between the texts of Hengwrt and Ellesmere might be attributed to Chaucer's own revisions. Invoking the parallel development in the works of such "romantic artists" as Wordsworth, Coleridge, Hölderlin, and Liszt, Fisher offered the explanation that the poet, "as he grew older and worked over the lines, made them both milder and more regular in rhythm" (p. 788). A number of considerations make this suggestion hard to accept. First there is the unlikelihood of the scribe as he wrote Ellesmere choosing always the later of the two sets of variants when other scribes did not and when he himself writing Hengwrt chose always the earlier. The consistency of the differences in Ellesmere is far more likely to have resulted from the editorial preparation that clearly preceded the copying of the manuscript, in contrast to the lack of such preparation in the case of Hengwrt.[10] Second there is the question of age. Chaucer started the *Canterbury Tales* in the final years of his life; he did not grow old over them. Furthermore his development as a poet shows a consistent tendency to sharpen and concentrate language rather than to make it bland and conventional.

What the manuscripts tell us is not of one copytext, preserved in a single place, available to scribes and editors in the years immediately following Chaucer's death. Rather it is of a collection of fragments, tales and groups of tales, reflecting the different stages of a developing plan for the whole work. After 1400, and to some extent even before, these fragments circulated among relatives and friends and on out into a fairly wide reading public. At first no one suspected that a collection would be especially meaningful. We owe, I think, to the Hengwrt editor the first effort to collect the tales – and the opportunity, for himself and for others, to read them all or almost all together for the first time. From this first collection came the inspiration for the other early efforts to collect the tales and arrange them in a more meaningful order. For the first twenty years after Chaucer's death we have a total of six collections. For the second twenty years we have certainly only four more collections. Between 1430 and 1450 the number increases, especially in the last ten years. But even if we accepted all the manuscripts whose earliest estimated dates in Manly-Rickert were pre-1440, we would still have a total of only twenty-one for these first forty years.[11] Two fragments, the Merthyr and the vellum part of Helming-

---

[10] See Owen, "Alternative Reading," 242 f., for the contrast between Hg and El in editorial preparation.

[11] The six for the first twenty years are Hengwrt (Hg), Ellesmere (El), Corpus Christi 198 (Cp), Harley 7334 (Ha⁴), Cambridge Dd.4.24 (Dd), and Lansdowne 851 (La); the four according to the Manly-Rickert estimated dates, certainly written before 1440, are

ham, were possibly parts of collections. The state of the text in two of the collections, Corpus 198 and Petworth, strongly implies the existence of two or three others. In addition two manuscripts not among the ones that we know of are mentioned in wills dated 1417 and 1420 (Manly-Rickert I: 606–608). How many others existed we can only conjecture. What we have by a kind of miracle is very probably the very first effort at a collected text in Hengwrt, two intermediate manuscripts, Harley 7334 and Corpus 198, and some early manuscripts that became models for the two orderings followed somewhat carelessly by a majority of the later manuscripts.

We do know from the textual relationships of the manuscripts we have that individual tales and groups of tales were circulating in great numbers throughout the manuscript period. Not as well bound as the collected tales, they had an ephemeral existence; they were constantly losing leaves at beginning and end and replacing them by copying from other manuscripts; they served at times as exemplars for collected manuscripts; they acquired from collected manuscripts and from each other the marginalia, especially the explanatory and commentary marginalia, that turn up sometimes in manuscripts with no other apparent connection. The textual tradition of the *Canterbury Tales* is thus an unusually complicated one. Germaine Dempster, commenting on Manly's conception of its early phase, called it "a picture of manuscript affiliations, or rather a compound of pictures, of extreme complexity, certainly without precedent in the history of textual criticism" (*PMLA*, 61, 409).

The contrast with Chaucer's other collection of tales within a frame story is instructive. All ten manuscripts of the *Legend of Good Women* with more than a single tale have the tales in the same order – this despite the fact that the work was unfinished, that the *Prologue* was rewritten some years later, and that the frame story of the *Legend* gives far less importance to the ordering than does the frame story in the *Canterbury Tales*.[12] Apparently, when the scribes were given an ordering of their materials with authority behind it, they did not wilfully derange it.[13] What Manly-Rickert concluded at the end of their work on *The Text of the Canterbury Tales* should give pause to the many scholars

---

Cambridge Gg.4.27 (Gg), Petworth (Pw), Bodley 686 (Bo[2]), and Paris Anglais 39 (Ps). The eleven with earliest estimated dates before 1440 are Royal 18 C.II (Ry[2]), Sloane 1685 (Sl[1]), Additional 25718 (Ad[2]) Additional 35286 (Ad[3]), Egerton 2726 (En[1]), Egerton 2863 (En[2]), Lincoln 110 = A.4.18 (Ln), Cambridge Ii.3.26 (Ii), Laud 600 (Ld[1]), Lichfield 2 (Lc), and Phillips 8137 (Ph[3]). Four more manuscripts were probably written by 1450: Holkham 667 (Hk), McCormick (Mc), Oxford (Ox), and Cardigan (Cn). Ox is in two parts, Manchester English 63 and Rosenbach 1084/2. Cn is now at the Humanities Research Center, University of Texas, Austin. Helmingham (He), now at Princeton, has an early vellum section (ff.166–202), dated 1420–30, and a later paper section (ff. 1–165, 203–15), dated 1450–60.

[12] Two manuscripts, Cambridge Ff.1.6 and Rawlinson C.86 (Bodleian), have single tales. Cambridge Gg.4.27 has the revised *Prologue*.

[13] When disarrangement occurred, as happened in the g ("gamma") manuscripts for the Proem to Book IV of the *Troilus*, the scribal errors are apparent and attributable to the state of the author's copy when the ancestor of the extant g manuscripts was made. In the cases of the *Monk's Tale*, Gower's *Confessio Amantis*, and *Piers Plowman*, different orderings result from authorial revision.

who continue to see manuscript arrangements as coming from Chaucer. According to Manly-Rickert only the text comes from Chaucer. The editors and scribes were responsible for the ordering, the explicits and incipits, the headings, and almost all of the marginalia and interlinear glosses.[14] Their purpose was not only to make the text more convenient for readers, but also to minimize its incompleteness.

[14] See M–R II: 41, 475, 488ff; III: 528. M–R entertain the possibility that some of the marginalia derive from Chaucer (III:525–27, especially 527).

II

The Six Earliest Manuscripts

The six collected manuscripts of the *Canterbury Tales* written before 1420 fall naturally into two categories. Three of them, Corpus 198 (Cp), Cambridge Dd.4.24 (Dd), and Lansdowne 851 (La), belong to what Manly-Rickert call constant groups. By this they mean that the exemplars from which the manuscripts were copied remained together and were used for more than a single manuscript. For each of the other three, Hengwrt (Hg), Harley 7334 (Ha[4]), and Ellesmere (El), the exemplars apparently did not remain together. Though individual exemplars from all three turn up in later manuscripts, no evidence of a manuscript using the same set exists. At the same time, interrelationships between all six indicate an awareness of each other's work on the part of those responsible. The marginalia that appeared in Hengwrt are largely repeated in Cambridge Dd and greatly expanded in Ellesmere. A few of these same marginalia appear in Corpus, but more important the Pausacio phenomenon in the *Clerk's Prologue* that makes what is probably its first appearance in Corpus turns up again in Ellesmere.[1] Corpus and Lansdowne, members of the constant group c, used the same set of exemplars. Finally Corpus and Harley, written by the same scribe, share, as we shall see, a number of other features.

Recent scholarship has both called into question and confirmed that a single scribe wrote both Hengwrt and Ellesmere and that another scribe wrote both Harley 7334 (Ha[4]) and Corpus 198 (Cp). The paleographical evidence set forth by Doyle and Parkes has been challenged by Vance Ramsey and confirmed by the evidence from dialect presented by M. L. Samuels.[2] Professor Samuels and

---

[1] Of the early manuscripts Hg has paraph marks at E 7, 15, 21, 31, and 39. Cp has a marginal "Pausacio" before lines 7, 15, 21, and 31. It lacks E 33–107 from loss of a leaf. El has a space with "Pausacio" at E 6, 14, 20, 30, 38, 46, and 56 (end of "prologe"), and a special capital for the initial letter of the next line. See M–R III:534, which however omits Cp's last "Pausacio".

[2] Ellesmere probably represents a second attempt by the Hg editor, using the same scribe; but the work of Samuels and Smith on dialect suggests it was some six years later. Roy Vance Ramsey, "Different Scribes," (1982) questions the identity of the

his student Jeremy J. Smith have gone further. They have been able to establish from their dialect studies the spelling used by Gower[3] and Chaucer and to bring

Hengwrt and Ellesmere scribes, confidently asserted by A.I. Doyle and M.B. Parkes in "The Production of Copies," (1978). See also their "Paleographical Introduction," (1979), especially "Handwriting: A, the Main Copyist," xxxiv–xxxvii.

M.L. Samuels, "The Scribe," (1983) answers Ramsey with evidence that indicates a development in the spelling habits of the scribe over a period of six to ten years from Hengwrt (1402–04), the Cecil fragment of the *Troilus* (1405–06), hand B in the Trinity Cambridge R.3.2 of Gower's *Confessio Amantis* (1407–09), to Ellesmere (1410–12). This period of time between Hengwrt and Ellesemere (six to ten years) would help to explain the difference in most of the exemplars used, the slight deterioration of the text provided by the exemplars, and the critical insights reflected in the Ellesmere arrangement and illumination of the text.

Ramsey has kept the question open with his response to Samuels, "Paleography and Scribes," (1986). J.J. Smith has responded with "The Trinity Gower D-Scribe," (1988) chiefly concerned with Ha[4] and Cp but pointing out what Smith considers flaws in Ramsey's method. One would have more confidence in the results of Ramsey's analyses if they did not always turn out to be negative. Not only are Ellesemere and Hengwrt and the Ha[4] and Cp scribes different but the portion of the Trinity Gower ascribed to B by the paleographers is not by either the Hg or the El scribe. The tests developed by Hinman to distinguish typesetters in the Shakespeare folio make no allowance for factors not present in the typesetting situation, for differences in the exemplars themselves, for the time element in the scribe's development, and for activities of an editor or supervisor in preparing the copy and instructing the scribe. A fourth factor in some instances would be the wishes of the patron. The editorial hand in Ellesmere is everywhere apparent; it alone could account for the 7:1 ratio in unique variants (243–35) as between El and Hg. As Ramsey himself points out, almost all the unique variants in Hg were inadvertent, while those in El show us a copyist "much more willing to deliberately change the text" (p. 130). For the D scribe, responsible according to Doyle and Parkes for stints in, or the whole of, twelve different manuscripts (eight of them Gower *Confessio Amantis*), a great deal of research remains to be done. We would seem here to have an ideal testing ground for Ramsey's methods.

[3] The order of D's manuscripts is more difficult than B's, because, as Samuels points out, he tends to copy what he sees before him. B on the other hand tends to use his own spelling. For the evidence about the handwriting of Hg and El, see note 2. For the scribe of Ha[4] and Cp and for the collaboration of five scribes on the Trinity Gower, see Doyle and Parkes, "The Production of Copies. . . ." M.L. Samuels and J.J. Smith take up the evidence for Gower's spelling in "The Language of Gower," (1981). For Chaucer's spelling see M.L. Samuels, "Chaucer's Spelling," (1983). The ordering of the twelve manuscripts identified as by the D scribe of the Trinity Gower is the subject of J.J. Smith's recently completed doctoral dissertation at Glasgow. I quote from a letter dated July 4, 1984: "To answer your query: I can give *tentative* sequence, from the linguistic evidence, for D's Chaucers and his *complete* Gower. This sequence is:

Harley 7334
Corpus B 67
Plimpton
Corpus 198   }   difficult
Christ Church}   to establish priority
Egerton 1991
Bodley 294

I believe D's stint in the Trinity MS comes at the end of this sequence, but the evidence important new evidence to bear on the temporal sequence of the early manuscripts. The collaboration of the two scribes (the Hg–El labeled B, the Ha^4–Cp labeled D) on a single Gower manuscript, the Trinity Cambridge R.3.2 (581) of the *Confessio Amantis*, promised new insight on the relative dating of all six early *Canterbury Tales* manuscripts. The evidence on the B scribe is unequivocal. Hg is clearly the first of the four manuscripts ascribed to B; Ellesmere the last. The Trinity Gower is in the middle, probably closer to El than to Hg.

Establishing a sequence for D's twelve manuscripts, eight Gower *Confessio's*, a *Trevisa*, and a *Piers Plowman*, as well as the two *Canterbury Tales*, is more difficult, but Jeremy Smith's tentative sequence places Harley 7334 before Corpus 198 and both before the Trinity Gower. Thus Ellesmere appears to be not only considerably later than Hengwrt, but later as well than Ha^4 and Cp. If these tentative findings hold, they will make it even more difficult to claim any special authority for the Ellesmere-a ordering of the *Canterbury Tales*.

Of course the new sequence does not establish the priority of Hengwrt. The excellence of the text and the special difficulties in acquiring and retaining exemplars for some of the tales and many of the links, apparent in irregularities of quire makeup, spacing of text, and the changes in quality of ink are consistent with Hengwrt's being the first effort to bring all of the tales together. Furthermore, the Hengwrt ordering cannot derive from any other early *Canterbury Tales* manuscript, whereas it can be seen as exerting an influence on both Ha^4 and Cp. Hg's spellings have none of the northern and midland forms found in Cp and Ha^4 and attributed by Samuels to "one or more Northern and Midland stages of copying."[4] The new evidence then does not call into question Hg's priority; indeed it tends to confirm it.

An intermediate position for Ha^4 requires correction of some of the statements made in my *PMLA* article.[5] To Ha^4 would go the discoveries of text there

is slight. D's stint in Bodley 902 is too short to place, and (as I may have explained in an earlier letter) I've been able to see only part of one folio of the Taylor MS. I base this sequence on (and this will probably seem much too crude) the number of SWM features in each text, since D appears to have originated in Worcs (probably NW Worcs). It is therefore difficult to place the *Piers Plowman* and the Trevisa in sequence, since both stem from SW/SWM traditions." J.J. Smith confirmed this sequence when I saw him at Kalamazoo in May, 1985. See also his "Linguistic Features of Some Fifteenth-Century Middle English Manuscripts," 104–12, in *Manuscripts and Readers in Fifteenth-Century English*, ed. Derek Pearsall (Cambridge, Engl., 1983), and his "Trinity Gower D-Scribe," (1988).

4   Samuels, "Chaucer's Spelling," 26. (p. 27 in Smith, *The English of Chaucer*).
5   The assumption of the priority of Cp was based on the absence of links in the three tales of the E–F fragment that follow D in the mansucript and on the inclusion of *Gamelyn* without evidence of the uncertainty shown in Ha^4. The influence of M–R also played a part. They refer to Cp as probably the "earliest representative . . . of the so-called 'New English Style' in MS illumination" (M–R I: 94), and attribute to Cp (perhaps) the inclusion of *Gamelyn* and the early placement of G – G C B^2 H I R (M–R I: 95, 96). A careful reading of Margaret Rickert's chapter on "Illuminations" strongly suggests that in her view Ha^4 is a less developed representative of the "New Style" than Corpus (M–R I: 567–69) and therefore earlier. The marginalia in Corpus, both

ascribed to Cp, the *Gamelyn* as *Cook's Tale* and the *Man of Law's* endlink. Ha⁴ would also be the first manuscript to include *CYPT* and to place the *SNPT* with the *CYPT* attached as fragment G after the *FkT* (the position for *SNT* alone in Hg). Ha⁴ thus would originate the sequence G C B² H I R that brings so many of the manuscripts and early printed texts to a close. Uncertainties in the ordering revealed by the way the manuscript was produced are more numerous than in Cp and thus reinforce the evidence presented by the dialectologists. The *Cook's Tale* comes to an end eight lines early with 4413 and 4414 written together on the last line of folio 58v. At the foot of the page well below the text and to the right occurs the director's scribbled note, "Icy comencera le / fable de Gamelyn." On 59r *Gam* starts with a demi-vinet and a five-line flourished capital but with no *explicit, incipit,* or *narrat.* The crowding of the text at the bottom of 58v suggests some irregularity. Did the editor leave out the last lines of the *CkT* realizing it was incomplete and desiring to start the *Gam* at the top of a folio? Did he then order the completion of the couplet with the writing of line 4414 on the same line as 4413? *Gam* begins on the third sheet of a quire and ends eleven lines from the bottom of 70v, the last page of an irregular quire of six leaves, a quire that has no catchword. The evidence points to *Gam*'s being a late insertion in the manuscript, in a gap purposely left for the conclusion of the *CkT.* The only other irregular quire, again a quire of six, is sewn between the fourth and fifth leaf. In other words it started out as a regular quire. It brings to an end the *Merchant's Tale* with a single line on the verso of the last leaf. The *Me–Sq* link occupies the rest of the page with a three-line gap for an *explicit* before and a four-line gap for *explicit* and *incipit* at the end. This spacing of a link is unique in the manuscript. *Explicits* and *incipits* ordinarily take no more than two lines. Many of the tales have no gap at all, with a marginal *narrat,* a demi-vinet, and a flourished initial to set off their openings. Manly-Rickert see in the short quire and the unusual spacing of the link at the end of the *MeT* the probability that the scribe had already begun copying the *SqT* before obtaining the *Me–Sq* link (I:224).

That Ha⁴ and Cp influenced one another can hardly be doubted, given the shared features, *Gamelyn,* the *Man of Law's* endlink, the ordering of the last five fragments, the scribe, the "new" style of illumination (M-R I: 567–69), and the fact of corrections, many of them indicated not made, in Cp, that seem to derive even to the spelling from Ha⁴ (M-R I: 93–94). The difficulty comes in the ordering and linking of the tales in the E–F fragment. Here Ha⁴ has the ordering associated with a-Ellesmere and a complete set of links, at least one of them derived from Hengwrt. Corpus on the other hand makes use of the *ML* endlink to introduce the Squire and places the other three tales in E–F after D.

commentary and explanatory, are with a single exception in Hg, when not original with Cp. The one not in Hg but in El, at D 54, is the one in the *Wife of Bath's Prologue* most commonly picked up in its complete form by other manuscripts, including the following early ones: Additional 35286, Paris Anglais 39, La, Lichfield 2, Laud 600, Petworth, and Sloane 1685: The four commentary glosses in Ha⁴ are all in Hg. One of the explanatory glosses in Cp, *latitantem* at G 186, occurs elsewhere only in Hg, Dd, and El. For my previous description and discussion of these two MSS, see *PMLA,* 97 (1982): 245f.

The *ClT* has its prologue and the envoy, but the leaf missing at the end of the envoy would accommodate neither Host stanza nor the *Merchant's* headlink. The *MeT* lacks the final hundred lines, coming to an end with Proserpine's last speech. The *FkP*, "Thise olde gentil Britouns. . . .", begins without the gap of a single line, but with a four-line capital fitted into a demi-vinet and a marginal title, "The prologe of the ffnkeleyn," to indicate the change from Merchant to Franklin. The tale itself has only a four-line initial, no gap in the text, no title in the margin. Throughout the manuscript the only indication of uncertainty comes at the end of the unfinished *Squire's Tale* with eighteen blank lines at the bottom of a verso page (99, not the end of a quire).

A distinction between the two manuscripts may have had an important effect on their relationship to one another. The exemplars from which Cp was copied remained together for at least two other manuscripts, Lansdowne 851 (La) and the ancestor for Sloane 1686 (Sl^2); many of them served as exemplars for the d manuscripts. The possibility that the exemplars were collected for another c manuscript earlier than Ha^4 and Cp cannot be ruled out. No evidence that the Ha^4 exemplars remained together after their use for Ha^4 exists. Quite the contrary. Ha^4 exemplars turned up randomly in other manuscripts, in Cambridge Ii.3.26 (Ii) for instances, for the tales in fragment A (M–R I: 296); in Laud 600 (Ld^1), for fragments B^2, H, and I (M–R I: 311); in Sion (Si), for the *ClT* (M–R I: 501).[6] Ha^4 and c then represent intermediate steps, the one between Hengwrt and the a-Ellesmere ordering, the other between Hengwrt and the d. After the original use of the Man of Law's endlink as Squire's headlink, the c director was apparently content to put the other three tales of the E–F fragment after D in the same order as in Ha^4. The *Clerk's Envoy* provides the only transition between the *ClT* and *MeT* and the lines about Breton lays between the unfinished *MeT* and the *FkT*.

The sequence suggested by Professor Samuels and Jeremy Smith would have no effect on Lansdowne. It is still clearly later than Cp and perhaps the last of the six extant manuscripts produced during the first twenty years after Chaucer's death. But it would reopen the question as to whether Ellesmere or Cambridge Dd.4.24 (Dd) was responsible for the most influential of the manuscript orderings of the *Canterbury Tales*. If Ha^4 was already in existence, the differences in the Ellesmere-a ordering are minimal. They involve rejection of the *Gamelyn* and the *Man of Law's* endlink and the positioning of the G fragment between B^2 (the longest connected fragment ending with the *NPT*) and H (the shortest fragment containing only the *McPT*). As to which came first, El or Dd, the evidence points both ways but the preponderance seems to favor Dd.

Dd, as we shall see in more detail later, shows in its makeup more of the uncertainties so evident in Hg and to a lesser extent in Ha^4. Not only does the scribe leave gaps at the end of the *Cook's* and *Squire's Tales*. He does the same between the *Pardoner's Tale* and the *Shipman's*. Between the *Nun's Priest's Tale* and the *Second Nun's Tale* he leaves a gap more than twice the length of the endlink, which he is the first to include. Ellesmere on the other hand has

---

[6] See M–R I: 222, the last paragraph of the section on "Affiliations" and textual character, for a general statment about the use of Ha^4 exemplars by later manuscripts.

only the spaces at the end of the unfinished *Cook's Tale* and *Squire's Tale*. Furthermore, the marginalia in Dd come almost exclusively from Hg. Only three of the commentary marginalia added by El appear in Dd, none of the explanatory ones. Two of the three might well involve accidental omission on the part of Hg of one of a clustered group, conveyed to Dd by the exemplar. The third was a Latin translation of an English proverb in the *CYP* (not in Hg). The Ellesmere is a much more formal manuscript, based on a carefully edited set of exemplars. The absence of any uncertainty as to text except for the two unfinished tales reflects the care and intelligence of the director, who is clearly aiming at a definitive *Canterbury Tales* in both what he includes and in what he rejects. The Dd scribe-editor has a more personal interest in his manuscript. He includes the *NP's Epilogue*, which does not connect with anything, and he does not mind the occasional signs of incompleteness, the provision in his manuscript for additional fragments of text should they turn up. He seems to have a scholar's interest in the text, not only correcting from exemplars other than the one he had used, but creating a text at times from more than a single exemplar.

The presence in Dd of passages not in Ellesmere, the first of the added sets of lines in the *Wife of Bath's Prologue* (D 44 a–f) and the *NP*'s endlink, might be construed as pointing to the priority of Ellesmere. On the other hand, they could well result from the editorial discretion so prominent in Ellesmere. The emphasis in the first passage on the virility of all five of the Wife's husbands conflicts with the later account of the first three; this conflict could have led to the decision not to include it. The *NP* endlink, like the *ML*'s, fails to introduce another tale; it thus calls attention to the incompleteness of the work, a quality the Ellesmere editor was seeking to deemphasize. What happens in the *Knight's Tale* is not so easily explained. Dd for the first 1022 lines (to A 1880) has a text closely related to that used by Ellesmere, so close as to suggest use of the same exemplar or at least of a copy of it. Thereafter, for the final 1228 lines, Dd shifts to a text derived from the earlier one used by Hengwrt.[7] Why the shift in Dd if the exemplar was available later for the whole of the *Knight's Tale* in Ellesmere? Possibly the Dd scribe-editor had a damaged Hg-related exemplar for the

---

[7]   Charles Moorman kindly sent me a copy of the paper entitled "Group and Independent Manuscripts of the *Canterbury Tales*" he read at Kalamazoo in May 1985. He and Vance Ramsey have been running computer checks of variants in the "landmark" mss. of the *Canterbury Tales*. Their checks have confirmed the close association of Dd and En^1 throughout the *Knight's Tale*. The coefficients of correlation for variants of the two manuscripts in the three parts of the *Knight's Tale*, A 859–1740, A 1741–2799, and A 2800–3108, are .99, 1.00, and 1.00 – in other words, practically perfect (1.00 shows a complete identity of variants). Dd and En^1 were clearly copied from the same exemplar. This exemplar had in the first part of the *Knight's Tale* a close association with Ellesmere, which resulted in a coefficient of correlation of .94 for El–Dd and .91 for $El–En^1$. For the last two parts this coefficient dropped to minus figures. On the other hand the coefficient for Hg–Dd, which in the first part had been –.77 became for the second part .99 and for the third part .76. In other words the association of Dd with Ellesmere in the first part is closer than it is with Hengwrt in the other two parts. The probability is that Dd was using for the first part the same exemplar as El. In the other two sections Dd was probably using Hg-derived text.

KnT, which lacked its beginning. He made up for this deficiency by copying from the exemplar later used by El.

The important thing to remember is the close association of those who produced not only Dd and El, but Hg as well. The marginalia, explanatory and commentary, developed in Hengwrt, present in Dd, and greatly expanded in Ellesmere, reflect this close association. The exemplars used in the three texts, while different for the most part, are usually affiliated. They show that those responsible for the Hg and Dd texts had some tales in their possession and access to others. Ellesmere may well result from the dissatisfaction with Hengwrt, as collections that were clearly better ordered emerged. The purpose of most of the early editors to give an impression of finish and completeness to the text reaches fulfillment in the Ellesmere and Lansdowne manuscripts.

These two manuscripts not only convey an impression of completeness, they also display the most artistic formats of any of the early manuscripts. Lansdowne has a title, "Incipit prologus fabularum Cantuar", entwined with a colorful vinet; the illuminated initial W encloses a full-length portrait of the author with pencase and book. It is perhaps the most impressive opening page of any of the manuscripts. No visual gap in the manuscript betrays incompleteness, and the scribe has added to the demi-vinets and champs that adorn the beginnings of the prologues and tales, rubricated headings, *explicits*, and *incipits*, that help guide the reader by presenting him with a visually articulated text. Adornment goes beyond guiding the reader. Some initial letters develop leaf extensions into the margin, and even more elaborate patterns such as faces.

Narrative completeness is also stressed; the tales are linked in every instance but one. The Cook is made to repent his harlotry and substitute for "Perkyn revelour" the tale "of a knyghte and his sonnes" (*Gamelyn*); the Squire out of consideration for the other pilgrims defers the conclusion of his tale to the next turn he will get at storytelling, and the spurious link goes on to introduce the Wife of Bath as speaker in preparation for her *Prologue*. The exception is the *Merchant's Tale*. It has links neither before nor after, and as in Corpus it is incomplete. Its sole introduction is the Clerk's song. It ends with Proserpine's vow to provide May with an answer (E2318). Then the Franklin starts talking of "thise olde gentil Britouns" without introduction but also without visual gap. The clear effort to plan in advance a satisfactory book, by the composition of spurious passages if necessary, is matched by a certain carelessness with the text.

Ellesmere, though almost as complete visually, takes a far more responsible attitude toward Chaucer's text. The only visual gaps occur with the incomplete *Cook's* and *Squire's Tales*. The editor did not use spurious links to connect the fragments but by judicious spacing and the consistent use of *explicits* and *incipits* within and between fragments minimized the appearance of incompleteness. Editorial preparation and control are everywhere apparent. There are no irregularities in quire makeup, no evidence of any doubt as to what was to go where. Indexing marginalia are consistent and helpful. Space is provided not only for the commentary marginalia in Latin (about half of them inherited from Hengwrt, where no advance provision was made for them) but for the colored paraphs as well that set off and adorn both text and marginalia.

The illuminated portraits at the beginning of each tale, showing as they do an intelligent reading of the *Prologue* and a critical appreciation of the importance of the frame story, give the manuscript its prime distinction. Restraint, intelligence, and good taste help make Ellesmere the most beautiful of *Canterbury Tales* manuscripts and lend authority to what is essentially a deceptive book. The editor of Ellesmere adopted for the fragments Chaucer left behind an ordering developed in whole or in part by the previous collections. He gave this ordering a form that has influenced all modern editions of the work.[8]

---

[8]   Plans for a Huntington Library Facsimile of the Ellesmere Manuscript have been announced. It will be accompanied by a volume of essays. Martin Stevens is chairman of the planning committee. Daniel Woodward represents the Library. Alan Gaylord has given a number of illustrated lectures on the Ellesmere, including one at the Vancouver New Chaucer Society Meeting in August 1988: "What do the Ellesmere Pictures Illustrate? (A dissenting View)".

III

The a Manuscripts

Dd differs from Ellesmere in one other important respect. The exemplars from which it was copied remained together and provided the text for the a family of manuscripts. To illustrate the general point about the manuscripts I am trying to make I should like to give two explanations of how the a manuscripts developed. First let us look at the problem. The first a manuscript, Cambridge Dd, has three sections that do not agree textually with other manuscripts in the a group. We have just taken note of the first of these, the shift in affiliation of Dd's text for just over half of the *KnT* at line A 1880 from the text used by Ellesmere to a text affiliated with that used by Hengwrt. This shift in affiliation Dd hands on to Egerton 2726 (En[1]), dated 1430–50, and through En[1] to Devonshire (Ds), dated 1450–60. The other arm of the a manuscripts, Cardigan (Cn), dated 1450, and Manchester English 113 (Ma), dated 1483–85, used a text affiliated with Ellesmere and Harley 7334 throughout the *KnT*. The other divergences from the a family's text are peculiar to Dd. The *WBT* and the first 686 lines of the *Clerk's* fragment derive from texts later used by Additional 35286 (Ad[3]) and the closely related Harley 7335 (Ha[5]), by Rawlinson Poetry 223 (Ra[3]) and by Trinity Cambridge R.3.3 (Tc[1]). Manly-Rickert erect the stemma reflected in Plate 1 to account for the irregularities of the Dd text.[1] This stemma has a number of implausible features. It adds three excellent complete manuscripts of the *Canterbury Tales* to the six we know existed at a time when the Hengwrt editor, the Cambridge Dd scribe, the Ha[4] editors, and the Corpus

---

[1] /Dd is never explicitly mentioned by Manly-Rickert, but they distinguish (M–R I: 132), between /En[1] and /Dd. They point out that Dd is "most frequently away from its associates, both by shift of exemplar, probably due to loss of leaves, and by extensive correction (usually invisible), partly independent, partly from an unknown source near the original" (I: 102). En[1] could not have been copied "from the same exemplar as Dd" (I: 131), if the exemplar had lost leaves (at the beginning of the *Clerk's Tale*) before Dd was copied. Dd, 1400–20, is certainly earlier than En[1], 1430–50. Manly-Rickert's /En[1] is /Dd in the stemma; their /Dd is /Dd in the stemma. For a discussion of a, see Manly-Rickert, II: 51–57.

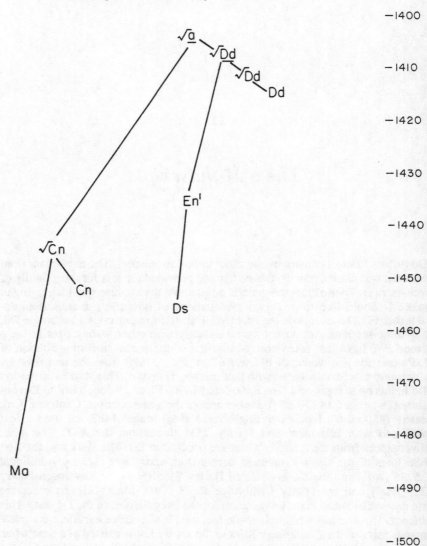

PLATE 1

Note: In the stemmata (plates 1–6), unbroken lines indicate textual derivation; √ = textual ancestor; underlining indicates a group of manuscripts derived from the text for the ancestor so designated. Thus √Dd = ancestor of the group Dd En[1] Ds; √Dd = ancestor of the single manuscript Dd; √a = the ancestor of the groups Dd Cn. Broken lines indicate influence. One or more short lines perpendicular to the unbroken line before the abbreviation for the manuscript indicate disarrangement of text and/or breakdown in the transmission of part of the text. In this stemma √Dd has Hg-related text for the *KnT* from A 1880 to the end. √Dd adds the further irregularity of non-a text for *WBT* and the first 686 lines of *CIT*. It uses text for *WBT* and *CIT* 1–686 that is used later in Ad[3]–Ha[5], Ra[3], and Tc[1].

editor had difficulty coming by elements of the text. It preserves two of these over long periods of time, separate from closely related manuscripts that in fact were derived from them. The only extant manuscript in the group from this period is the most flawed, while the one that serves for exemplar, as Manly-Rickert put it, half a century later, survives unflawed. During this short period of not more than ten years manuscripts derived from /a suffer the loss of an unlikely amount of text from, first, the end of the *KnT*, and then the beginning of the *ClT* (approximately half in each case), as well as the whole of the *WBT*. They supply this text not from the manuscript most closely associated with their exemplar but from another. Note that these two manuscripts are assumed to be undamaged except for the loss of text specified. Of course any effort to add texts between the ones necessary to the theory would simply add to the unlikelihood of such an abundance of collected texts in this period of manifest difficulty, however much it might bring the egregious losses suffered more in line with the laws of probability.

Let us assume instead that there are many tales and groups of tales circulat-ing, that the Dd editor gets wind of the Hengwrt editor's success in doing a collected edition, gathers together exemplars for his own collection, arranges them in an order also used by Ellesmere, adopts the Hengwrt marginalia, and unlike his fellow editor serves as his own scribe. Among the texts he has collected is a *KnT* that suffered some drastic accident, an accident that had forced replacement of the first 1022 lines of his text from an exemplar derived from the one used by Ellesmere. Then, while he was at work on the *ClT*, at about the time he had written line 686, something happened. Either he came on a copy of the *ClT* much easier to work with than the exemplar he had been using, or the owner demanded the return of the exemplar. The shift in exemplar in the *ClT* is related to the text the Dd scribe-editor had used for the *Wife of Bath's Tale*. None of the four other a manuscripts use the text for the *WBT* and for lines 1–686 of the *ClT* used by Dd. On the other hand these appear in a group of later manuscripts (Ad[3], Ha[5], Ra[3], and Tc[1]) with the *ClT* complete.[2] Whatever happened to cause the change of exemplar in the *ClT* affected also the *WBT* in the collection of exemplars used by the a family of manuscripts. This collection, with texts for the *WBT* and lines 1–686 of the *ClT* different from those used by Dd, remained together for some thirty to forty years after the writing of Dd. Perhaps given some sort of binding, it served first as copy-text for Egerton 2726 (En[1]), dated 1430–50 by Manly-Rickert, and somewhat later for the ancestor of the Cardigan group of manuscripts, which includes Cardigan (Cn), dated 1450, and Manchester English 113 (Ma), dated 1483–85. By the time the editor for the ancestor of Cn used the collection, the exemplar for the *KnT* where the text changes from El-derived to Hg-related at line 1880, had either disappeared entirely or deteriorated to the extent that it was difficult to read. The Cn editor substituted El–Ha[4]-related copy for the section of the

---

[2]   The presence of the exemplar of the first 686 lines in later texts for the whole of the *Clerk's Tale* (Ad[3], Ha[5], Ra[3], and Tc[1]) shows that the reason for shift of exemplar in Dd was not loss of leaves.

KnT in making his own copy of the manuscript materials.[3] This copy served as exemplar for both Cn (1450) and Ma (1483–85). But the collection of exemplars first brought together around 1410 for Dd, which served the Cn editor as copytext between 1440 and 1450, disintegrated shortly afterwards. Some of the individual texts survived, tougher, perhaps on vellum as opposed to paper, and formed the basis for the a portions of the b set of exemplars.[4] (See Plate 2)

This second explanation has certain advantages over the first. It makes fewer assumptions. The assumptions it makes are less drastic. That two otherwise complete manuscripts should lose from their midsections so soon after being written such large segments of text strains credulity. Furthermore the close relationship postulated between Hengwrt, Ellesmere, and Cambridge Dd has the evidence on marginalia developed in the *PMLA* article to confirm it. These three manuscripts share a number of explanatory and commentary glosses. The number and nature of the glosses eliminates coincidence as a possible explanation.[5]

One other characteristic of Cambridge Dd supports this theory. The scribe-editor, as we have seen, shows uncertainty as to text on a number of occasions. He leaves the last twelve lines of a verso page blank after the unfinished *Cook's Tale*. At the end of the *Squire's Tale* he leaves more than a page and a half blank, writing first "Explicit Secunda pars," and then "Here endith the Squieres tale as meche as Chaucer made." Similarly at the end of the *Pardoner's Tale* he leaves a page and a half blank and at the top of f. 150v writes, "Here bigynneth the Shipmans tale next folwyng the Pardoner." His handling of the *Nun's Priest's Epilogue*, which he is the first to include, betrays an original uncertainty as to its length. He leaves a blank of three lines at the end of the tale, writes the epilogue without a heading, and then in a gap of nineteen lines before the start of the *Second Nun's Tale* writes on lines 15 and 17 the following rubric: "Heere endeth the Tale of the Nonnes Preest & bigynneth the / Secund Nonnes Tale of Seynt Cecile With oute a Prologe." If the Dd scribe-editor was copying an already assembled text, it is difficult to explain these features. Furthermore the text itself, as we have seen, is not entirely an a text. We find exemplars being used for the *WBT* and for the first part of the *ClT* that belong to another tradition; we find readings in the *Friar's* and *Summoner's Tales* that reflect consultation of other manuscript materials, as Manly-Rickert repeatedly put it, "independently corrected" (M–R II: 193, 208f., 218, 236). The Dd scribe-editor had a different attitude toward his text from those who produced the later a manuscripts. He combined the functions of compiler,

[3] Dan Mosser in his computer work on the texts of what he has named the alpha manuscripts has discovered the relationship of the Cn exemplar for the *KnT* with Ha[4]. This is part of Chapter 6, "The Origins and Development of the Alpha Text of the *Canterbury Tales*" in his work in progress, *The Alpha Text*, on every aspect of the a constant group.

[4] The copy used by Cn, however, remained intact, was used as copytext by Ma in the early 1880s, and had an influence on En[3], the last constant group, (an independent influence even on Ad[1] which supplied some missing lines in the *KnT* from Cn), and To. Cn was possibly an unbound manuscript, possibly a set of exemplars.

[5] *PMLA* 97 (1982) 243f.

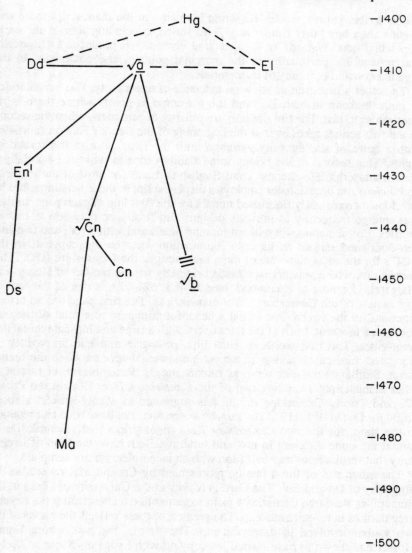

PLATE 2

In this stemma **a** is the collection of exemplars assembled for Dd, later used for
En¹ and for the copytext used by Cn and much later by Ma.

editor, scribe, patron, reader. He wrote his name in the manuscript more frequently than any other *Canterbury Tales* scribe, concluding four of the early
tales with "quod Wytton," or "Amen quod Wytton." He produced a manuscript
that reflects his personality in the marginal pointers and comments, in the
organization and economy of its materials.

The other a manuscripts show no evidence of uncertainty. The irregularities
of quire makeup in both En^1 and the Cn come at points where there is no
question as to text. For En^1 the only irregularity occurs early, when the second
of the two scribes takes over at the beginning of the *Reeve's Tale* on folio 49a,
with a quire of six, the only variation until the final quire in the format of
eights. This second scribe brings some flamboyance to what is essentially a
plain manuscript. He changes from English to Latin for most of the *explicits*
and *incipits*, he occasionally employs a display script in these headings, and he
develops incrementally flourished initials for the first line of each page, initials
that emerge frequently as intricate designs and finally on occasion as human
profiles. En^1, a manuscript without running heads and with three- and two-line
pen-flourished initials as its only illumination, became the copytext in the
1450's for the most elaborate of the a manuscripts, the Devonshire (Ds).[6] This
manuscript, which was perhaps made originally for the mother of Henry VII,
Margaret, Countess of Richmond, (see M–R I: 621–22), is one of the four or
five richest of the *Canterbury Tales* manuscripts. The first page has an ornate
vinet and in the twelve-line initial a beautiful miniature of a man sitting out-
doors on a low seat. Each of the tales opens with a large and intricate initial in a
demi-vinet. The first words of each link, prologue, and tale are written in
elongated miniscules, giving an almost monumental appearance to the manuscript. Similar miniscules serve as running heads. Resemblance in format to
other manuscripts, including two of the *Canterbury Tales* (Rawlinson Poetry
223 and Trinity Cambridge R.3.3), has suggested to Manly-Rickert a shop-
origin for Ds (M–R I: 119).[7] The text, however, must not have been one retained
in the shop, for the two *Canterbury Tales* manuscripts that resemble Ds in
format are quite different in text and ordering. Both have the kind of irregularity that results from improvisation with an incomplete set of exemplars.

The other arm of the a family, represented by Cn and Ma, reverts to the
simplicity of Dd and En^1. The Cardigan, now at the University of Texas in the
Humanities Research Center, is a plain workmanlike manuscript. It has several
irregularities in its quire makeup. The greatest of these reflects the habits of the
two scribes involved in its production. The first of the two, whom Daniel
Mosser has shown to have started his copying with Lydgate's *Siege of Thebes*

---

[6] Devonshire is now in Japan in the library of Professor T. Takamiya.

[7] The Devonshire manuscript is one of a group of fourteen in the same or similar
hands with the same kind of running titles. These include the two *Canterbury Tales*
manuscripts mentioned in the text, six manuscripts of Lydgate's *Fall of Princes*, two of
the *Polychronicon*. See *Sixty Bokes Olde and Newe*, pp. 109, 110, for a plate of a leaf
from one of the *Fall of Princes* manuscripts and a list of manuscripts in the set of
fourteen. The plate is of the leaf in the Philadelphia Free Library, MS T15/487.
Fifty-four additional leaves from the same manuscript are Columbia University Library
MS Plimpton 255.

now bound at the end, wrote most of the manuscript in quires of twelve.[8] The second, who took over on the fourth leaf of quire 16 in the midst of the *MkP*, changed immediately (with the quire he started on) to quires of eight. He corrected quire 10 (which had the mistake in sequence caused by the shifting of a double-leaf between the writing of the two leaves) by excision of a leaf and the insertion of folio 109 recopied. Each of the scribes was responsible for an irregular quire of ten (A for number 3 in the midst of the *KnT*, B for number 19 which contains a section of the G fragment). It is worth emphasizing that none of these irregularities reflects uncertainty about text. Cardigan derives from an already assembled set of exemplars. The two scribes apparently worked on it separately and were responsible, as Daniel Mosser has shown, for the corrections and for the "ex" marks that indicate proofreading. They developed as they worked on the manuscript the elements of organization and format that are present. The manuscript has no illumination at all. In this respect it resembles Ma made from the same set of exemplars as Cn some thirty years later. Ma does have a red and blue W for its initial capital and red and blue paraph marks on its first page. But though it leaves space for three-line ornamental initials at the beginning of about half the tales, no illumination or colored ink occurs after the first page. A manuscript on paper, it has running heads except in the *General Prologue*, gaps of two to five lines for *explicits* and *incipits* at the junctures, unobtrusive paraphs to mark rime royal stanzas, and a reasonably consistent set of indexing marginalia. That the set of exemplars for Cn and Ma remained intact for more than thirty years suggests that like the original a collection it was not a shop-copy but remained in private hands.

All of the a manuscripts adopt some of the special features introduced by Cambridge Dd. They include five passages added to the *Wife of Bath's Prologue* as well as the renumbering of husbands during the description of her fourth marriage that permits a spurious individualization of all five. The renumbering begins at D 452 (fourth to first) and ends with D 525 (fifth to fourth). The first added passage, perhaps cancelled by Chaucer when he developed the Wife's dialogue with the senile composite of her first three husbands, makes better sense with the renumbering of the Wife's husbands, most likely initiated by the Dd scribe-editor, but possibly copied from an already edited exemplar. This passage (D 44 a–f) illustrates again the consultation by Dd of more than a single exemplar of his text. The Dd scribe corrects his manuscript, but not the exemplar, to what is clearly a better reading, leaving the other a manuscripts the reading he had originally copied himself.

All the a manuscripts include the *Nun's Priest's* endlink. They all designate the Man of Law "Legis Periti" in the rubrics. They all include the Clerk's song without the indication so frequent in the manuscripts, "Envoy de Chaucer." They all have the information in the *incipit* that the *Physician's Tale* is without a prologue. All but Cardigan do the same with the *Second Nun's Tale*. The Cardigan editor, having extended the *Nun's Priest's* endlink into a prologue for the *Saint Cecilia*, not only included it in his manuscript with the rubric altered accordingly, but managed to insert the six lines he had composed into the set of exemplars later used by Manchester. The Manchester scribe included this six-

---

[8]   See Daniel Wayne Mosser's dissertation, "The Cardigan Chaucer Manuscript."

line "prologue" and copied as well the now inaccurate "without prologue" inherited through Cn from the exemplars for Dd. Further indication of a common heritage comes in the rubric for the *Retraction*. Here all the manuscripts except Dd, which breaks off in the midst of the *Canon's Yeoman's Tale*, leave out the phrase "of this book:" "Here takith the Maker his leve." Cambridge Dd shows every sign of resulting from an independent gathering together of exemplars under the influence of the Hengwrt operation, a collection which then became the basis for the other a manuscripts.[9]

---

[9] Mosser does a thorough study of rubrics in the Cardigan, as they relate to other *Canterbury Tales* mss. and especially as they relate to the other a mss. and Hg and El (pp. 106–35). He takes up the points made here (a copy in an earlier version had been sent to him). His study confirms the conclusions reached here (see Chapter 6, "Conclusions," pp. 136–41, especially 140f. See also Appendix C, pp. 163–77).

IV

The Four Manuscripts
Certainly Written Before 1440

The early history of the *Canterbury Tales* manuscripts should further take into account the four manuscripts certainly written before 1440, Cambridge Gg.4.27 (Gg), Petworth (Pw), Bodley 686 (Bo²), and Paris Anglais 39 (Ps). The most important of these manuscripts is the Cambridge Gg. Parkes and Beadle in their commentary for the facsimile edition suggest a much earlier date than Manly-Rickert; they lean toward a date before 1420.[1] Cambridge Gg is the first extant manuscript to include an extensive collection of Chaucer's works. Not only does it precede *Canterbury Tales* with *Troilus and Criseyde*, it also includes the *Legend of Good Women* and *Parlement of Foules*; it opens with some lyrics, the *ABC*, the *Envoy to Scogan*, the *Balade de Bone Conseyl*, and two non-Chaucerian lyrics; and it ends with Lydgate's *Temple of Glas*. No other fifteenth-century manuscript brings together so much of Chaucer's work. Furthermore the texts are comparatively unedited. The manuscript provides us with the unique copy of the revised Prologue to the *Legend of Good Women*. The *Envoy to Scogan* appears in only two other texts. As Manly-Rickert point out, the makers of the manuscript had access to "special sources".[2]

The dialect is East Anglian and the spelling has peculiarities that led Manly and Rickert to suggest the possibility that the scribe was Flemish or Dutch. Parkes and Beadle in the introduction to the facsimile compare carefully three repeated passages, and come to the conclusion that the scribe is translating into East Anglian as he produces the manuscript.[3] They further conclude that he

---

[1] M.B. Parkes and Richard Beadle, "Commentary," Vol. 3, "The Date," pp. 6ff. See Samuels, however, "Chaucer's Spelling." On p. 30 Samuels presents the evidence for an intermediate stage of copying between Hengwrt-Ellesmere and Cambridge Gg. See note 2, Chapter II (p. 8) for Samuels's later conclusion that Hg is six to ten years earlier than El.

[2] Manly-Rickert I: 179.

[3] M.B. Parkes and Richard Beadle, "Commentary," "Scribal Practices and Ortho-

worked over the manuscript for a considerable time, rereading and correcting the parts he had already written. The exemplars he used are many of them independent, and in a number of other instances closely associated with the texts used by Hengwrt and Ellesmere. No other manuscript is copied from Gg, but portions of the exemplars used by Gg provided text for such manuscripts as Jean d'Angoulême's Paris manuscript, the Douce d.4 fragment of the *Prologue*, the Sion manuscript in the D fragment, the fragments of Phillips 6750 (Ph[1]), and the latter portions of Harley 7333 (Ha[3]). The textual relationships suggest that Gg got the ordering of the text from Ellesmere rather than Cambridge Dd,[4] and that the exemplars the editor provided for the scribe had not been used before for a collection and did not remain together after their use by the scribe of Gg.[5]

Once elaborately illuminated, the manuscript has lost large sections of text at the beginnings and ends of tales. It had once a complete set of portraits of the pilgrims, which it used as did Ellesmere to illustrate the tales. The miniatures are cruder than Ellesmere and suggest like the text a provincial origin. The six pilgrims whose likenesses remain in the text – the Reeve, the Cook, the Wife of Bath, the Pardoner, the Monk, and the Manciple – show less attention on the part of the artist to Chaucer's *Prologue* descriptions than the Ellesmere illuminators and also considerably less skill, especially in the depiction of horses. Here, as in the ordering of the text and the textual affiliations, the relationship to the Hengwrt-Ellesmere operation appears fitful. The Gg editor got the idea of the portraits but none of the detail, just as he got the Ellesmere ordering and some exemplars closely related to or actually those used by Hengwrt and Ellesmere. He also restricted himself to the elements of text used by Ellesmere, including the *Host* stanza as well as the *Envoy* at the end of the *Clerk's Tale*, but not the *Man of Law's Epilogue* or the *Nun's Priest's Epilogue*. He includes all but four of the 26 lines in the *WBP* that Ellesmere adds to Hengwrt, but apparently did not have the six present in Dd and the other a manuscripts not in Ellesmere. On the other hand he did not use the Hengwrt-Ellesmere marginalia; he frequently used texts not used by other editors of collections. He had the original idea of collecting a number of the works of Chaucer in a single manuscript, he had his texts translated into an East Anglian dialect, and he went

graphy," 46–56; Manly-Rickert I: 176ff. Manly-Rickert acknowledge evidence assembled by Robert Caldwell, the basis for his article, "The Scribe of the Chaucer MS, Cambridge University Library Gg.4.27," *MLQ* 5 (1944): 33–44.

[4]   The text is not, as Parkes and Beadle say it is, p. 3, "the A text." Manly-Rickert call it "independent of the other manuscripts" in about half the text (M–R I: 175f). In the rest of the text it is most frequently closely associated with Ellesmere and Hengwrt. It represents, according to Manly-Rickert, "in the main, the El tradition without the El editing" (M–R I: 176).

[5]   A possible exception is the copytext for Phillipps 6750 (Ph[1]). The two fragments of 12 leaves each that survive include a sequence from the end of the *PdT* to the middle of the *Mel*, and the end of the *PsT* and the *Retraction*. All the text that survives derives from Gg. Ph[1] was once, in all probability, a big anthology, with space for more literature than Gg itself. Whether it was based on another copy of the exemplars used for Gg or a bundle of exemplars copied from them, whether all of Ph[1]'s text for the *Canterbury Tales* was Gg-derived, cannot be determined. All we can be sure of is that Gg-derived text survives in the two fragments.

beyond Ellesmere (and indeed all other editors of *Canterbury Tales* manuscripts) in his program of illustrations. He included in the *PsT* miniatures of the virtues and vices. He had at the beginning of the *Canterbury Tales* at least one full-page picture.[6]

Of the other three manuscripts, which according to Manly-Rickert were certainly written before 1440, two were what they term "pick-up" manuscripts. That is, they got their text from a variety of textual traditions. Bodley 686 (Bo[2], 1430–40) has a very mixed textual background with relationship in the different tales to "the large composite group," to *c*, to a, to Hengwrt, to Ellesmere, and to Cambridge Gg. The *Cook's Tale* in Bo[2] boasts the most elaborate conclusion to be found in the manuscripts, mixing in with heavily edited genuine lines sections of inept original verse and bringing the two riotous heroes to the satisfactory penalties of death and perpetual imprisonment. This conclusion, we can deduce from codicological evidence, constitutes a probable expansion of the text provided by the exemplar. The *CkT* starts with eighteen genuine lines, which fill out the penultimate folio of quire six. A different handwriting, which Manly-Rickert identify with the hand in some of Bo[2]'s corrections, then copies on the final leaf of the quire the eighty lines of the conclusion, starting out with a passage of inept rhetorical vituperation and ending with another of lame moral admonition to young men eager to improve on their humble origins. This last folio of the quire has ruling for forty-one lines to the page instead of the usual forty in order to accommodate the eighty lines of text and the *explicit* with the gap of a line between.[7] Presumably the editor noted the incompleteness of the *CkT* and had the scribe leave the final leaf of the quire blank while he

---

[6] Parkes and Beadle, "Commentary," "Illustration and Decoration," 58–62. They see clear evidence of one full page illustration and the possibility, as reported by Bradshaw, of a second (see also pp. 9f.). Parkes and Beadle raise the possibility of more than a single illuminator. The virtues and sins (*PsT*) are more skillfully done than the pilgrims. Richard Beadle kindly called my attention to a description of Gg in Urry's edition of Chaucer, which included, when he was shown it by Dr Jenkins, Master of St John's, Cambridge, "before it," "the picture of *Chaucer*, drawn by *Sir Thomas Occleve* on a leaf of his book, *De Regimine Principis*." Beadle points out that this could well have been a full-page picture at the beginning of the *Canterbury Tales*.

[7] Manly-Rickert list Bodley 686 as having thirty-nine lines to the page (M–R I: 65). This is true of the first page with its full vinet, and of folios 11–14, 17–24. The norm is 40. Folio 90b has four extra lines on the page, clearly below the final ruled line which always extends to the outer vertical lines for marginalia and paraphs. The four lines on 90b appear crowded; they bring to an end the *FrT*. The other exceptions are 55a and b with their forty-one lines. Manly Rickert, II: 169, give forty-four as the number of lines added to the *CkT*. A few lines are so altered as perhaps to qualify as new. But parts at least of all the forty remaining lines (after the eighteen on 54b) appear in the Bo[2] conclusion. The *CkT* in Bo[2] has a total of ninety-eight as opposed to the fifty-eight composed by Chaucer. The M–R list of the additions (I: 68) is also faulty. The hand that begins on 96 is not the one that adds the lines on f. 55; see the account under handwriting on I: 65. The lines on 55 start not with 4382, but with the six spurious lines following 4382; they continue as follows: 4383–88 plus eight; 4389–98 plus six; 4399–4410 plus four; 4411–12 plus four; and 4413–22 plus twelve. (M–R have 4390 instead of 4398 and leave out the final twenty-two lines.) In the chapter on glosses they omit the one in the *MLT* at 197 (III: 492).

arranged for a conclusion to be written. A further problem occurs after the *explicit*. Five ruled lines in an ink different from the normal rulings appear below the text. Similar ruling at the bottom of other pages provides for insertion in the text of lines originally omitted (eight lines on folio 84a, five lines on folio 17b, and four lines on folio 144b). Had the editor planned to add verses to his already padded conclusion? Or did he simply make a mistake? Single rulings with no text appear at the foot of folios 48b and 174b. We have here in any event a brace of anomalies. An editor who as we shall see brings the *Canterbury Tales* to no closure at all works hard to give the *CkT* a "suitable" ending. Readers who could afford superior craftsmanship had little sensitivity to the quality of Chaucer's verse.

Bodley 686 shows a curious connection with Cambridge Dd. It repeats the marginal joke of the Dd scribe-editor for the line in the *Merchant's Tale*, "If he be povre, she helpeth hym to swynke" (E1342). "Or to drynke," writes the Dd editor. "Vel drynke," echoes Bo², and goes on to write "vel Deus est" at line 1345: "Al that hire housbonde lust, hire liketh weel; / She seith nat ones 'nay' whan he seith 'ye' " (E 1344–45), implying perhaps that the husband is her God. This relationship with Dd may account for the ordering of the manuscript to the point at the end of *Sir Thopas* and the prologue of the *Melibeus* – the Ellesmere-a ordering – that with no warning breaks off. Instead of *Mel*, the *MkT*, and the *NPT*, occurs the rubric: "Here endeth Chaucers tale and begynneth a lytel tretys of the Crowe." The *Manciple's Tale* follows, without *Prologue*, but with a running head throughout the tale that assigns it to Lydgate. No mention of the Manciple occurs at the end either: "here endeth the tale of the Crowe / and here begynneth the Nonnes Tale." At folio 184v this beautifully appointed and thoroughly controlled manuscript brings the *Canterbury Tales* to an end without fanfare: "Here endeth the Nonnes tale of the storye of the blessed lyfe and Martirdome of the glorious Virgine and Martir Seynte Cecile translated into englysse tonge." Two lines only separate this *explicit* from the following *incipit*: "Here begynneth a lytel Tretis made and compyled in Balade be Dan John Lydgate Monke of Bury of al the kynges that hath regned sethen Wylliam Conqueror." At the top of this and the following pages occurs again the running head, "Lydgate."

Manly-Rickert detect the possibility of three handwritings in Bo². The two changes would occur at the end of quires, with the new scribe taking over at the beginning of 13 (folio 96) in the midst of the *Summoner's Tale*, and at the beginning of 22 (folio 167) in the fourth stanza of the *Prioress's Prologue*. No sudden changes in format occur, though the manuscript shows slight steady increments in the richness of its decoration. Vertical lines throughout provide space for the text, for marginalia on both sides of the text, and for flourished paraphs that help articulate both text and marginalia. Though a full vinet with a miniature of a man standing in the initial W sets off the first page of the *General Prologue*, only champs mark both prologues and tales, until folio 86b, where the *Friar's Tale* has a demi-vinet. From then on the demi-vinets appear for all but two of the tales, the champs for the prologues and subdivisions. Display script distinguishes the headings and running heads throughout. Almost from the beginning (folio 15b) ascenders in the first line of a page extend above normal height; when the second scribe takes over, they develop more intricately, sometimes to the extent of four or five in a single line (97b), reaching to the level of the running heads (117b), and occasionally elaborated into designs (120b). Paraphs mark each of the rime royal stanzas, but not until the *Prioress's Tale* does a one-line space separate them. It is worth stressing that this change, though it occurs on the first folio of the third scribe's stint (167a), precedes by two tales or a full quire the abandonment of the Ellesmere-a ordering. Except for loss of leaves there is no irregularity in the quiring.

What happened? An editor who up to this point had experienced no difficulty in acquiring exemplars and who had as model a manuscript with an Ellesmere-a arrangement of the text would surely have been able to get exemplars of more than two of the seven tales remaining. The end of the B² fragment and the *Parson's Prologue* and *Tale* had been among the more easily acquired sections of the *Canterbury Tales*. The editor appears to have lost interest at the point where he was faced with a long tale in prose. He gives no sign of uncertainty, no evidence of making any special effort. He allows the *Canterbury Tales* to dwindle to a close with the "Tale of the Crow," which he attributes to Lydgate, and the "Nun's Tale of Saint Cecilia," which he recognizes as a translation. He does not even acknowledge that the great collection of stories has come to an end. He gives us no clue for his motives.

A similar quixotism marks the Paris manuscript, made during his years of captivity in England for Jean d'Angoulême. Here the motives are clear. Jean finds the *Squire's Tale* "valde absurda" after 28 lines and the *Monk's* "valde dolorosa" after 32. He has them both terminated. He also disliked the *Canon's Yeoman's Tale* and took similar measures with it. Manly-Rickert surmise that he was unable to find a copy of the *Melibeus*. He certainly left space for it in his manuscript, two blank double-columned pages (180 lines) at the end of an irregular quire (ten instead of twelve leaves). But since the *Parson's Prologue* and *Tale* are also missing, it is at least as likely that he purposely had the prose tales left out. He also omitted without comment the *Cook's Prologue* and *Tale* and most of *Sir Thopas*. He apparently used as model a manuscript with the Ellesmere-a ordering. The only deviation has the *CIT* preceding the D fragment rather than following it. This deviation coincides with a second quire-irregularity in the manuscript, a 14-leaf quire that includes the *MLPT*, the *CIT* and the beginning of the *WBP*. Jean d'Angoulême's influence, evident throughout the manuscript, extends to personal correction of the text. His 300 corrections, made "without regard of the look of the MS" (M–R I: 402), are well over double the number by the scribe, who names himself Duxwurth in a note at the end of the manuscript. Written on paper in double columns, with little room for decoration and with a text constantly changing textual affiliation, the book suggests commitment on the part of its original owner over a long period of time, during which he acquired exemplars, read and reread, corrected and emended, and even added in one instance verses of his own composition (after A 3208). His influence perhaps extended to the tendency not to use capital letters at the beginnings of lines. Even more clearly than in the Bo² editor's "Lydgate" as running title for the "Tale of the Crow", the Paris manuscript reflects the taste of a contemporary reader.[8]

---

[8] For a full account of Jean d'Angoulême and the Paris manuscript, see Martin Crow,

The only manuscript that definitely uses a number of Paris exemplars is the Harley 1239 (Ha[1]) with its collection of five. Some one, possibly Jean himself, who had found the *Knight's Tale* "valde bona", picked out the exemplars for the *KnT*, the *MLT*, the *WBT*, the *CIT*, and the *FkT* and kept them together over a period of years. If it was Jean, he must have given them away or lost track of them, for when he returned to France, they were left behind and were copied out sometime after 1450 by a man who called himself in a Latin colophon the hermit of Greenwich. The result is unique among *Canterbury Tales* manuscripts. Elongated and narrow Ha[1] could have been designed as a "holster book" for traveling (M–R I: 191). It contains in addition, before the five *Canterbury Tales*, a much more professionally written *Troilus and Criseyde*, the product of three scribes doing fairly equal stints. The drop in skill and handwriting with the beginning of the *Knight's Tale* is unmistakable. The scribe makes no mention of the *Canterbury Tales*, and in fact leaves out the first 34 lines of the *Knight's Tale*, beginning with "This duke of whom I make mencioun" (A 893). That this did not result from an accidental loss of text reveals itself in other omissions of frame material – the introduction of the *Man of Law's Tale*, the prologue of the *Clerk's Tale*, and the link for the *Franklin's Tale*. In all probability the hermit-scribe was not responsible for restoring the *Clerk's Tale* to its position after the *Wife of Bath's*. That "correction" would have more logically resulted from Jean's demonstrably assiduous reading of the Paris manuscript. The hermit's intention in Ha[1], to bring together a number of courtly narratives and present them to some powerful noble, finds expression, however inadequately, in the florid eloquence of the already noted colophon, where the prospective patron is addressed, "Vestre magnifice et generossissime dominacionis ..."

The last of the manuscripts certainly written before 1440 (see Plate 3), Petworth (Pw), has peculiarities in its ordering which reflect a combination of carelessness and attention to detail. The oldest manuscript of the ₫ family to survive, it has the B[2] section of its text broken up, with the *Shipman's Tale* and the *Prioress's Tale* following *Gamelyn* and preceding the *Man of Law's Tale*. The rest of the manuscript agrees with the normal ₫ ordering. The *explicits* and *incipits* at the junctures, at the end of *Gam*, at the end of the *PrT*, at the end of the *PdT*, where the *Prologue* to the *Thopas* opens with response to the *PrT*, have only one slight irregularity, which betrays haste or impatience rather than uncertainty. This comes at the beginning of the *ShT*, where the line of the *incipit* precedes the line for the *explicit*. The fact that the *and* at the end of the

---

"Jean of Angoulême and his Chaucer Mansucript," *Speculum* 17 (1942): 86–99. He dates the manuscript as most likely written between 1422 and 1430 (p. 86 and 88n.4). In discussing the relationship with Ha[1] (p. 98), he does not take note of the long interval in time between the two manuscripts. His explanation of the shifting textual relationships in the two manuscripts sees them as dependent on a manuscript prepared in a shop where multiple exemplars of passages were available and scribes shifted at will from one to another in their copying. For references to Crow's work on the dialect of the scribe, corrections by the scribe and Jean, and variants of the manuscript, see the footnotes in the *Speculum* article. His University of Chicago dissertation (1934) was entitled *Scribal Habits in the Paris Manuscript of the Canterbury Tales*. The scribe's first name John comes to us from a note at the end of the Tabula Capitulorum in *Dialogus Anselmi*, Bibliothèque Nationale, fonds Latin 3436 (M–R I: 403).

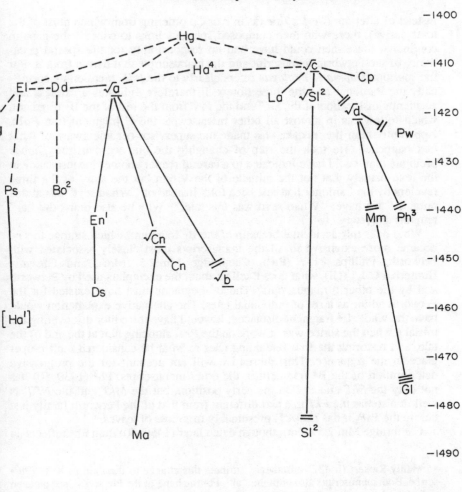

PLATE 3

explicit remains in the text, a dangling connective, indicates that the scribe was copying rather than composing the rubrics and carelessly got the second one first. The rest of this elaborately illuminated manuscript shows a beautifully ordered text with ruled space for marginalia, with the *explicits* and *incipits* in rubric within the text invariably taking up two lines, and with only occasional inconsistencies in the running titles and the handling of the stanzaic verse.

The image of the scribe copying from material he had no part in composing or ordering finds confirmation in the details of his text. Those who gathered the texts together that make up the d exemplar, those who devised the d ordering, deciding to move the *Merchant's Tale* to a position before the *Wife of Bath* instead of after the *Clerk's Tale* (as in *c* or Cp ordering from which most of the texts derive), those who then composed spurious links to conceal the gaps in continuity, these men could have had no responsibility for the special peculiarity of the Petworth manuscript and the manuscripts that derive from it. For the spurious *Shipman's Prologue* refers clearly to the *PdT*, mentioning specifically the Pardoner and the three rioters. It therefore indicates a careless and accidental dislocation of the *ShT* and the *PrT* from the rest of the B² fragment, which follows as in almost all other manuscripts the C fragment (the *PdT*). Apparently after the mistake was made the supervisor became aware of what had happened. He took the step of changing the one word in the *Thopas* prologue that would have indicated to a careful reader another inconsistency in the text, namely that not the miracle of the Virgin but the story of the three revelers by the Pardoner had just been told. Instead of "Whan seyd was al this miracle," we have, "Whan seyd was this tale."⁹ Why he also omits the "al" remains a mystery.

What does this accidental breakup of the B² fragment, which strange to say, became more extensive in all the manuscripts most closely associated with Petworth, Phillips 8137 (Ph³), Cambridge Mm.2.5 (Mm), and Glasgow Hunterian U.1.1 (Gl), what does it tell us about the exemplars used by Petworth and by the other d manuscripts? The B² fragment must have existed for the Petworth editor as a set of individual tales. The alternative explanation would have the whole B² fragment displaced; it would have the editor discovering the mistake when the scribe was at work on the *PrT*, stopping him at the end of the tale, and restoring the four remaining tales to what he considered their proper place in the sequence. This alternative will not account for the progressive deterioration of the B² fragment in the other manuscripts. Ph³ (1430–50) has not only the *ShT* and *PrT* in the early position, but the *MkT* and the *NPT* as well. It also has the *FkT* in a text different from that of the Petworth family just before the *PsP*; it has no *McT*, presumably from loss of leaves.¹⁰

Cambridge Mm.2.5 (Mm), though dated later (1450–60) than Ph³ reflects an

---

⁹ Manly-Rickert (I: 432) mistakenly attribute this change to the Phillips 8137 (Ph³) scribe. Both manuscripts also omit the "al". For the hand of the Ph³ scribe, see plate on p. 6 of Anderson, *Sixty Bokes Olde and Newe*. The manuscript is described on pp. 5–7.
¹⁰ The *McPT* were almost certainly present in Ph³ originally, though not a trace of them remains in the manuscript as we have it. The text skips from F 1406 in the *FkT* to I 515 in the *PsT*, the gap being caused by the loss of three quires. Superficially it might appear that there is no room for the *Manciple* segment. The 216 lines remaining in the *FkT*, the 362 lines of the *McPT*, and the seventy-four lines of the *PsP*, with an allowance of two lines each for the four junctures, would take up a total of sixteen and a half pages, leaving thirty-one and a half for the 441 lines of *PsT* prose. But at the rate of twenty-five lines per folio for *Parson's Tale* prose, derived from the fifteen leaves of the *Parson's Tale* present in the manuscript, we would need 17.64 leaves or 35.28 pages, almost four more than would be available. It turns out, however, that the line numbering of the *Parson's Tale* prose, erratic at best, changes rather drastically in the course of the work. At I 166 and again at I 286, the average of what is included in a line increases. The average for a leaf over the passage in question, I 75–514, would have been more than twenty-five lines per leaf and would just have fitted the space available.

earlier stage of the dislocations associated with the Pw family. As study of the quire makeup reveals (M–R I: 367f.), those responsible for ordering Mm decided midway through the copying of the *Man of Law's Tale* to insert the *MkT* (*e* of the B^2 fragment) between the *PrT* and the *MLT*. The *NPT*, also separated from B^2 (as in Ph^3), turns up immediately after the *FkT*. The rationale of those responsible is difficult to recover. Both the *Monk's Prologue* with its references to Melibeus and Prudence and the *Nun's Priest's Prologue* that starts with the Knight's interruption of the Monk's tragedies reveal their proper places in the B^2 sequence after *Thopas* and *Melibeus*. Yet the Mm supervisor seeing the two tales adrift goes to some trouble to insert the *MkT* after the *PrT*, and finds a place for the *NPT*, not after the *Monk's* where it clearly belongs but after the *FkT*. The only other deviation on the part of Mm from the Pw set of exemplars involved the substitution of a text for the *SuT* more closely associated with ḏ than the one used by both Pw and Ph^3.

Ph^3 dependence on the Mm ordering seems clear. The supervisor detected not the proper place for the *ShT* and the *Monk's Tale* but the position for the *Nun's Priest's Tale* after the *Monk's Tale*. His care resulted in the first two and last two of the tales in the B^2 fragment occurring in sequence after *Gam* and before the *Man of Law*. The fragility of the set of exemplars used by the Pw family finds confirmation in Ph^3's loss of most of the *FkT*, which as we have seen appears just before the *Parson's Prologue* in a text independent not only of the Pw family but of ḏ as well. This text has the regular *Sq–Fk* link to introduce it and 572 lines of link, prologue, and tale before reverting to a ḏ tradition for 72 lines. At line F 1406, the end of the quire, the manuscript breaks off, to resume some three gatherings later with line 515 of the *PsT*. Evidence for the use of a single set of exemplars by Pw, Mm, and Ph^3 involves not only the Pw textual tradition and the progressive displacement of the tales in the B^2 fragment but also the sharing of a set of linking passages which in one instance, the variants in the *Thopas* prologue, are peculiar to the three, and in another instance, the *Cl–Fk* link, are peculiar to Pw and Mm because by the time Ph^3 came to be copied the exemplar for the *Franklin's Tale* had to be replaced. There is in addition the presence in the three manuscripts of a curious numbering system for the tales, that originated in the *c* text. Pw shows discretion in the use of the numbers, copying only those where the differences in ḏ from the *c* ordering and its own displacement of the two tales in B^2 will not show as inconsistent. For instance the scribe wrote the word "Cap" for the *PrT* but no number. But Mm and Ph^3 betrayed their inattention by going on to copy the number "xviii," appropriate to the *c* position for the *Prioress* but not to its place in the Pw family where it is the sixth tale. Mm has five other numbers appropriate to the *c* ordering rather than its own out of a total of eight. Ph^3 confines itself to only the one.[11]

---

[11] The numbering in Cp is most extensive. It involves 12 tales. Blake, *The Textual Tradition*, p. 97, feels this numbering reflects a different attitude toward the work as a whole, chapters replacing the "link-tale formula found in Hg." Thus *Gam* fills out "the Cook's chapter"; it does not receive a number of its own. The other manuscripts with the Cp numberings, beside the Pw family, are Fitzwilliam McClean 181 (Fi) with two out of the three numberings wrong and Sloane 1685 (Sl^1), which numbers only the

After Mm and Ph³ the Pw set of exemplars apparently broke up. But contact with the Pw tradition continued to have somewhat the same effect as partaking of the insane root. Many years later in 1476 a father-and-son team named Geoffrey and Thomas Spirleng completed their work on Glasgow Hunterian U.1.1 (Gl). They had used Mm as their copytext through the Pardoner's interruption of the *Wife of Bath's Prologue* (D192). They then turned to a manuscript closely associated with Rawlinson Poetry 223 (Ra³) which had an even more dislocated ordering. When they came to the end of the *Retraction*, they discovered that though they had done two versions of the *Shipman's* and *Prioress's Tales*, they had left out two others. They returned to the still available Mm for the text of the *Clerk's Tale* and the *Canon's Yeoman's Tale*.

What motivated their shift from Mm in the midst of the *Wife's Prologue*? A possible answer occurs when one considers the group of manuscripts to which Ra³ belongs. These manuscripts, easily recognizable, all employ elongated miniscules for the first words of prologues and tales and have programs of illumination more elaborate than Mm. Written in the third quarter of the fifteenth century, some of them by the "hooked g scribe", they include Ds, Trinity College Cambridge R.3.3 (Tc¹), and the Clumber Gower (Lyell 31). If, as seems likely, the manuscript used by Gl as copytext belonged to this same group, sharing with Ra³ exemplars and a wildly irregular ordering, the Spirlengs' motivation in shifting to it is plain. They were responding to the imposing format; they felt the change was to a manuscript of greater authority. None of those responsible for the Pw family over its span of fifty years saw fit to restore the first two tales of the B² fragment to the position indicated in the spurious *Shipman's Prologue*. The story of Pw reflects the d editors' desire to make a book of the *Canterbury Tales* by bridging every gap in the text, yet it ended by producing seventy-five years after Chaucer's death a manuscript with the ordering, A X B²ᵃᵇᵉ B¹ Fᵃ Eᵇ D Gᵃ Cᵇ H B²ᶜᵈᶠ Cᵃ B²ᵃᵇ Fᵇ I R Eᵃ Gᵇ. (See Plate 3 for relationships of the manuscripts so far discussed.)

KnT. Royal 17 D.XV (Ry¹) carries a Roman numeral system of its own as rubric running heads.

V

The d̲ Family of Manuscripts

The d̲ family, including the Petworth subdivision, has the closest connections with the c̲ manuscripts. In fact d̲ uses Corpus exemplars for all but the following sections: the larger portion of the *Knight's Tale* from A 1740 through the first half of the *Miller's Tale* to line A 3480, the *Clerk's Prologue* and *Tale*, the first 400 and the final 100 lines of the *Merchant's Tale*, the last eighty lines of the *Franklin's Tale*, the *Pardoner's Prologue* and *Tale*, and the first 200 lines of the *Shipman's Tale*. These exceptions add up to two full tales, sizable portions of four more, and a small part of one. In addition some of the d̲ manuscripts split off in most of the *Summoner's Tale* and the *Monk's Tale*:

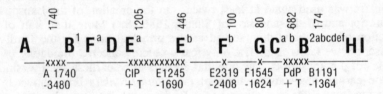

Underline = c̲ and d̲ closely related   xxxx = c̲ and d̲ clearly separate.

In SuT and MkT part of the d̲ family is separate.

Numbers above represent the number of lines in each of the separate passages.

This pattern suggests that quires in the middle of the A fragment were lost, that the D fragment was damaged at the end, that the E–F, C, and B² tales were separate, and that the B² fragment was damaged at the beginning. The Corpus was the first extant manuscript to have the tales numbered. This numbering survived, as we have seen, in the Pw family and two other manuscripts.[1] It no doubt helped to preserve the c̲ arrangement in the d̲ texts. Since the d̲ manu-

---

[1] Fitzwilliam McClean 181 (Fi) and Sl¹, which has only *KnT* numbered. Royal 17 D.XV (Ry¹) develops its own system.

scripts used many of the exemplars previously gathered together in the set employed by the c scribes, the assembly of the d exemplars must have occurred after the break-up of c, in other words after the copying of La and the ancestor of Sl². The only change the d editor made in the ordering was to move the *Merchant's Tale* from a position after the *Clerk's Tale* to one between the *Squire's Tale* and the *Wife of Bath's Prologue*. Manly-Rickert attribute the change to the discovery of the *Squire-Franklin* link adapted as in Hg to the *Squire-Merchant* connection (M–R II: 485). Mrs Dempster agrees and attributes much of the c ordering to the influence of the Hengwrt manuscript.[2] Both see the d family as radiating from the $/d$ exemplar into four constant groups and three single manuscripts, as in Plate 4.

In accounting for the peculiarities of Corpus and the c text, for its lack of links and its wide textual affiliations, Manly-Rickert implied another stemma – an $/c$, which was incomplete before Corpus was made from it and to which are attributed the positioning of the linkless tales of the E–F fragments, an $/cd$ behind both $/c$ and a later derived $/d$ to account for the fact that Corpus's texts are closely related not only to the small family of c but also to most of the text behind the much larger family of d manuscripts. Whether there should also be added an $/b*cd$ to account for the fact that "$/c$ was itself derived from the same sources as $/d$ and $/b$ and others" is not clear. (See Plate 4)

Fortunately there is a simpler way of accounting for the resemblances than this elaborate stemma that assumes a number of collected texts behind Corpus 198, derived from one another, but in the instance of $/cd$ more complete than Cp and surviving in other manuscripts much later than Cp in the more complete form. The Corpus editor made an independent effort to collect the tales and groups of tales into a complete collection of the *Canterbury Tales*. He used the same pool of fragments available to the other early editors. His collection of exemplars was used again at least twice – in the creation of the Lansdowne manuscript and of the ancestor of Sloane 1686 (Sl²) More than half of his collection of exemplars then served as the principal basis for the family of manuscripts we know as d. The only real problem concerns the dating of the families of d manuscripts. The one that appears to be earliest, the Pw, since it has the earlier, non-stanzaic form of the *Clerk-Franklin* link, shows in its derivation from $/d$ the breakdown of the B² fragment. We have already seen in the relationship of the d tradition to the c slight indications that the B² fragment was not entirely secure. Three of the other d manuscripts will be seen to be missing text in the B² fragment, and all the others have at least some part of the B² fragment from a non-d tradition. But the three other families and the three separate manuscripts in the d group, later on palaeological evidence than Pw as well as in their use of the revised, now almost wholly spurious link, show no signs of the special break-up of the B² fragment associated with Pw.

The evidence strongly suggests two sets of exemplars, $/d$ and $/d'$, the second

---

[2] Germaine Dempster, "A Chapter," and "Fifteenth Century Editors." As Mrs Dempster points out, M–R are not entirely consistent, attributing the order in E and F sometimes to arrangement of the tales before obtaining the links (II: 489; I: 275). At II: 485, M–R attribute the position of *MeT* in d to "discovery" of the adapted link. See *PMLA* 63 (1948), p. 473 n.57.

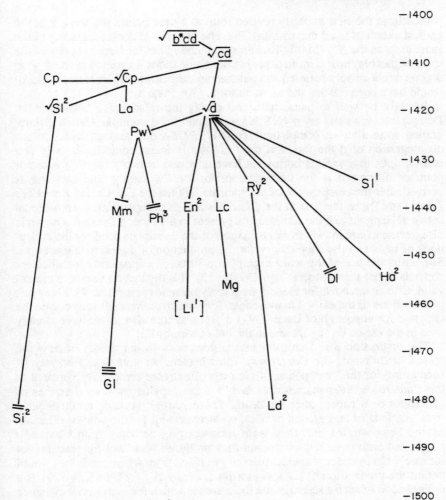

PLATE 4

copied from the first in partly revised form at a time before the writing of the earliest extant of the d manuscripts, Pw. The fact that /d contained many of the same texts as the /Cp (Manly-Rickert say /c and /d are for large sections of the text inseparable) makes more plausible the dislocations it suffered as the /Pw. /d was no doubt a badly battered and patched up collection of exemplars, while /d' would have been fresher and more uniform. (See Plate 5)

It might be well to pause here and clarify the relationship between Mrs. Dempster's views and my own. She agrees that "the d exemplar started disintegrating soon after its completion" (p. 447, *PMLA* 63), and attributes to the disintegration of d the fact that the "link-set is found complete in only two manuscripts, that various borrowers have only one or two." (p. 483) A minor point of difference is the time element for the Pw family. She sees Pw as derived after the composition of the stanzaic link for the *Clerk's* and *Franklin's Tales*. I see Pw as the first of the d families and the couplet link as transitional between Hengwrt and the stanzaic link present in the other d families. Our main disagreements are in two areas, the nature of the exemplars used for the collections of tales and the shop theory for the production of the early manuscripts. She limits the use of the word exemplar to "Mss . . . apparently intended for copyists rather than readers." (p. 459, fn. 12) This distinction seems to me not valid. Copies intended for readers frequently became exemplars. We know this is true of one of the early d manuscripts, Ry^2, which as we shall see became the copytext for almost all of Laud 739 (Ld^2). It was true also as we have already seen in the use of En^1 by Ds and in the use of Mm by Gl.

The distinction Mrs Dempster makes goes back to her theory of how the textual tradition of the *Canterbury Tales* became so complex. Her way of accounting for the "compound of pictures, of extreme complexity" present in the *Canterbury Tales* manuscripts involved the copying by several scribes of Chaucer's own papers after his death. These scribes worked simultaneously from single tales and groups of tales, no arrangement for the whole collection having been worked out; they were soon copying not only from Chaucer's papers but each other's copies; what they produced was "not for readers, not for sale", but intended "as exemplars to be copied from when conditions would permit the preparation of *CT* manuscripts for readers." (*MLN* 63, p. 329) The unlikelihood of such a scenario and the extent to which the manuscript evidence itself did not support it were taken up in my article, "Early Manuscripts," pp. 104–110. Mrs Dempster's theory cannot accommodate the two important elements in the early history of the *Canterbury Tales* previously noted as tests for any theory – the Hengwrt manuscript and the disparate numbers of textual traditions for the different parts of the work. If the scribal activity she envisaged had occurred, the history of the early manuscripts would have been quite different: The Hengwrt editor would have had no difficulty finding exemplars for the links and the tales, and he would surely have taken the trouble to plan his collection in advance. Furthermore the scribal activity would have produced a relatively equal number of independent textual traditions for the different parts of the *Canterbury Tales*. Mrs Dempster's theory leads her to emphasize copytexts as a whole rather than the collections of exemplars the history of the d families would seem to require.

Mrs Dempster and Manly-Rickert assumed that many of the early *Canter-*

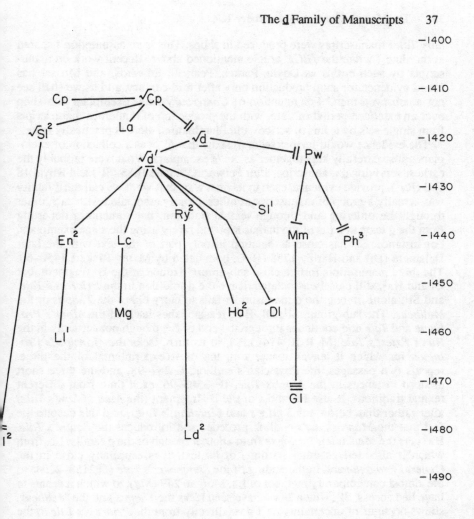

PLATE 5

bury Tales manuscripts were produced in shops. This is an assumption I shared at the time I wrote the *JEGP* article mentioned above. Recent work on manuscripts by such critics as Doyle, Parkes, Pearsall, Edwards, and Mosser has found evidence for shop production only after mid-century, and as we shall see not much even then.[3] For retention of *Canterbury Tales* exemplars in a shop over an extended period of time, with the production of numerous manuscripts from single sets by teams of scribes and illuminators, there is practically none.

The evidence would further seem to show that /d' was a collection of exemplars not so carefully kept together as the /a exemplars. What were probably the earliest surviving d manuscripts after Petworth, Sloane 1685 (Sl[1]) and Royal 18 C.II (Ry[2]), provide evidence, each in its own way, that what we call the d family was actually a group of manuscript families, closely associated with each other through the ordering and through textual tradition, but sometimes departing from the d texts in parts of the manuscript and rarely using the same exemplars. For instance, Sl[1] has close association in only part of the text with the later Delamere (Dl) and Harley 1758 (Ha[2]), both dated by Manly-Rickert 1450–60. The three manuscripts form a close sub-group in much of the B[2] fragment, but Dl and Ha[2], still closely associated, leave the d tradition in the *Prioress's Tale*, and Sl[1], alone among the d manuscripts fails to carry either the *Thopas* or the *Melibeus*. The sub-group, Sl[1], Dl, Ha[2], reestablishes itself in the *Monk's Prologue* and *Tale* and continues through the end of B[2], though not certainly in the *Nun's Priest's Tale* (M–R II: 414f.). Dl, in its turn, lacks the *Manciple's Prologue*, for which it leaves space, and, the most experimental of the three, repeats two passages, the Physician's endlink, C 287–98, and the three short modern instances in the *Monk's Tale*, B[2] 3565–96, each time from different textual traditions. It also has most of the B[1] fragment (the *Man of Law's Tale*) after rather than before the *Squire's* and *Merchant's Tales*, and this despite the fact that the *Man of Law's* endlink precedes and introduces the *Squire's Tale*. Ha[2] gets the *Manciple's Prologue* from another branch of the d family, Lc, from which it also derives other portions of its text. It is especially close in the *General Prologue* and in the ending of the *Summoner's Tale* (D 2158–2294) to the almost contemporary member of Lc, Morgan 249 (Mg), to which it seems to have had access. Sl[1], which as we have seen lacks the *Thopas* and the *Melibeus*, shows no signs of uncertainty as it goes directly from the *Prioress's Tale* to the *Monk's Prologue*, despite the Host's reference to Melibeus's wife Prudence. In fact Sl[1] has no gaps, and though it lost many leaves shows no irregularities in quire make-up. It breaks off twenty-two lines from the end of the *Nun's Priest's Tale*, at the end of a quire, an estimated six quires (M–R I: 504) having been lost. Apparently the text was assembled in advance, and one scribe, the third or fourth to work on it, was responsible for all but the first sixty-two of the 223 folios. Modestly decorated, the manuscript has champs but no demi-vinets; it has for the most part rubricated running titles, *explicits*, and *incipits*, and

---

[3] For the classic statement on *Canterbury Tales* manuscripts in general, see Doyle and Parkes, "The Production of Copies," pp. 196–203. For a more recent assessment, see Edwards and Pearsall, "The Manuscripts", pp. 257–278 in Griffiths and Pearsall, *Book Production*. Mosser shows in "The Two Scribes" that Cardigan is not, as M–R say it is (I: 72), shop-produced.

marginalia. In format reasonably uniform, it has always a well-ruled page and a professional controlled handwriting, with running titles (a few of them mistaken) and never more than two lines for the rubrics at the junctures. Nothing in the text suggests incompleteness; each tale has what the manuscript terms a prologue, sometimes as in the *Wife of Bath's* and the *Second Nun's* not actually a link, sometimes when a link, spurious, as in the *Canon's Yeoman-Physician* and the *Pardoner-Shipman* links, sometimes contradictory as in the *Prioress-Monk* link with references to a preceding *Tale* not in the manuscript.

Ry^2 resembles Sl^1 in its modest appearance, with only champs for decoration and with running heads, *explicits* and *incipits* in red. Its pages have not quite the same controlled appearance for both ruling and handwriting as do Sl^1's, and almost every page has in the top line at least one extended, highly decorated ascender. Ry^2 and Sl^1 were probably the earliest surviving *Canterbury Tales* manuscripts with the text written by more than a single scribe.[4] As in Sl^1 one of the scribes did most of the work. The change of hand in Ry^2 does not occur until the *Parson's Prologue*, where, as Manly-Rickert deduce from the quire make-up (M–R I: 485), the second scribe fitted the first quire of an already written *Parson's Tale* into the quire in which the *Manciple's Tale* had come to an end. The text of Ry^2 has almost all the links developed by the d editors, and includes one to connect the *MeT* to the *WBP* present in only two other later manuscripts. It lacks the *McP*, also missing in the later Dl and as we shall see in the almost contemporary En^2. It lacks as well the comments of the Friar and Summoner at the end of the *Wife's Prologue*, and at the end of the *SuT*, the visit of the angry friar to the lord's house. The text is d through the *MeT*, but departs from the d tradition in the *WBPT* and in the first part of the *FkT* (to F 1050); in the last three tales of B^2 and in the *McT* Ry^2's close relationship with another d manuscript, Egerton 2863 (En^2) includes a 361-line segment (B^2 2748–3108) where the pair leaves its d tradition and associates itself with the group of manuscripts that includes Ellesmere, the a group, Gg, and Ad^3.

Evidence that Ry^2 served as exemplar in the copying of Laud 739 (Ld^2) some forty-five years later raises some interesting questions. The Ld^2 scribe copied mindlessly the Ry^2 text for folios 69–72, where the two central sheets of the quire were reversed, ignoring the notes at the bottom of each verso that gave the proper order. Since the Ld^2 scribe has a smaller folio of thirty-three lines to the page as opposed to Ry^2's forty to forty-two, he produced a text that breaks continuity five times at intervals of eighty lines, all in mid-page, making nonsense of a ten-page segment of the *MLPT*. As in Ry^2, a scribe or editor made an effort to unscramble the situation with instructions in the margin for turning forward or back a number of pages to the line with a special mark by it. Ld^2 also followed Ry^2 in leaving out, as no other manuscript does, the comments of Friar and Summoner at the end of the *Wife's Prologue*. Manly-Rickert attribute the omission, peculiar to these two manuscripts, to a twenty-eight-line eye-skip (M–R I: 317) from "wol heere" on D 828 to "wol heere" on D 856, presumably on the part of the Ry^2 scribe. Ld^2 also copies Ry^2's sixteen-line *Merchant-*

---

[4] Probably contemporary was Bo^2. Slightly later were the second a manuscript En^1, Lincoln 110 = A.4.18 (Ln), Additional 25718 (Ad^2), and Phillips 8137 (Ph^3). Lichfield 2 (Lc) and Cardigan (Cn) were later still.

Wife of Bath link, the only manuscript other than Bw to do so. The failure of the Ld² scribe to use the Ry² text for the first 531 lines of the *General Prologue* and for 1165 lines from E 298 in the *Clerk's Tale* to F 944 in the immediately following *Franklin's Tale* is most puzzling. Manly-Rickert call these passages one quire and two quires respectively. But the first is more than one hundred lines short of the first quire in Ry² and even more of the first quire in Ld² (which has quires of twelve). The second passage comes closer to the requisite quire length, but is still short. Furthermore, it is more than one hundred lines longer than double the length of the first passage. For some reason a scribe started copying the *General Prologue* of the *Canterbury Tales* from an exemplar closely related to the one used by Ad³. After 531 lines he shifted to Ry², almost contemporary with Ad³, which he continued to copy for the rest of the manuscript that survives (through B² 2056, fifty-two lines from the end of the *Thopas*) with the single exception of a passage that starts in mid-stanza 298 lines into the *Clerk's Tale* and ends at a point in the *Franklin's Tale*, where Aurelius's love for Dorigen is first being described. This passage, some 1165 lines in Ry², has text in Ld² derived from the same exemplar as Ry¹ through most of the *Clerk's Tale*. It omits the Clerk's address to the Wife of Bath (E 1170–76), includes the Clerk's Song without the common designation "Envoie de Chaucer" and with the ordering that has the "archewyves" stanza (E 1195–1200) at the end; in these features the two manuscripts agree (though from different textual traditions); Ld² omits the Host stanza present in Ry² and includes (as does Ry²) the fourteen-line d link to the *Franklin's Tale* with the cd* text. The motivation for the abandonment of Ry² for approximately three quires must have some special explanation. We have the Ry² manuscript, as presumably the scribes and editors of Ld² did. The two passages in Ry² show no apparent justification for the failure to copy them. Possibly three quires survived from an earlier manuscript and led the owner to repair the damage to his manuscript by having the scribe copy from Ry² except in the passages that survived. The Ld² omits Ry²'s *explicits* and *incipits*; it has running titles and spaces for capital letters, some of which have been penned in with flourish, some of which have only a small-letter indication of what the capital should be.

Clearly the two early d manuscripts Ry² and Sl¹ were not copied from the same set of exemplars. Though the ordering is constant, these manuscripts and the manuscripts later copied that were most closely related to them lack different portions of the text with no indication that the omissions were noticed. Shifts take place in textual tradition within the d family and occasionally outside in an arbitrary way. Anomalies occur as in the copying of Ld² from Ry² for which no entirely plausible explanation can be given. Yet Sl¹ was owned by Sir Thomas Neville with close connections to Chaucer's granddaughter and niece, and Ry² belonged to people closely connected with the Nevilles, perhaps Sir Thomas's aunt, Anne Neville, Duchess of Buckingham (M–R I: 489ff. and 509).

Egerton 2863 (En²), which we have already seen as having close textual associations with Ry² in the *Melibeus*, the *Monk's*, the *Nun's Priest's*, and the *Manciple's Tales*, shares the 361-line departure from the d tradition at the end of the *Melibeus*. Originally a more elaborate manuscript, it has lost the demi-vinets that once illuminated the beginnings of the tales, and it never had room for the *McP*. Like some of the other d manuscripts, its exemplars lacked the end of the *SuT*, but the ending appears in a text closer to c, later used by Barlow 20 (Bw), a manuscript associated in the *SuT* with the other arm of d, the one that includes Lichfield 2, Morgan 249, and Cambridge Mm. The manuscript, like Sl[1] and Ry[2], has no gaps or irregularities in the make-up of the quires to indicate uncertainty as to the ordering or text. *Explicits* and *incipits* take up one or two lines and like the running heads are always in rubric. The commentary marginalia, which En[2] carries only in the *Man of Law's Tale*, also appear in rubric and within the text in the hand of the scribe. The evidence would seem to show that the scribe had marginalia in his exemplar but waited ordinarily to copy them until it was convenient for him to use red ink. The gaps for the commentary vary from two to five lines to fit the length of the gloss. The glosses sometimes run over three to five words, which appear to the right of the text in the subsequent lines. One marginalium, at B 421, never got copied, though it appears in other manuscripts. Four blank lines precede the stanza beginning "O sodeyn wo, that ever art successour," on folio 53b. This manuscript might well be the one bequeathed by William Knoyell in 1501 to his cousin William Carraunt, "for I had him of his grandfather" (M–R I: 614). The Carraunt family had connections with Thomas Chaucer, similar to those enjoyed by the owners of two other d manuscripts, Sl[1] and Ry[2]. En[2] or its exemplars served as copy some twenty years later for the two tales in Longleat 257 (Ll[1]). Called "Arcite and Palamon" and "Grisild" in the running titles and the *explicits*, the two tales have no prologues, but the first retains the references to the storytelling contest with the supper as prize at A 889ff. and the second has the Clerk's song labeled "Lenvoie Chaucer," though the stanza in which the Clerk addresses the song to the Wife of Bath is missing as in all the other d manuscripts. The choice of these two tales in a section of manuscript that also contains Lydgate's *Siege of Thebes* and the prose *Ipomedon* shows an interest on the compiler's part in a far narrower range of narrative than if he had been trying to bring together the available Canterbury material.

Lichfield 2 (Lc), contemporary with En[2] and with Ry[2] and Sl[1] as well, is the most regular of the early d manuscripts. It has the d ordering and the d text; its only deviations are its failure to have the *Monk's Prologue*, and its substitution in a 550-line section of the *Clerk's Tale* (E 210–760) of text with a close association to c. Here its closeness to c has the paradoxical effect of separating it from the d tradition, the *ClT* being one of the sections of the *Canterbury Tales* where the two traditions are separate. The only other d manuscript to be associated with c in this portion of the *ClT* is Ld[2], the manuscript copied from Ry[2] except for segments that approximate three quires (see above). The limits of the affiliation with c are different in the two manuscripts (Lc and Ld[2]). Curiously, the affiliation in both cases breaks off before the *Wife of Bath* stanza (E 1170–76), missing from both manuscripts (as in all other d manuscripts). Lc places itself among the more elaborate d manuscripts with a generous ruled space on every page for marginalia and with demi-vinets for the beginnings of the tales. A curious note on 104b that summarizes the work of the first of the two illuminators includes "j hole venett," undoubtedly for the first folio of the manuscript, one of only five missing from the text. The running titles, *explicits* and *incipits*, and the marginalia start out uniformly in red, but first the indexing marginalia and then some of the others appear in the ink of the text, often with red underlining. At one point, beginning at f. 192 b, we get a golden ink for the running titles. On some pages the marks for paraphs have been disregarded. Despite these occasional inconsistencies, the manuscript gives no impression of uncertainty even at the point where the prologue (the *Monk's*) is missing. Lc served as exemplar apparently for Morgan 249 (Mg), which shares Lc's omissions, and many of its spellings. Mg, dated 1450–60, some fifteen to twenty years after Lc, has very simple illumination. It gives the impression of being a not very professional product. The Ha^2 scribe apparently used it not only for corrections, but also for sections of the text in the *General Prologue* and the *Summoner's Tale*.

Certain features of the d manuscripts show that they go back to a common origin, collections of exemplars derived from one another that we have called /d and /d'. All d manuscripts share the ordering, sometimes disarranged as in Petworth and the manuscripts derived from it. They share the *Gamelyn* as conclusion of the *Cook's Tale*, the *Man of Law's* endlink as introduction for the Squire and his tale, and a set of spurious links including the one that connects the *Squire's* and *Merchant's Tales*. They all omit the *Wife stanza* at the end of the *Clerk's Tale* and have the "archewyves" stanza at the end of the Clerk's song. At the same time, it is clear that the four early manuscripts derived from /d' do not share the same set of exemplars. Rather they derive from a common pool of exemplars, each manuscript in its own way departing from what one might call the d tradition. At the end of the *Summoner's Tale* the manuscripts definitely form two groups, one derived from an exemplar with the complete text – Lc and Mm (though Mm's exemplar had only through line 2224) – the other derived from an exemplar that lacked the final episode (D2159–2294): Pw–Ph^3, Ry^2, Sl^1, En^2, and Ha^2 (though En^2 picked it up from an exemplar in the c tradition and Ha^2 picked it up from Lc). The *Manciple's Prologue* seems also to have been missing from some of the d exemplars. It is missing in Ry^2, En^2, and the later Dl; Sl^1 breaks off before the end of the B^2 fragment; and the later Ha^2 picks up the *Prologue* from the Lc tradition; only Lc and Pw seem to have had it with their exemplar for the tale. Some of the manuscripts have surprising additional omissions, the *Thopas* and the *Melibeus* in Sl^1, the *Monk's Prologue* in Lc. Of the later manuscripts, outside the Pw group, two, Mg and Ld^2, are in all probability copied directly from previous manuscripts; one, Ll^1, contains only two of the *Canterbury Tales* in a collection of narratives; Dl is a highly experimental manuscript with spaces left for text and two passages repeated; and Ha^2 used a contemporary d manuscript Mg as a source for both corrections and text. Though fragments of the d text survived and were sometimes copied, no evidence indicates that a d set of exemplars was used after 1460. The d tradition of course continued to exist in the ordering of such manuscripts as Bw (1450–80), Royal 17 D.XV (1450–70), Fitzwilliam McClean 181 (1450–69), and Rawlinson Poetry 149 (1450–70), as well as all the manuscripts associated with the b ordering. The evidence taken as a whole would indicate that the original d set of exemplars produced the Pw line of manuscripts only after it suffered the dislocation of some of the tales from the B^2 fragment and the d' set of exemplars survives intact in none of the extant manuscripts. Sl^1, Ry^2, En^2, and Lc were copied in the period around 1425–40 from related but distinct sets of exemplars.[5] Portions of the text associated with d circulated freely and provided text for manuscripts of mixed origin. The order associated with d carried some authority throughout the fifteenth century.

It might be well to pause at this point and review what had happened to the *Canterbury Tales* in the thirty-five years after Chaucer's death. By the year 1435 twelve of the surviving collected manuscripts had probably been written. Evidence is strong that others existed that have not survived, for instance an ancestor for Sloane 1686 (Sl^2) that would transmit the c text and arrangement to that very late manuscript. It is also evident that some copies of the Petworth exemplars must have been made before the dislocation of the first two tales of the B^2 fragment. How many others existed we can only conjecture. But it would be my guess that the number is not large. We have what appears to be a first effort at collection in Hengwrt; we have two manuscripts that apparently build on Hengwrt, Harley 7334 and Corpus 198; they serve as transition to the two most complete of the early manuscripts, the Cambridge Dd with authentic and the Lansdowne with spurious materials.

We have evidence that two early collections of exemplars remained together over a period of time. Corpus 198 is an early copy of the first of these collections; its text was used for at least two other early manuscripts and provided the exemplars for over two-thirds of the d collection. Cambridge Dd was almost certainly the first of the a manuscripts; it not only shows signs of uncertainty, but uses text in two of the tales from a different tradition; it corrects its text extensively from independent sources, some of them close to the original (M–R I: 102). Ellesmere uses the same arrangement as Cambridge Dd and through its marginalia reveals an association with both Hengwrt and Dd. It shows in its format and in its text the most careful preparation of copy, the most responsible choice of what to include, and the most beautiful execution of any of the manuscripts. The supervisor made detailed plans in advance of the actual copying. He had little occasion to alter or change. Even the use of two illuminators for the portraits of the pilgrims does not obtrude itself on the reader's attention.

The influence of the a-Ellesmere arrangement would seem to be the stronger in these early years. Not only does Cambridge Gg use it without change, but it is clearly the model for two eccentric manuscripts, Bodley 686 (Bo^2) and Paris. These two manuscripts show a willingness on the part of patron and supervisor to pick and choose, to follow in the copying out of tales Chaucer's advice for reading them: "Turne over the leef and chese another tale." The evidence on the strength of the traditions may, however, be illusory. The collection of exemplars used by Petworth must have produced at least one manuscript with the ordering the spurious *Pardoner-Shipman* link was designed to make firm. The second d collection of exemplars with revised and additional links must also have been in existence before 1435 and have already been copied. Sloane

---

[5] The neatly radiating lines in Plate 5 for En^2, Lc, Ry^2, Sl^1, Ha^2, and Dl are oversimplifications of what really happened. A better visual parallel might be offered by a circle for d' with lines for the actual d manuscripts and families of manuscripts starting at different points on the perimeter. The time element, which is an important part of the plates in this book, could still be retained.

1685 (Sl[1]) and Royal 18C.II (Ry[2]) probably belong to this period. Representatives of the two other early strands of the $\underline{d}$ family, Lichfield 2 (Lc) and Egerton 2863 (En[2]) perhaps qualify or were copied soon after 1435. There is also the vellum section of the Helmingham dated 1420–30. This section includes the last part of the B[2] fragment beginning in mid-*Melibeus*, the H fragment, and part of the *Parson's Prologue*. Gaps and a change of textual affiliation show it to be experimental rather than an early copy of the $\underline{b}$ family of exemplars. It does, however, reflect the $\underline{bcd}$ arrangement in its failure to place the G fragment between B[2] and H, and it once included more text, perhaps a complete collection. This cannot be said for the three leaves of Merthyr, which give no indication as to ordering or extent.

Though there is only one clear instance of an early manuscript with a single tale, Longleat 29 (Ll[2]), the textual tradition of the early manuscripts points to the circulation of single tales and groups of tales in great numbers. Ll[2] itself used an exemplar for the text of the *Parson's Tale* closely affiliated with the one used by Ellesmere. Nothing associates the treatise on penitence in Ll[2] with the Parson, with the *Canterbury Tales*, or with Chaucer. It appears as much the longest in a collection of religious writings. Apparently the exemplar was circulating by itself. The exemplars used by Hengwrt show shifts of textual affiliation with later manuscripts from one section to another. A few of the exemplars, as we shall see later, did remain together; many others circulated, being copied and sometimes replaced. Copies and copies of copies occasionally served as exemplars in other collections, in one instance (Py) almost exclusively. A similar situation holds for Ellesmere, Harley 7334 (Ha[4]), Cambridge Gg, Bodley 686, and the Paris manuscript. In the case of the last named, exemplars of five of the tales, as we have seen, remained together for at least twenty-five years and were used by an incompetent copyist in the *Canterbury Tales* section of Harley 1239 (Ha[1]). Cambridge Dd used as text for the *Wife of Bath's Tale* and for the first part of the *Clerk's Tale* exemplars that turn up many years later in a group of four manuscripts. The evidence shows a wide circulation of tales and groups of tales and suggests that this circulation led some readers to seek out a complete collection of the Canterbury materials. By the end of the period exemplars of all the tales were not hard to come by.

VI

Eight Additional Manuscripts

The other manuscripts before 1450 fall into two groups. One is a set of highly irregular manuscripts. Additional 25718 (Ad²) (1430–50), Holkam 667 (Hk) (1440–50), and the constant group Mc, consisting of McCormick (Mc) (1440–60) and Rawlinson Poetry 141 (Ra¹) (1450–60). The other group consists of four manuscripts: one with a b ordering, Lincoln 110 = A.4.18 (Ln); one with an a ordering, Additional 35286 (Ad³); one with a d ordering, Cambridge Ii.3.26 (Ii); and one with the Ha⁴ ordering, Laud 600 (Ld¹). Manly-Rickert date the last four manuscripts 1430–50. All four are eclectic in textual tradition and all but Ln show independence with respect to tale order at some point in the manuscript. This independence is most interesting in the case of Additional 35286 (Ad³). Though the manuscript has a predominantly Ellesmere ordering and gets small sections of its text from the same sources as Hg, El, Gg, and a, it draws primarily on the c and d traditions and shows closest affiliation with Ha⁴ and with Rawlinson Poetry 223 (Ra³). It has more of the commentary marginalia developed in Hengwrt and Ellesmere than any other manuscript. It shows some curious lapses. The *Cook's Tale*, absent from its normal position at the end of the A fragment, turns up after the *Manciple's Tale* as if to satisfy the dramatic situation created in the *Manciple's Prologue*. The only other displaced section, the G fragment, breaks in two, with the Second Nun telling her tale after the Summoner and before the Clerk, and the Canon's Yeoman overtaking the pilgrims between the *Cook's Tale* and the *Parson's Prologue*. No irregularity in the manuscript at the junctures gives any indication of uncertainty. The text of the *Second Nun's Prologue* has no awkward references, nor does the *Clerk's Prologue* that follows *Saint Cecilia*. But the *Cook's Prologue* refers to the *Reeve's Tale* explicitly, the *Canon's Yeoman's Prologue* to the saint's legend that should precede it, and the *Parson's Prologue* to the Manciple. If the supervisor or the scribe felt any uneasiness at these moments, he has left no sign of it in the manuscript.

Some remarkable similarities in the marginalia suggest that Ad³ had a close relationship with Ellesmere. It includes for instance most of the commentary marginalia in Ellesmere that do not appear in the Hengwrt – those in the *FkT*, the *WBPT*, and the *SuT*. These three tales alone account for sixty-nine of the seventy-seven that Ellesmere adds to the sixty-eight shared with Hengwrt. Of these sixty-nine Ad[3] has sixty-three. Furthermore, unlike Cambridge Dd and Christ Church, which show in their marginalia a closer relationship with Hengwrt, it has none of the six in Hengwrt that Ellesmere fails to carry. Confirmation of the close association with Ellesmere comes from certain details of the indexing marginalia – the Pausacios that punctuate the verse paragraphs of *Clerk's Prologue* at exactly the same lines in the two manuscripts;[1] the four English titles for the temple orisons of *Knight's Tale* repeated almost word for word, the "argumentum" at Egeus's platitudes, and two "exemplums" for the oak and the hard stone from Theseus's final speech; the "nota malum quid" at the description of adultery in the *Manciple's Tale* (unique at this point to these two manuscripts as opposed to its appearance at Absolon's kiss in Hengwrt, Christ Church CLII, Cambridge Dd, and Royal College of Physicians 13).[2] This relationship suggests ready access on the part of Ad[3]'s makers not just to Ellesmere materials but to the manuscript itself.[3] The commentary marginalia in Ad[3], which include all but thirteen of the possible 139 in Ellesmere (Ellesmere has a total of 145 but Ad[3] lacks text for six because of loss of leaves), these marginalia must have appeared in the exemplars copied by the scribe, for they match in every instance the ink of the text (one of the marginalia even appears twice, in the margin and a few lines later in the text). With this full knowledge of Ellesmere the makers of Ad[3] must have deliberately chosen to alter its arrangement of the fragments, a choice that we can see to be not entirely misguided. The *Second Nun's Tale* makes some sense in the midst of the tales associated with the Wife of Bath and marriage. The *Manciple's Prologue* strongly suggests that the Cook will have to be called on again before the Host can address the Parson with the words, ". . . every man, save thou, hath told his tale. . . ." And who is to say that for a fourteenth-century Canterbury pilgrim Bobbe-up-and-down should not precede Boughton on the Canterbury

---

[1]   For the Pausacio phenomenon in the early manuscripts (Hg, Cp, El) see Chapter II, fn.1 (p. 7). Ad[3] follows El, marking the divisions with a marginal "Pausacio," a space as if for a stanza, and an initial capital. The other member of Ad[3]'s constant group, Harley 7335 (Ha[5]) has lines but no space to mark the divisions (at lines 7, 15, 21, 31, 39, and 47). The rime royal stanzas in Ad[3] normally have a space as well as the line, but in the ensuing *ClT* the space diminishes, until it disappears completely. Because of the displacement of *SNPT* (after D), *ClT* is the last part of the *Canterbury Tales* in rime royal. Rawlinson Poetry 141 (Ra[1]) has the word "Pausacio" at all but line 47 and paraphs at all the divisions. The small collection Sion has spaces before lines 9, 15, 29, 35, and 47 with lines 21 and 41 at the top of a page. Another division of the *ClP* occurs in Dd, Ha[2], La, Lc, Mg, Ps, and Ph[2] at "This worthy clerk," E 21, with a paraph, a capital, or both.
[2]   Trinity Cambridge R.3.15 (Tc[2]) has "nota malum quid" at line 247 (instead of 257) in the *McT*.
[3]   Rawlinson Poetry 141 (Ra[1]) and Trinity Cambridge R.3.15 (Tc[2]) on the other hand contain almost all the El marginalia from the *WBP* and the *SuT* but few of the others that El adds to Hg's. Ra[1] lacks the *PdT* glosses shared by Hg, El, Ad[3], Tc[2], and others. Probably the El glosses came to Ra[1] and Tc[2] through individual exemplars, in contrast to Ad[3], which apparently had direct access to El and could copy the marginalia directly into its own exemplars.

way? The Ad³ editor, like his predecessors who presided over such manuscripts as Ps and Bo², had no apparent hesitation in altering the arrangement of materials he found in Ellesmere. In other words he found the Ellesmere ordering helpful but not authoritative. The materials used in Ad³ remained together, except for a section of the E–F fragment, long enough to provide the text for Harley 7335 (Ha⁵, 1450–70). Curiously, for a part of the section, where the two manuscripts are apart, Ha⁵ got its text from the same exemplar as the Paris manuscript.

Contemporary with Additional 35286 is another composite and highly edited manuscript, Lincoln 110 = A.4.18 (Ln). Manly-Rickert list the ordering as type b, which means that it is the same as d without the *Gamelyn*. The text is highly eclectic, a manuscript for which a set of exemplars was assembled on an *ad hoc* basis. No evidence indicates that the exemplars remained together after Ln was copied. Its chief affiliations are with a and with the same pool of exemplars drawn on by d. At a few places the manuscript has gaps as if in the expectation of further copy – at the end of the *Canon's Yeoman's Tale* and at the end of the *Pardoner's Tale*. At another place, between the *Merchant's Tale* and the *Wife of Bath's Prologue* there was once a gap. But it has now been more than filled with the *Merchant's Epilogue*, added after the D fragment was copied, with the last five lines running beyond the beginning of the *Wife's Prologue* in the left margin. At still another point the manuscript labels the *Man of Law's Epilogue* as the *Prologue* of the *Squire's Tale*, but retains the reading "Sompnour" in line 1179 for the pilgrim who takes over from the Parson. Under the influence of other manuscripts, from which, as Manly-Rickert note, it derives its tale order and numerous corrections, it remains in part experimental, uncertain at times of the copy it would be able to acquire.

The style of the manuscript more than matches the uncertainties already noted. In the beginning the manuscript often lacks space for *explicits* and *incipits* to mark the division of its tales and prologues; it resorts instead to marginal titles, to page headings, sometimes to flourished initials only (end of *MiT*, beginning of *SqT*), even to nothing at all in one instance (*MLT*). In the end it adopts a three- to seven-line gap with *explicits* and *incipits* spaced in the gap as a standard. But with the *MkT* and the *NPT* the script of the headings becomes more formal and monumental. *Explicits* and *incipits* no longer take a single line, though short in number of words. The *McT* fills a three-line gap with "Heere bigynneth the maunciplis tale of the Crowe," and the *PsP* fills a five-line gap with "Heere bigyneth the prolog/Off the persouns Tale. . . ." The *PsT* reverts to a single non-differentiated and combined *explicit* and *incipit* followed by the Latin quotation from Jeremiah in three lines of the same undifferentiated script. Meanwhile, the manuscript has experimented with emphasizing letters by backing them with what looks like a brown wash. The brown background appears in running heads, marginal notes, *explicits* and *incipits*, and especially in first letters of lines. Most frequently the brown appears with a flourished initial, backing the first letters of the rest of the lines on the page. Another experiment occurs at the start of the *MeP*, with the flourished initial "I" in red and the next two letters of the first line and the "And" of the second in red as well. Lincoln 110 shows the kind of uncertainty and independence one encounters throughout the manuscript period. Few manuscripts enjoyed the convenience of a completely assembled and ordered set of exemplars.

Cambridge Ii, which Manly-Rickert describe as an augmented b̲ manuscript, usually very near the top of the line, has sections of its text related to Ha⁴, to the augmented d̲ tradition, and to Rawlinson Poetry 149 (Ra²). Earlier by at least a decade than Helmingham or any of the regular b̲ manuscripts, it picked up texts from a number of traditions, included the *Gamelyn* as the conclusion of the *Cook's Tale*, and placed the *Franklin's Tale* after the *Merchant's Tale* and before the *Wife of Bath*. If the complete b̲ text had already come into being, Cambridge Ii would presumably have taken a different form. As it was, sections of its text became the ancestors of exemplars used in assembling the b̲ text. It confirms what we shall see in the next chapter – the lateness of the b̲ text. The manuscript shows a number of inconsistencies. The scribe conscientiously left spaces for lines of text apparently missing in his exemplar. But he failed to notice an eighty-four-line gap in the *Monk's Tale* that took out all but the opening four lines of "Balthasar" and extended through the first three stanzas of "Zenobia". In the *Monk-Nun's Priest's* link he managed to displace by two lines the twenty lines that distinguish the long from the short form of the link. Thus we go from B² 3960 to 3981,2 to 3961–80 to 3983. The running titles, the *explicits* and *incipits*, and the many indexing marginalia (including ones for most of the proper names in the text) are in red, each with its own colorful paraph, blue with red trim or gold with brown. But the running titles are occasionally wrong; and the first lines of a number of the tales – the *Knight's*, the *Miller's*, and the *Merchant's*, for instance – have no spacing, no rubrics, only a three-line initial to set them off. The *explicit* at the end of the *Cook's Tale* (before the *Gamelyn*) calls it the *Prologue*, and for the *Man of Law's Tale* there is a three-line capital for the poverty stanzas, nothing at all for the tale. The surface evidence of scrupulous attention to detail is thus deceptive in Cambridge Ii, a manuscript that despite its inconsistencies of format and single-line omissions gives no sign of uncertainty as to ordering.

Laud 600 (Ld¹) reflects in its ordering the Harley 7334 arrangement. B¹, however, instead of appearing after *Gamelyn* and before the *Wife of Bath*, splits the *Clerk's Tale* from the *Merchant's Tale* in the sequence after the D fragment. The text belongs prevailingly to the augmented d̲ tradition, but has sections in close relationship to b̲*, to Ry¹, and c̲, to cd̲*, to Ha³, and ends up deriving from the exemplars used much earlier in Harley 7334 (Ha⁴) for B², H, and I, the final eight tales. An elaborately illuminated manuscript, Ld¹ has lost numerous pages to vandals, many of them replaced in the seventeenth century. Still remaining are many of the *explicits* and *incipits* in red with initial capital in blue, the alternating red and blue capitals at the start of each rime royal stanza in the *Clerk's Tale*, the incorporation of commentary in the text, always set off in red, and many flourished capitals and illuminated pages. But the manuscript shows frequent lapses. The gaps in text proved too small frequently for rubricated commentary, necessitating a one- to two-line runover in the margin. In two instances the heading initials stand alone without further text, in another all but the initial appears. In several headings the colored initial is followed by a second capital in the ink of the text. The colored capitals that mark off the stanzas in the *Clerk's Tale* seem too small for the spaces left in the text for them.

Both vellum and ink were irregular in quality. But though the manuscript with its seventeenth-century additions presents a highly varied appearance, it shows no evidence of uncertainty in its ordering. Short gaps in the text accommodate the *explicits* and *incipits*, with no spaces left for additional passages. The anomalous position of the *Man of Law's* fragment caused no apparent uneasiness on the part of the editor or scribe.

Each of the four really irregular manuscripts shows a close relationship with at least one later manuscript. Holkham presents the interesting example of a manuscript itself disarranged yet providing text or sharing exemplars with two manuscripts with the Ellesmere-a arrangement. Holkham's arrangement is unique:

$$A^{bcd} \quad G^a \text{ (1--119)} \quad G^b \quad H \quad F^b \quad F^a \quad B^1 \quad D^{ab} \quad E^a \quad E^b \quad D^{cd} \quad B^{2abcd}$$

The make-up suggests the random putting together of exemplars as they came to hand rather than the copying from a finished collection. Though the manuscript has suffered from being long unbound (until 1814) and has lost quires at beginning and end, it is professionally written in double columns on a large well-ruled page and it has a moderately elaborate program of illumination. Multicolored champs with two- to four-line gold capitals mark the beginnings of prologues and tales (the "I" at the beginning of the *Franklin's Tale* on 32a is exceptional; it variably indents eight lines of text). Two-line gold capitals signal important passages and divisions within tales. Red and blue paraphs and numerous pointing hands serve to articulate the text with paraphs setting off the stanzas in rime royal passages. Occasionally the system breaks down and signs for paraphs have gone unnoticed (80a, for instance).

Hk seems to combine improvisation and an erratic commitment over a period of time. It may once have included almost all of the tales. There is no hint that scribe or editor expected a *Cook's Tale*, and they left a page and three-quarters at the end of a quire blank for the *Second Nun's Tale* (they had obtained the *Prologue*). The only other extensive gap came at the end of the *Squire's Tale* (one and a half pages). As one might expect from the ordering, those responsible for Hk engaged in very little editing. They brought exemplars together that show almost no affiliation textually with earlier manuscripts. The only exception is in the *Summoner's Tale* with Ry^2. An anomaly of textual history that will require later consideration involves what happened to some of the Hk exemplars. Those for ten of the tales and the *Second Nun's Prologue* remained together and served as copytext for two very late manuscripts with a-Ellesmere ordering – Egerton 2864 (En^3) and Additional 5140 (Ad^1).

The badly mutilated Additional 25718 (Ad^2) has an arrangement that puts the C fragment between the *Summoner's Tale* and the *Clerk's Tale*: $A^{bc} \ B^1 \ D^d \ C$ $E^a \ B^{2abd}$. Losses within quires as well as the evident losses of quires make the manuscript little better than a collection of fragments. Each of the sections is separate; the *Summoner's Tale*, incomplete at both ends and in a quire of its own, is in a distinctly different handwriting; the only complete section, the C, fills exactly two quires; the B^2 section has gaps. The decoration is confined to red and blue penwork and includes flourished initials in two colors as well as red and blue paraphs, used to set off rime royal stanzas. Marks for paraphs, however, were frequently disregarded. Some of the *explicits* and *incipits*, in the ink of the text, were enclosed in red rectangular boxes gargoyled at either end (32a); the language shifts from Latin to English and back to Latin; the *incipit* for folio 52a for the *Pardoner's Prologue* reads *Shipman's Tale*, corrected with the start of the tale two pages later. The text of Ad^2, like that of Hk, has almost no close relationships with earlier manuscripts. An exception is the *Physician's Tale* with Ln. Exemplars for many of Ad^2's fragments provided text for Hatton Donat 1 (Ht); they may also have influenced its highly irregular arrangement. Ad^2's heavy losses of text and the complex textual relationships with Ht and of Ht with the almost contemporary Rawlinson Poetry 149 (Ra^2), with Ph^3 of the Pw family, and surprisingly with Hengwrt, will raise interesting questions about the break-up of constant groups and the way exemplars circulated in the second half of the fourteenth century.

Similar questions emerge from consideration of the constant group Mc, consisting of McCormick (Mc) and Rawlinson Poetry 141 (Ra^1). These two manuscripts, written around 1450 from the same set of exemplars, had the tales arranged in a unique way:

$$A \ B^1 \ F^a \ E^a \ B^{2abcde} \ D \ B^{2f} \ H \ G$$

The manuscripts were mutilated at beginning and end: Mc is missing the first eight quires (A 1–3858; into the *Reeve's Prologue*), Ra^1 the first five (A 1–2566; into Part IV of the *Knight's Tale*); Mc breaks off in the middle of the *Canon's Yeoman's Tale* (G 1057) at the point where the canon is first duping the priest with his "multiplication"; Ra^1 ends even earlier at the beginning of the *Manciple's Tale* (H 140). Ra^1 has suffered further damage, losing batches of leaves that add up to eleven, plus one full quire just before the end. Except for these losses the quiring in both manuscripts is a regular sequence of eights.

The text for the constant group probably continued beyond G and included some of the missing fragments, E^b, F^b, C and I.[4] The order reflects in part the way the exemplars became available. Close relationships with previous manuscripts are almost as rare as in Hk and Ad^2. For the *Squire's Tale* Ad^3–Ps–Ha^4 are related; for parts of the *Summoner's Tale* and the *Clerk's Tale* Lc is close; for the *Canon's Yeoman's Prologue* and *Tale* Ln–Tc^1 and Mc have a common ancestor. Clearly the exemplars collected for Mc were single tales, or as in the case of A and B^2 small groups of tales. With D those responsible either acquired a recently assembled fragment or made the connections themselves. The textual associations do not provide evidence for the Manly-Rickert opinion that the ancestor of Mc was an "obviously picked up manuscript which was put

---

[4]   M–R (I: 451) misrepresent this aspect of the constant group. Their statement that G was lacking in Ra^1's ancestor is clearly wrong, since Mc has 1057 lines of G. In view of what happened to the text shortly after Ra^1 was copied, it is probable that Mc's copytext was a collection of exemplars and that Ra^1 was copied from the exemplars rather than from Mc itself. Tc^1 was able to use only *Th*, *Mel*, and *MkT* from Mc in the B^2 fragment. Both Mc and Ra^1 have the first five tales of the fragment intact. *ShT* and *PrT* had clearly become detached before the others were copied by Tc^1. Mc exemplars were later picked up by St (*Mel*), Hl^1 (*PrT*), and Sl^2 (*SNPT*).

together early" (M–R I:357), despite the fact that the texts used in many of the tales are high in their respective textual traditions.

The manuscripts show no signs of uncertainty. The tales follow along after one another with gaps only big enough for rubrics. They share the four-line conclusion of the *Cook's Tale* that hangs the two miscreants and draws the appropriate moral in a commercial metaphor. In the endlink to the *Man of Law's Tale* Mc has the Summoner, Ra[1] the Squire as the interrupter. Mc has a single running title, in the cursive hand that furnishes a number of the headings, "Somoners tale". The much more formal Ra[1] has an *incipit* for the "Squyers tale" at the beginning of the endlink and a running head for the *SqT* throughout. The two manuscripts include a complete version in *Mel*, B 2525–26, found in no other manuscript. They also follow the Monk's tragedies with the *WBP* but give no evidence of uncertainty; yet Mc, and presumably Ra[1] before its mutilation as well, place the Knight's interruption of the tragedies at the end of the *SuT* as an introduction to the *NPT*.

Mc was originally a very plain manuscript, lacking page headings and *explicits* and *incipits*, lacking in some instances even space for them (41a, 175b). Blue initials with red pen trim and red and blue paraphs give the text its only contemporary decoration. Later scribbled headings for pages and tales, sometimes in margins, provide an unattractive further articulation of the text. Ra[1] has a much more attractive appearance. *Explicits*, *incipits*, and running heads are in rubric; paraphs alternate red and blue, often with pen trim in the opposite color; initial capitals for tales and prologues are two to four lines in blue with red pen trim. Only occasionally does the system break down, as when the running heads for the *Clerk's Tale* and the *Shipman's Tale* are reciprocally misplaced (73a and b; 78a and b), or when some headings are omitted.

The Ra[1] editor makes a number of efforts to correct or complete Mc's text. We have already seen his work on the *Man of Law's* endlink and the *Squire's Tale*. He also did not follow Mc in calling the *Shipman's Tale* the Merchant's. He tried to supply missing words and lines in his copytext. He supplemented what he found in the Mc exemplars with a large number of the marginalia present in El and Ad[3]. The evidence would seem to show that he did not have access to either of those manuscripts. For while he includes most of the marginalia from the *MLT*, the *WBP*, and the *CIT*, he apparently found none of the ones from the *MeT*, the *FkT*, and the *PdPT*.

Perhaps the most important thing about the constant group Mc is what happened to the exemplars shortly after Ra[1] was made. The editor of Trinity College Cambridge E.3.3 (Tc[1]) found himself forced to supplement the exemplars he inherited from the almost contemporary Ra[3] and the earlier Ln, turned to a set of five from Mc, then finished his manuscript by copying the final four tales from En[1]. This situation is best shown graphically:

$$\text{Tc}^1: \quad \text{A}^{abcde} \; \text{B}^1 \; \text{F}^a \; \text{E}^b \; \text{E}^a \; \text{D} \; \text{G} \; \text{C} \; \text{B}^{2f} \; \text{H} \; \text{B}^{2cdeab} \; \text{F}^b \; \text{I}$$

$$\underset{(X)}{\text{———————}} \cdots\cdots \underset{\text{xxxx}}{\cdots\cdots} \cdots - - - - - - - - - - \;\; |||||||$$

$\underset{\cdot}{(X)} = Ad^3 \quad - = Ra^3\text{-Ln}; \quad \cdots\cdots = Ra^3 \quad xxx = Ln; \quad - - - - - - - - = \underline{Mc}; \; ||||||| = En^1$

If the Tc[1] editor had had access to all the Mc exemplars or to either of the manuscripts, he would have seen the *Shipman's Tale* and the *Prioress's Tale* (B[2ab]) in their proper order at the beginning of the B[2] fragment. One can reach an additional conclusion with respect to timing. He must have come upon En[1] after his work with the Mc exemplars. Despite the peculiarities of his ordering he managed to gather copytext for all of the tales.

One further note on the Mc exemplars: Stonyhurst used the one for the *Mel* in this same period, c. 1450. Somewhat later, 1460–1470, Harley 1704 (Hl[1]) used the one for the *PrT*, apparently not in the set available to the Tc[1] editor. Later still Sloane 1686 (Sl[2]) replaced the *SNPT*, missing from its c-derived copytext, with an Mc exemplar (Ra[1] breaks off before G in the Mc ordering and Tc[1] had Ra[3]-derived text for *SNPT*).

It is surprising to find manuscripts as disordered as Mc, Ra[1], Ad[2], and Hk appearing approximately fifty years after Chaucer's death. Not since the very first manuscript, Hengwrt, had such disordered collections of the *Canterbury Tales* appeared. The decades after 1450 will find a number of important manuscripts produced with equally disordered sequence of tales.

VII

The Decade of the Fifties

None of the manuscripts so far discussed shows any sign of having been produced in a shop by a team of scribes turning out manuscript copy to meet heavy demand. The shop theory, which for earlier textual critics explained the complexities met with in the *Canterbury Tales* manuscripts, has received critical review by the new school of English textual critics led by A.I. Doyle and M.B. Parkes. They have found no evidence for the commercial production of *Canterbury Tales* manuscripts by teams of scribes and very little for the retention of an exemplar by a stationer for vernacular works most commonly in demand. For Chaucer's *Canterbury Tales* the earliest evidence of retention Doyle and Parkes would date in the fifth and sixth decades of the century, and the manuscripts they name as examples, Devonshire, Rawlinson Poetry 223 (Ra^3), and Tc^1, Manly-Rickert assign to the sixth decade.[1]

We have already seen one of these three, Devonshire, as the most elaborate a manuscript, and we have seen that it used Egerton 2427 (En^1) as copytext. Some paleographers assign all three of these manuscripts to a single scribe whom they call the "hooked g" scribe. Dan Mosser, who has been studying the a manuscripts, would assign them instead to three separate scribes, so closely associated that they adopted a common format and developed similar handwritings. In Mosser's view each was responsible for other manuscripts includ-

---

[1] See Chapter V, fn.3, where articles by Doyle and Parkes, Edwards and Pearsall, and Mosser are cited. The "bespoke" trade favored by recent scholars involved scribes, stationers, and limners working in their own shops on an *ad hoc* basis. Evidence that Gower and possibly Occleve had some influence on the way their texts were produced is presented by Edwards and Pearsall, "The Manuscripts," but they question "commerical production" (p. 260) of any literary texts in the first half of the fifteenth century, and of Chaucer texts at any time. Derek Pearsall in his "Introduction" to *Book Production* finds that copy made at the author's instigation or initiated by the consumer "were still widespread, indeed dominant," (p. 2). C. Paul Christianson, "Evidence," describes the geographical concentration in the area around St Paul's of those connected with the London book trade.

ing at least one *Confessio Amantis*.[2] What gives these manuscripts their distinguishing characteristic is the use of elongated miniscules at the beginnings of sections of their texts. They also shared a rather elaborate style of illumination. Their interrelationships throw light on the way exemplars of the *Canterbury Tales* were handled in the period around 1450.

We saw at the end of the last chapter that in even those manuscripts with comparatively regular orderings, Ad^3, Ii, and Ld^1 for instance, those responsible did not hesitate to make slight changes. In the case of four manuscripts, Hk, Ad^2, Mc, and Ra^1 the ordering is quite irregular. What appears to be happening is a return, on the part of some editors and supervisors, to the uncertainties that characterized the earliest efforts at putting together collections of the *Canterbury Tales*. This holds true for two out of the three surviving *Canterbury Tales* manuscripts with the "elongated miniscule" format. A closer look at what happened will be illuminating.

The most disordered and therefore presumably the earliest of the three manuscripts is Ra^3. Textually a pick-up manuscript, it derives from a tradition that includes Ln through the *Prologue*, the first six tales, and part of the seventh, and from the Ad^3 tradition for the next five. It then draws on the same sources as the contemporary Rawlinson 149 (Ra^2) for some tales, as Ad^3, as Ha^4, as Mc, and as Pw for others. In the *Franklin's Tale* it is independent. It fails to include the *Monk's Tale* and the *Canon's Yeoman's Prologue* and *Tale*. The order starts out like Ln and the b manuscripts through the *Merchant's Tale* – A B^1 F^a E^b. But the *Clerk's Tale* precedes the D fragment and the *Second Nun's Prologue* and *Tale* follows it. So far the order has precedents. But after G^a it runs as follows: C^b H B^{2cdf} C^a B^{2ab} F^b I R. From the quiring Manly-Rickert (M–R I: 462f.) conclude that the *Merchant's Tale* with its link was inserted between the already copied *Squire's Tale* and *Clerk's Tale*, and that when the *Clerk's Prologue* was obtained an extra leaf had to be provided and the text, now too short, spaced out.

Despite these uncertainties and a tendency to vary the running titles, sometimes even to get them wrong, Ra^3 is an impressive book, monumental in size and rich in execution. The signatures indicate that the manuscript was in the fifteenth century even more monumental. Over the centuries it has lost its first 14 quires plus the first seven leaves of quire p. With gatherings of twelve and with 34 lines to the page, the lost quires could have included an anthology almost the size of Cambridge Gg and with the same proportion of the total (approximately 60%) given over to the *CT*. Illumination in Ra^3 includes paraphs in two different two-color combinations, demi-vinets for the beginnings of tales, and elaborate initials that, for the *Friar's Tale* and the *Melibeus*,

---

[2] The Ds scribe was responsible for the Magdalen Oxford 213 and for the major portion of Folger Vb29. The Ra^3 scribe and the Tc^1 scribe ("hooked g") were also responsible for *Confessio* manuscripts (Ra^3, Harley 7184; Tc^1, Lyell 31): Forthcoming in Mosser's study, *The Alpha Text of the "Canterbury Tales."* Edwards and Pearsall, "The Manuscript," p. 277, n.74, n.75, ascribe all three *Canterbury Tales* manuscripts to the "hooked g scribe." The reference there to Edwards, "Lydgate Manuscripts," p. 19 and note 19, is to Lydgate's manuscripts and to a list given Edwards by Prof. Takamiya that contained unspecified non-Lydgate manuscripts.

enclose two handsome miniatures. Not only are initial capitals often touched with yellow at the start of tales but the practice continues over succeeding lines, once even to later pages (folios 130f). *Explicits* and *incipits* are in red, as are also the Latin glosses in the *Man of Law's Tale*, these last in space provided within the text. Original response to the text is occasionally apparent. The special treatment accorded the *Thopas* versification continues through the couplets of the *Thopas-Melibeus* link. The division into parts of the *Clerk's Tale* starts with the end of the second part; it thus results in a misnumbering of parts. Enthusiasm for the Clerk's song leads to the rubric, "Respice quomodo cantat Clericus Oxonie prout sequitur," and to the inclusion of the words "and his good song" in the *explicit* of the tale.

It was a manuscript with the same ordering and a similar text that the scribes of Glasgow Hunterian 1.1 shifted to after the Pardoner's interruption in the *Wife of Bath's Prologue*. One small difference confirms the opinion of Manly-Rickert that it was not Ra^3 that served as copytext for the second part of Gl (M–R I: 185). Appended to the displaced *Prioress's Tale* in Gl, with no gap and no contemporary rubric, is the twenty-one-line stanzaic link to *Thopas*. These lines stand out because they perform no function, coming as they do before an also displaced *Franklin's Tale*. They do not appear in Ra^3. That the ordering of Ra^3 after the *Wife of Bath's Tale* is exactly followed by Gl suggests a second manuscript produced by the same team.[3] No conceivable set of coincidences could have produced independently the Ra^3 ordering.

Heavily influenced by Ra^3 is the second of the extant elongated miniscule *Canterbury Tales* manuscripts, Trinity College Cambridge R.3.3 (Tc^1). The relationship of the manuscripts will be clarified by the following graph:

Ra^3-Tc^1 = underline. Ra^3-Gl = overline. (Gl not copied from Ra^3)   xxx = Mc - - - - = En^1

(Ln) From E 1795 (half way thru MeT) Ra^3- Tc^1 are no longer derived from Ln. They are closest to Ps for the rest of MeT.

---

[3] The *Pr–Th* link continues the textual associations of the *Sh–Pr* link and the *PrT* (minus of course Ra^3): Ad^3–Ha^4–Ld^1 (M–R VII: 152). Gl shares variants with Ad^3–Ha^4–Ld^1 at B 1881, 1888,1889 (space for place), 1891; see also 1896 and 1899. Gl clearly got the passage from its main copytext.

Manly-Rickert trace Tc^1 back to an ancestor of Ln–Ra^3 for the text to E 1795 (M–R I: 524), but it seems clear that Ra^3 resulted from an *ad hoc* effort, that Tc^1 used the same exemplars or their immediate derivatives in the same order for the first twelve tales, and that even in the later part of the manuscript where Ra^3 exemplars were no longer available Tc^1's ordering was influenced by Ra^3. It is worth noting that Ra^3's uncertainties about order begin with the *Merchant's Tale* at the end of the Ln-derived text and continue through the rest of the manuscript with the possibility of Ad^3 influence on the D G^a sequence. Exemplars inherited by Tc^1 include only the *PdPT* (C^b) not derived from either the Ln or the Ad^3 traditions. Both Ln and Ad^3 were made from ad hoc collections. That exemplars derived from theirs remained together in small groups suggests private ownership and the "bespoke" nature of the book trade before the advent of printing.

Between Ra^3 and Tc^1 there must have been a time-interval. The two manuscripts are extremely close over the first twelve tales. In addition to ordering and text, they share such details as the misnumbering of parts in the *Clerk's Tale* and the Latin admonition to take note of the Clerk's song. After the *Second Nun's Prologue* and *Tale* the relationship changes. Apparently the exemplars for all but one of the subsequent tales (*Pardoner's Prologue* and *Tale*) were no longer available. Tc^1 substitutes others, picks up the two tales missed by Ra^3, and makes complete the G and C fragments by attaching the *CYPT* to the *SNPT*, and the *PdPT* to the *PhT*. But its ordering clearly influenced by Ra^3 is almost as confused, and its *Thopas* gives out after thirty lines at B 2156. This truncated *Thopas* is introduced by four spurious lines. The *Th–Mel* link is followed by some further spurious lines. Additional signs of confusion and uncertainty occur in the fifty-six-line gap at the end of the *MLT* (folio 31a) and the seventy-five-line gap between the *CYPT* and the *PhT* (folio 75b), with in each case only a two or three-line rubric to fill the gap.

It is of course conceivable that Tc^1 was the first of the "elongated miniscule" manuscripts. Not quite as big as Ra^3 despite its double-column format, it is also not as elaborately decorated as either of the other *Canterbury Tales* manuscripts. It might therefore be regarded as a first experiment in the development of the style. The patterns of borrowing favor slightly the priority of Ra^3. The real difficulty arises in the two tales Ra^3 lacks and in the completeness in Tc^1 of the C and G fragments. The two efforts at a collection of the tales are clearly connected; it is difficult to see them resulting in such egregious mistakes as the loss of two tales and the break-up of two fragments. Two other considerations carry weight. The Ln-derived text for the *Prologue* was apparently no longer available when Tc^1 came to be made. Those in charge substituted an Ad^3-derived exemplar. The last four tales in Tc^1 derive their texts from En^1. They therefore bring the scribes and supervisors responsible for the elongated miniscule style into contact with the copytext they were to use on the most elaborate of their *Canterbury Tales* manuscripts, Devonshire.

What does this set of associated manuscripts tell us about the state of the book trade in mid-fifteenth century England? A group of scribes and illuminators cooperated in developing a costly and impressive format for noble and royal patrons interested in such vernacular texts as the *Canterbury Tales*, the *Confessio Amantis*, and the poems of Lydgate. They may have worked together in a single scrivener's shop. The collection of exemplars for each of the *Canterbury Tales* manuscripts was apparently not retained in the shop (if there was a shop) over any considerable length of time. Two texts were probably produced from the same set of exemplars. We have one of these (Ra³) and a mindless copy, Gl, of the last fourteen tales of the second. But when Tc¹ came to be made, all the exemplars, apparently sent back to their owners, were no longer obtainable. For the last nine tales the supervisor had to make a fresh collection. He soon found five exemplars of tales he had not yet copied, all derived from Mc. Later En¹ became available and made it possible for him to complete his work on Tc¹. He or an associate then used this a manuscript as copytext for Ds perhaps intended for Henry VII's mother, Margaret of Richmond. Dialect evidence places these scribes east of London but south of the Norwich area, where Gg, the early a manuscripts, and Gl were produced. The contrast with the *Confessio Amantis* manuscripts is striking. The *Confessio Amantis* was never assembled from exemplars of single tales or small groups of tales. Many of the *Canterbury Tales* manuscripts were.

The decision to use En¹ as copytext for Ds shows the recognition by those involved of the superiority of the a ordering over the somewhat careless makeshifts they had previously developed. The decade of the fifties saw the production of a number of comparatively regular *Canterbury Tales* collections. At the very beginning (c. 1450) there was another a manuscript, the Cardigan (see pp. 20f). The decade of the fifties saw the development of a new constant group, the b. Manly-Rickert describe the family as having an enchained rather than a radiating arrangement with the development occurring in this order: Helmingham (now Princeton 100) to New College D314 (Ne) to Caxton's first edition (Cx¹) to Trinity College Cambridge R.3.15 (Tc²).[4] Helmingham, the first, has a short vellum sequence, dated 1420–30, enclosed in a much later paper text. The vellum extends from mid-*Melibeus* through the final two tales of B² and the *Manciple's Prologue* and *Tale* into the *Parson's Prologue* (line 45). It shows signs, as Manly-Rickert point out (M–R I:260), of being put together as successive tales over a period of time. Two of the three completed junctures between tales have blank spaces of twenty lines or more, the first at the end of a quire, the second with the *incipit* repeated at the end of the gap. The vellum part of Helmingham suggests either tales written out before their place in the sequence was determined or blanks left for linking passages that when obtained turned out to be shorter than expected. Neither alternative is consistent with an already established b text. The paper section, arranged in d ordering without the *Gamelyn*, has no gaps. But it lacks the *Shipman's Tale* and the *Canon's Yeoman's Tale*. The *Pardoner's Tale* ends with the deaths of the three revelers, leaving out the moral apostrophes, the efforts to peddle relics, and the exchange with the Host. Uncertainty with the rubrics also marks the *Pardoner's Tale*. The link is labeled a *Prologue* and the *Prologue* his tale. At the end of the *Prologue* occurs the *explicit*, "Here endith the Pardonere his Prolog." The paper section, dated 1450–60, shows a b text in the process of being assembled rather than one already complete. New College D314, almost contemporary and closely related to Helmingham, includes the missing tales and the missing

---

4   Manly-Rickert II:57. The manuscripts, however, are not copied from one another.

section of the *Pardoner's Tale*. Since earlier texts associated with b̲ do no more than pick up bits and pieces related to later manuscripts, the reality of an early ancestor for the b̲ manuscripts has little evidence to support it. The Oxford fragments (Manchester English 63, consisting of two folios, and Rosenbach 1084/2, consisting of eleven folios), dated 1440–50, are a case in point. Decorated with fine ink portraits of the pilgrims at the beginning of the *Miller's*, *Cook's*, and *Man of Law's Tales*, the fragments have a text and ordering (A B¹ Fᵃ. . . Gᵇ. B². I) that identify with b̲ to some extent. However, a third of the text shows different affiliation and the b̲ ordering has only the absence of *Gamelyn* to distinguish it from d̲. Lincoln (1430–50) has the b̲ ordering but a text that has no close connections with Helmingham and New College. The reality of a b̲ family of manuscripts may indeed be confined to the b̲ manuscripts we have, and almost certainly belongs to the period after 1450. This would help to explain the variable relationships of the texts, much edited and of little value, according to Manly-Rickert.[5] (See Plate 6)

We should perhaps credit the He editor, responsible for the b̲ collection of exemplars, with the contribution of 10 spurious lines to the final scene of the *Merchant's Tale* – soft pornography of a high enough order to attract the attention of the Ha² editor, who had them copied as marginal additions in his text.[6] Ha² itself, a late d̲ manuscript, its illumination dismissed by Manly-Rickert as "conventional mid-fifteenth century shopwork, coarse and ugly," lacks the miniatures for which spaces are provided, but is still the most elaborately illuminated and certainly the most edited of all the d̲ manuscripts. It has a full vinet at the beginning with an interesting title between the foliage of the vinet and the eight-line capital W: "Ere begynneth the book of the tales of Caunterburye compiled by Gef/fraie Chaucers of Brytayne chef poete". In addition the running title Prologus Libri, underlined in red, appears in spaces of the foliage, and a three-line capital A for the beginning of the Knight's portrait fits into the bottom of the page. This system continues throughout, with demivinets for the beginnings of tales (some of them pilfered, the Knight's, the Miller's, and the Cook's, for instance), with running titles and marginalia in red, with eight-line flourished capitals for the beginnings of tales and three-line ones for the prologues, with rime royal stanzas set off by two kinds of two-colored paraphs. Corrections and additions to the text come from a number of sources – from Ii for corrections in the *WBP*, from b̲ (He?) for the Host stanza and the previously mentioned pornographic lines in *MeT*; and especially from

---

[5]   Manly-Rickert I:258. Helmingham is described as a "careless copy of a very bad and much edited ancestor . . . worth little in the making of the text." See Anderson, *Sixty Bokes Olde and Newe*, pp. 7–9, for a description of the Helmingham, and a plate of the hand in the paper section. For the portraits in the Rosenbach leaves of Oxford, see *Sixty Bokes*, frontspiece (in color) and p. 4. The Oxford fragments are discussed, pp. 3–5.

[6]   A problem results from these lines. He has 10 lines, but Ha² and N̲e have 14. The lines seem to have their origin in b̲, since they all occur in the margin in Ha². For similar lines in *ShT*, two seem to be inherited by N̲e from Ii (before B 1509). Two others appear first in Ne (before B 1507) and are picked up by Cx¹. Tc² is based on a non-b̲ exemplar for *ShT* and does not have the lines. See M–R, CV, VI: 493–96; VII: 139,40.

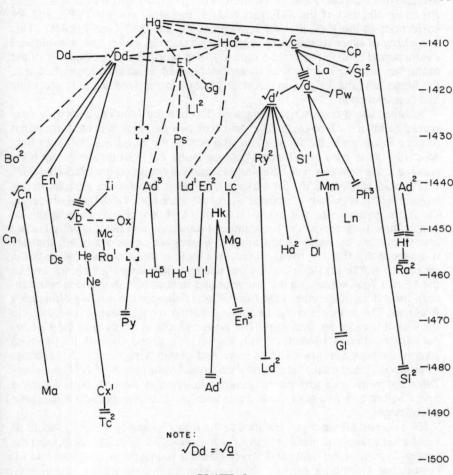

NOTE:

$\sqrt{Dd} = \sqrt{\underline{a}}$

PLATE 6

Morgan (contemporary and the plainest of the d manuscripts for the texts of the *Prologue*, the end of the *SuT*, part of *Mel*, the *McT*, and the *PsPT*, and for corrections in the *KnT*, the *MiPT*, fragment G, the *ThPT*, and the *MkT*. This consulting of other manuscripts suggests special preparation and commitment over a period of time rather than ordinary shop-work. If the poor quality of the exemplars and the carelessness of scribes resulted in an undistinguished text, the format and the decoration made for what on the surface is a fully articulate and beautiful book.

Another late d manuscript, Delamere (Dl) had the *Man of Law's Tale* misplaced (after the *Merchant's Tale*) and had two passages repeated, the short modern instances in the *Monk's Tale* and part of the *Physician-Pardoner* link. Modestly ornamented, the manuscript has double columns on a page not quite so wide as Ha²'s with single columns. Occasionally couplets are bracketed (*GP*, *CYPT*, and spurious *ShP*, for instance); at other times extra paraphs occur, suggesting the regularity of stanzas where there are none (*WBP*) and obscuring the stanza pattern where it exists (*MLT*, 68b and 69a). Flourished capitals of two or three lines set off the beginnings of prologues and tales, usually but not always marked by *explicits* and *incipits*. Spaces are occasionally left that are not adequately filled – twenty-three lines before the *Melibeus* for instance, containing a four-line spurious linking passage, fifty-seven lines at the end of the *Monk's Tale*, containing the four repeated stanzas (the short modern instances), forty lines at the end of the *Nun's Priest's Tale* for the missing *Manciple's Prologue*. The manuscript has throughout a tentative appearance, borne out in the way it became an anthology. The twelve pieces in addition to the *Canterbury Tales* include six selections from Gower's *Confessio*, the end of a poem on Joseph, a unique *Speculum Misericordie*, and a unique fragment of 308 lines on "Partinope"; they total a little more than a quarter the length of the *Canterbury Tales* and were once apparently designed to come at the end. Now arranged seven before and five after, they create with the *Canterbury Tales* a disparate miscellany.

Two other d manuscripts, assigned to the fifties by Manly-Rickert, should be mentioned again. The plainest of the d manuscripts, Morgan 249 (Mg), used the earlier Lc as copytext, and itself served Ha² as a source for missing text and for corrections. Cambridge Mm.2.5 (Mm) reflects the second stage in the disintegration of the B² fragment in the Pw family, a disintegration that started before the first extant d manuscript Pw was copied. Since we can see this second stage developing in Mm itself with the insertion of the *MkPT* between the *PrT* and an already started *Man of Law's* headlink, the copying of Mm must have preceded Ph³ (dated by Manly-Rickert 1430–50). Ph³ carries further the reordering of B² by placing the *NPPT* after the *MkT*. The fact that Mm replaced the text for the *SuT* used by both Pw and Ph³ is countered by the fact that Ph³ not only used a different text for the *FkT* but placed it with its regular prologue (rather than the one developed by the Pw editor to connect it to the *ClT*) just before the *PsPT*. (See M–R II: 68 and 483, where the assumption is clear that Ph³ was later than Mm.) Manly-Rickert speak of an unbound ancestor of the Pw family (M–R I: 430). Many of the collections of exemplars used as copytext for *Canterbury Tales* manuscripts were gathered together only so long as they were needed. In the case of a collection like the one for Pw, which apparently remained together for more than a decade, perhaps for two, some sort of binding must have been provided; either that, or, less likely, the exemplars were kept together in the possession of a scrivener.

The last two of the manuscripts for the decade of the fifties, Hatton Donat 1 (Ht) and Rawlinson Poetry 149 (Ra^2), shared exemplars over the *Prologue* and the first six tales. Ht also has an interesting relationship textually with the earlier irregular manuscript, Ad^2, and with the earliest of all, Hg. The following graphs will clarify the textual relationships of the four manuscripts.

Ht A$^{a\ b\ c\ d}$ B^1 A^e X F^a E^b F^b D$^{a\ b\ c\ d}$ GC$^{a\ b\ c}$ E^a B$^{2\ a\ b\ c\ d\ e\ f}$ HIR

A$_d^2$ A^b ^{c} B^1 D^d C$^{a\ b\ c}$ E^a B$^{2\ a\ b\ d}$

$3^2\ 7^7\ 8^0 - 11^0$ 12^8 $14^0\text{-}21^0$ 22^7 23^8 25^8 fragments
4^4 13^2 24^8 26^8
$5\text{-}7^2$

Ra^2 A$^{a\ b\ c\ d}$ B^1 F^a E^b X D$^{a\ b\ c\ d}$ E^a G C$^{a\ b\ c}$ B$^{2\ a\ b\ c\ d\ e\ f}$ H I R

$1^3\ 2^6\ 5^2\ 6^1\ 7^8$ 8^1 10^8 11^0 13^6 $13^3\ 14^1\ 15^5\ 15^3\ 16^2$ 18^7 $19^4\ 19^3\ 19^2\ 19^1\ 20^1\ 21^1\ 22^3\ 22^4$
$2^2\ 3^7$ $7^1\ 8^7$ 9^7 12^0 $14^7\ 15^2$ $16^7\ 17^7$ 19^1 $21^1\ 22^3$ 23^7
4^0 18^2 24^5
5^2

Underlining = Ht-Ra^2 xxx = Hg   ○○○ = Ad^2 - - - - - - - - = Ph^3

Ht has Hg text from A2200; Ra^2 has lost all but the last 159 lines of this part of KnT. The numbers represent the quiring

Ad^2 and Ra^2 have quires of 8. Ad^2 has lost many quires and leaves. In Ra^2 quires 1, 2, 3, 5, 6, 8, 9, 17, 21, 23, and 24 are defective; 4, 11 and 12 are lost.

Mutilations of Ra^2 and of Ad^2 obscure the probable extent of the interrelationships that once existed. For instance almost all of the extant text of Ad^2 relates closely with the corresponding text of Ht. The exceptions are two late tales, the *Pardoner's* (but not the *Prologue*) and the *Melibeus*, and the four bits of Fragment A still present in Ad^2, which include two-thirds of the *Knight's Tale* and the first half of the *Miller's*. At precisely the point in the *Miller's Tale* where Ht and Ra^2 join the group of manuscripts to which Ad^2 belongs Ad^2 has lost the rest of its text for the A fragment. Lack of specific textual evidence should not rule out a number of possibilities: 1) That for the second half of the *MiT* Ht and Ra^2 used an Ad^2 exemplar. 2) That they even continued to use Ad^2 text for the *ReT*, as they certainly did for the immediately following *MLT*. 3) That as Manly-Rickert suggest (M–R I: 455f.) Ra^2 once included after the *MeT*, in two lost quires, the *FkT*, the *CkT*, and the first 266 lines of *Gam*; if so, in the *FkT* it may have continued to use Hg-derived text, as in the *MeT*, perhaps extending the close relationship with Ht to the seventh tale. 4) That Ht may have used other Ad² text between the *MLT* and the *SuT*, but if it did in any tale other than the *CkT*, a close relationship of Ad² with Hg would be established that is present nowhere else.

Ht is one of the few intact manuscripts of the *Canterbury Tales*. Not only are there no losses of text; the one sign of uncertainty comes at the end of the unfinished *Squire's Tale*, where the last five leaves of a quire were originally left blank. The question naturally arises: did those responsible for Ht or for Ra² make the collection of exemplars on which the two manuscripts base the *Prologue* and the first six tales? The presence of Hg and Ad² exemplars in both manuscripts offers some evidence as to priority. The copytext for Ht includes six exemplars from each of the earlier manuscripts. Since one of each appears in the part of the collection shared with Ra², the breaking up of the collections used by Ht would seem to be the simplest way of accounting for the pattern of textual affiliations. The borrowing of text by Ht from Ad² involves the succession B¹ Dᵈ Cᵃᵇ Eᵃ, almost the exact composition of Ad² itself over this series of tales. Only the absence of Cᶜ, the *Pardoner's Tale*, breaks the sequence and makes clear that the borrowing is from exemplars rather than the manuscript. A similar sequence, this time in Ht, characterizes the borrowings from Hg – Eᵇ Fᵇ Dᵃᵇ. This sequence confirms that the original collection was made for Ht, rather than for Ra² which has a different textual tradition for each section of the D fragment. Because the sequence ends in the middle of the D fragment, it also confirms that as in the case of Ad² the borrowing is from exemplars rather than from Hg itself. If Hg had been available (as Manly-Rickert surmise in I: 253; II: 77, 201, 216, 307, 386), Ht would hardly have made the shift in the middle of the D fragment to other exemplars for the *Friar's Tale* and the *Summoner's Tale* (and then returned to Hg for the *Melibeus* and the *Parson's Prologue* and *Tale*).

Ht is an impressive looking manuscript. Decoration includes a vinet for the opening page in gold, green, blue, and violet with an *incipit* for the *Prologue* of the whole work in bright red; it also includes demi-vinets for most of the tales, flourished initials of two to four lines in gold, white, and blue, rubric headings for pages and tales, rubric marginalia (most of the commentary marginalia in Hg), and paraphs in two colors liberally if somewhat erratically used. Despite the colorful format and the evidence in some of the *incipits* and *explicits* that the supervisor was at least reading the tales ("the Squiers tale of the horse of Brasse," "the Franckeleyns tale of the Rokkes of Bretaigne"), the manuscript betrays some inattention to detail and an underlying lack of insight. The flourished initials for the pilgrims' portraits in the *Prologue* are occasionally omitted (Squire, Cook, Shipman; others have the flourished initial in the second line: Second Nun, Pardoner). The eyeskip of forty-four lines, already present in the copytext, goes unnoticed; it takes us from the door the Miller heaves off its hinges to the Reeve's skill in a ·granary, ascribing the latter's guile to the prize-winner at wrestling matches, and skipping over the Manciple entirely. Capitals for stanzas in the *Man of Law's Tale* are sometimes omitted, and, more serious, some of the stanzas lack lines. The *Cook's Prologue* with its references to the Reeve's performance follows the *Man of Law's Tale*, and the spurious *Prologue* to the *Shipman's Tale* with its reference to the Pardoner follows the misplaced *Clerk's Tale*, without disturbing the apparent equanimity of those responsible. The Clerk's song has the amusing marginal rubric, "len voit de/Chauncere".

The most important conclusion to be drawn from Ht concerns the textual tradition at mid-century. The survival of six exemplars used in the earliest collected manuscript some fifty years before is truly surprising. That these contain the marginalia copied into Hg but none of the additional ones that appear in Ellesmere (El has thirty-five in the *Wife of Bath's Prologue*; Hg and Ht none) throws light on the way the marginalia were composed. The fact that the same holds true for the nine in the *Man of Law's Tale* and twenty-four of Hg's twenty-five in the *Clerk's Tale* suggests that the collection of Hg exemplars might have included ones for those tales as well and that the supervisor gave preference to the more recent and perhaps better preserved Ad^2 exemplars where he had a choice. Also worth noting: The effort to collect exemplars of all the *Canterbury Tales* was successful. But those responsible did not turn to complete collections for copytext nor did they derive their ordering from them in any but the loosest way. Apparently in some instances complete manuscripts were either not as available or not as convenient for copying as smaller collections and individual exemplars. The Ht scribe got more than half his copytext from small collections of Ad^2, of Hg, and perhaps of Ph^3 exemplars. For the remainder of the tales and links, the Ht editors found copy in the b*, cd*, and d* traditions, some of it close to Mc, to Ii, to Ha^4, some of it not close to any extant manuscript collection.

Ra^2 is even more dependent on single texts. After the six tales based on Ht exemplars Ra^2 changes affiliation with almost every tale except in the fragment B^2. There though Ra^2 maintains a consistent position in the d* tradition, it is close to other manuscripts only in the *Melibeus* (to the later Barlow, and for the first three-fifths to the earlier En^2–Ry^2). That it is still sharing exemplars with Ht in the *Merchant's Tale* (despite the Manly-Rickert opinion in M–R II: 77, 280 that their relationship is one of contamination) the list of variants shared by each with Hg (M–R II: 279) makes probable. What settles the issue beyond any reasonable doubt is the presence in the two manuscripts of every one of the ten marginalia present in Hg (and not the one added by El) with every Hg variant (the single exception being an abbreviated *et cetera* at the end of the marginalium for E 1371; the two manuscripts may even provide the correct reading of the marginalium for E 1327, where rats have made Hg defective). Ht and Ra^2 share two misreadings of the Latin commentary, the only ones that either manuscript makes. They clearly copied this commentary from the same exemplar.

Six scribes contributed unequally to Ra^2, giving it a variety of formats, especially at the beginning. Lines to a page vary from thirty-eight to seventy-four. The fifth scribe copied only the *Merchant's Tale* of the extant text, but Manly-Rickert see him as finishing the *Merchant's Tale* and adding the *Franklin's Tale* and the *Cook's Prologue* and *Tale* on thirteen of the sixteen folios of the two missing quires (M–R I: 455f.). The sixth scribe finished the job by copying eighty-five of the 137 leaves; he then identified himself in a mirror-writing signature as William Stevenns. Ra^2's irregularities concentrate at the beginning where the manuscript was using Ht exemplars. It repeats the Ht eyeskip that conflates the Miller's and Reeve's portraits. It gets the *Gamelyn* even more displaced than Ht, putting it just before the *Wife of Bath's Prologue* and *Tale*. But when the Ht copytext gives out, probably near the start of the final scribe's stint, the ordering becomes the d̠, the only change being the omission of the presumably already included *Franklin's Tale*. The handwriting is cursive throughout, the final scribe's painfully small and crowded on the page. The illumination, plain and inexpensive, consists of rubric headings for pages and tales (occasionally left out, as on 83a for the beginning of the *Second Nun's Tale* and as for most running heads from 69a to 83b), two and three-line capitals in blue with red trim (but note the five-line capital on 59b for the Wife's resumption after the Pardoner's interruption), and red and blue paraphs liberally distributed (they imply rime royal stanzas for the couplets of the "squiers prolog" on 36b and are twice misplaced in the Clerk's song on 83a). Ra^2 impresses one as being made for personal use rather than for sale.

VIII

The Decade of the Sixties

The tendencies that were developing in the forties and fifties reached fulfillment in the decade of the sixties. Irregularity became a kind of standard among
the eleven manuscripts ascribed by Manly-Rickert to that period. Three of the
manuscripts – Christ Church CLII (Ch), Selden Arch. B.14 (Se), and Northumberland 455 (Nl) – have completely irregular orderings. Se, described by
Manly-Rickert as "mainly a d* manuscript" (M–R I: 496), has a list of thirteen
sections where the text departs from the d tradition, often in mid-tale, sometimes twice in the same tale. Nl and Ch present texts as disordered in textual
tradition as in sequence of tales. Of the four manuscripts with regular orderings,
Harley 7333 (Ha³), Royal 17 D.XV (Ry¹), Phillips 6750 (Ph¹), and New College D 314 (Ne), only the last two derive their texts from a single tradition.

New College D 314 is the first "complete" b text that we have. Since the b
family is different from the other constant groups in developing by "enchainment" rather than by "radiation" (M–R II: 57), New College did not simply
add exemplars to the incomplete set used by Helmingham. Rather the Ne editor
or possibly an intermediary between him and the man responsible for making
the He collection added texts for the *Shipman's Tale*, the *Canon's Yeoman
Prologue* and *Tale*, and the end of the *Pardoner's Tale* to the manuscript or the
set of exemplars derived from the one used for He. This b chain could involve
at any point a single manuscript or a set of exemplars made up of single tales
and/or small groups of tales. It is a fair assumption that at least at one point the
b tradition involved a set of exemplars rather than a single manuscript. For we
know that the b tradition, like the earlier d, incorporated text for some tales
from another constant group, in this case a. Ne picked up the *Canon's Yeoman's
Prologue* and *Tale* from a Hk exemplar which was also used by the later
constant group En³; Ne's *Shipman's Tale* came less certainly from an exemplar
derived from the one used by Gg and Ph¹; its complete *Pardoner's Tale* is from
the same c tradition from which Helmingham got its incomplete version.

Ne is a very modestly produced manuscript. Its main decoration consists of
rubricated running heads with blue paraphs to set them off. Initials are invariably two-line blue capitals outlined in red with red pen flourishes. Often the

first word of a prologue or tale will be in large script and once (*Squire's Tale*, 69b) the first line was written as two lines in half the writing space with the rubric *explicit* and *incipit* taking up the same two lines in the other half (cp. 255b, start of prose *Parson's Tale*). No notice of the stanzas is taken in the rime royal sections, but proper names often underlined in red and authorities are sometimes noted by index marginalia also underlined in red.

The text of Ne betrays no signs of uncertainty. *Explicits* and *incipits* were copied as they came, before the text, as evidenced by the fact that their runover in the right margin will occasionally displace the final word of the first line of a tale (80a, *MeT*; 122a, *SuT*; 260b, *McT*). The three short quires of six instead of eight leaves are purely mechanical. A Latin *explicit* on 310a (perhaps inherited from Ii) shows an interesting response to the *Parson's Tale*, recognizing it as a treatise by Chaucer assigned to the Parson (the only tale of which this is said in any of the manuscripts): Explicit tractatus Galfridi Chaucer de vii / peccatis mortalibus ut dicitur pro fabula Rectoris. The boxed colophon for the *Retraction* on the next page, in red display script with an elaborate blue paraph, calls the *Canterbury Tales* a "tractate", cancelling some of the implications of the *Parson's Tale*'s *explicit*. Names written in the text suggest that the manuscript was produced in Suffolk, the same area as the earlier b manuscript He.

Phillips 6750 (Ph[1]), the other manuscript in the sixties with a regular ordering and a single textual tradition is a series of contradictions. Two fragments of twelve folios each, the sequence of tales – C B[2] . . . I R – would fit any of the orderings associated with a constant group. Two plausible assumptions can be made of the manuscript: (1) from the colophon at the end, that it once contained a complete collection of the tales; (2) from the signatures on the first five leaves and the derivation of the text from the biggest anthology in the *Canterbury Tales* tradition, Cambridge Gg, that it was itself at some point in its history an anthology. For a time it was bound with a mutilated *Legend of Good Women*, now Additional 9832 in the British Library. Both manuscripts are paper in quarto with quires of twelve, but the paper has different watermarks and the handwriting is different. It is thus a moot question whether the two belong together. Manly-Rickert (M–R I: 416f) calculate that the v signature of the first quire would permit inclusion of all the *Canterbury Tales* to the point where Ph[1] begins (only six of the nineteen or twenty quires indicated) plus the *Troilus*, the *Legend of Good Women*, and Lydgate's *Temple of Glass* (pieces other than the *Canterbury Tales* that appear in Gg) with spaces left over for additional material.

The text of Ph[1], derived from Gg exemplars, has none of the editing and none of the "translation" into East Anglian that characterize the earlier copy. It is one of the two best of all post-1450 manuscripts. Yet the appearance has signs of improvisation and haste, somewhat tempered by intelligence. The handwriting is cursive throughout and uneven. The double-column format gives way in mid-*Thopas* to single columns, providing more space for the presentation of the stanza pattern with the single trimeter lines out to the right of the octosyllabic couplets. After the heading across the whole page for the Host's interruption of Chaucer the text reverts to double columns for the first twelve lines of the link (folio 7a). For the prose *Melibeus* the format remains double-column but for the prose *Parson's Tale* it is single.

A spontaneous response to the text characterizes the totally unadorned set of indications for the beginnings and endings of links, prologues, and tales. A mid-column "*explicit*" brings to an end "the myrie Wordes of the Worthy hoost to the Shipman and to the Prioresse" as well as "the myrie talkyng of the hoost to Chaucer", both introduced by "Biholde". Thus a nice distinction is maintained between links on the one hand, prologues and tales on the other, the latter having their beginnings and endings marked in English with "Heere . . ." always the first word. On the other hand a square space four lines deep and twelve letters wide invites an otherwise unemployable illuminator to start the *Melibeus* with a capital A.

The question inevitably arises: did the complete Ph[1] base its text for all the tales on Gg exemplars? If the question could be answered affirmatively, it would have considerable importance in the way we view the textual tradition some sixty years after Chaucer's death. Even the limited and I think justifiable assumption that the text from the C fragment to the end is derived either from Gg exemplars or from very closely related ones contemporary with Gg has important implications. As in the case of the Hg exemplars used by Ht, a collection of early *Canterbury Tales* exemplars remained together over a period of approximately fifty years and then provided copytext for a "complete" collection of the tales.

Royal 17 D.XV (Ry[1]), another paper text, follows the d̲ order for the tales but gets its text from a variety of sources. Manly-Rickert call it "a conglomeration of tales"; they also make clear that as a rule it got "exemplars of good tradition" (M–R I: 479). This usually means exemplars derived from early independent manuscripts like Ha[4], from the early constant groups a̲ or c̲, or from manuscripts "high" in the b̲*, d̲*, or c̲d̲* lines With Ry[1] it means all of these in a constantly changing set of affiliations. The relationship of some of its exemplars with the later Royal College of Physicians 388 (Py) will turn out to be especially interesting.

The d̲ ordering of the tales in Ry[1] must have been intentional. For the text is full of discontinuities. After the *Man of Law's* endlink, labeled the *Squire's Prologue* in the rubric (95b) but with the Summoner as the speaker at line B 1179, there is a two-line gap followed by the *Merchant-Squire* link with its reference to a preceding *Merchant's Tale*. The two-line rubric at the end (96b) is clear that what we have been reading is the *Prologue* and that what follows is the *Squire's Tale*. Apparently, the two scribes are copying all the links they can find and, as we shall see, they provide space for missing text when they are aware of it. They do not, however, alter the links to fit the context. Thus the *Clerk-Merchant* link in the first scribe's stint connects the *Squire's Tale* to the *Merchant's Tale* (106a, b) without changing the references in the link to the Clerk's song. The scribe is apparently not aware of the incompleteness of the *Squire's Tale*. Then the second scribe leaves unnecessary space for a continuation of the interrupted *Thopas*, short its final twenty-seven lines (241b). He obtains the spurious *Canon's Yeoman-Physician* link (213a) and the useless *Nun's Priest's Epilogue* (284a), but not the *Clerk-Franklin* (176b) or the spurious *Pardoner-Shipman* (227b) links, for which he leaves space but in his uncertainty omits *explicits* and *incipits*. The difficulties with junctures and links are the more surprising for scribes who knew the d̲ ordering and obtained all the tales.

Written by the two scribes in nearly equal stints, the manuscript gives a deceptively controlled appearance. Running heads after the *Prologue* consist exclusively of rubricated roman numerals that indicate the number of the tale. Ry[1] is the only manuscript to use this system. Both scribes write their *explicits* and *incipits* in red, and have blue initial capitals of two to four lines with fine red pen trim in the left margin, extending at times the length of the writing space and even below and above the text. The scribes must themselves have been in control, for the format alters in two important ways when the second scribe, whose hand has been identified in two other *Canterbury Tales* manuscripts, Py and Harley 2251 (Hl[2]), takes over on folio 167 in the midst of the *Clerk's Tale*.[1] The attitude toward stanzaic verse changes, and the format for the headings of prologues and tales as well. Paraphs now mark the beginning of each rime royal stanza, and the rubrics, which up to this point have been included in the text, are with three exceptions (*Fk–SN*, 190b; *ShT*, 234a; *McT*, 285b) expelled to the margin. The second scribe's understanding of metrics has its limits: he does not recognize the stanza pattern in the Clerk's song (176a, b); he tries to make triplets of the decasyllabic couplets in the Host's interruption of Chaucer (242a) by the kind of bracketing he had earlier experimented with in the *Thopas* stanza. A third scribe with a later hand added the final twenty-seven lines to *Sir Thopas* in a different, two-column format, and was perhaps also responsible for adding to the rubrics on 238a,b and 242b the words "by Master Chaucer". Two other questions about Ry[1] remain unanswered: Was the modest display script used for the running heads of the *Prologue* and for most of the rubrics in the first part of the manuscript the work of the first scribe? Whose was the hand that added the two-line rubric between the *Cook's Tale* and *Gamelyn* on folio 66b? Ry[1] had no difficulty collecting exemplars for all of the tales and putting them in the d̲ order. The links and rubrics were another matter.

Some time after its completion as a *Canterbury Tales* manuscript two political tracts, a poem on Edward IV, sixteen folios of a *Book of Nature*, and a printed tract (later removed) were attached to Ry[1] at first to the beginning and later shifted to the end. The additional material is in a number of different hands and on paper with different and, except for the poem, later watermarks. The protection of a binding is sufficient to account for the association of these two incompatible collections of text.

The fourth manuscript with a regular tale order, Harley 7333 (Ha[3]), is a true anthology of secular literature, containing seven "books" of varying length and including beside the *Canterbury Tales* a number of poems by Chaucer, Lydgate,

---

[1]   The second scribe is identified as John Multon by C. Paul Christianson, "Evidence," p. 107n.43. Christianson adds to the list of manuscripts in M–R I: 477 the following: Trinity Cambridge R.14.52; BLMS Cotton Claudius A.VIII, fols. 175–97; BLMS Harley 78, fol. 3r; Bodley MS Rawl D.913, fol. 43; Worcester Cathedral MS F. 172. The list in M–R includes BL Harley 2251, mislabeled in Christianson as 2551, and with fols. 144–293 not specified. Also Trinity Cambridge R.3.21, fols. 33–50 (corrected in C. to 34–49v); BL Add 34360; BL Arundel 59; Royal College of Physicians MS 13 (now numbered 388); and of course fols. 167–301 of Ry[1]. Harley 2251 (Hl[2]) includes only *PrT* in an anthology. *PrT* is in the first hand of the two, not the one named Multon. The first scribe of Hl[2] also did BL Add. 34360 and Trinity Cambridge R.3.2, fols. 34–79. Hl[2] is also mislabeled 2551 in the M–R "Contents," xix–xxi, vol. I.

Gower, Occleve, and others. Written in double columns on the largest size page of any of the *Canterbury Tales* manuscripts,[2] Ha[3] was produced over a period of years by perhaps nine different scribes, all of whom were connected with the house of Austin canons, St Mary de Pratis at Leicester. Among them they created the biggest anthology that includes the *Canterbury Tales*, the only extant one in which the *Canterbury Tales* represents less than half the book (here an unmutilated Ph[1] would perhaps also have qualified).

The manuscript bears the marks of its origin in its censorship of parts of the *Canterbury Tales*. This occurs most blatantly in the revision of Malyne's ancestry in the *Reeve's Tale*. Instead of a parson for grandfather she has the "swansherde of the towne" (A 3943); her mother was "yfostred" in a dairy rather than a nunnery. Further changes make her father rather than her grand-father ambitious to marry her well (3977). They also remove all mention of holy church from lines 3983–86. The omission of two later sections, the end of the *Pardoner's Tale* (his misguided offer to sell pardons and the use of his relics to pilgrims) and the ensuing *Shipman's Tale* (with its exposure of a Monk's misconduct) have been attributed to the same ecclesiastical censorship (M–R I: 212).

The Austin canons lavished a great deal of effort on their manuscript. Illumi-nation includes some very handsome initial letters, three or four lines high, usually blue with red pen trim. Red and blue paraphs abound in some sections, marking rime royal stanzas, for instance, in the *Man of Law's Tale*. *Explicits* and *incipits* are sometimes in red, sometimes underlined in red with red tracing for some of the letters. The impression is of a group effort, somewhat recre-ational in the writing as well as in the purpose of the written product.

Of the three scribes involved on the *Canterbury Tales* section the first did all but one of the first twenty-eight and a half folios, another did all but one of the final fifty-four and a half folios, a third did approximately one in each of the other scribe's stints. The one who started the *Canterbury Tales* was responsible for the other items in the "book", which included the one French poem in the anthology, Charles d'Orléans' "Mon cuer chante joyeuxsement", a product no doubt of his long imprisonment in England. Even the censorship is intermittent: No effort has been made to eliminate religious satire in the *Prologue* or the *Canon's Yeoman's Tale* where it is at least as strong as in the *Shipman's Tale*.

The Shirley influence is evident in the long wordy preface at the beginning of the *Canterbury Tales* and in the tautological headings for the first prologues and tales. It becomes explicit in the marginal comments, "Nota per Shirle", that call attention to such pithy lines as "Ther for he was a prikasour a right", or "That first he wrought and Afftirwardis he taught".[3] This influence must have been exerted through the exemplars for it comes to an end in the *Miller's Tale*.

Mainly a b* manuscript textually, Ha[3] starts out in the *Prologue* and the first

---

[2] Ha[3] is 17.75″ x 13″. The biggest single-column manuscript is Rawl. 223 (Ra[3]), 16.25″ x 11.25″. El is 15.75″ x 11.125″.
[3] For an excellent assessment of Shirley's role, see Julia Boffey and John Thompson, "Anthologies and Miscellanies," in Griffiths and Pearsall, *Book Production*, pp. 284–87 and fn. 26–54.

two tales as a member of the $\underline{d}*$ group. It also changes affiliation at the end of the *Monk's Tale* and the three tales that follow. In the *Monk's Tale* Ha[3] is at first associated with what Manly-Rickert call the "$\underline{Bo}$[1] sub-group of d*" (M–R I: 211). Among the earlier manuscripts in this sub-group is Dl, the only other manuscript to repeat the modern instances. But Dl uses a different text for its second version and does not repeat the *Hugelino*. Ha[3] not only has the *Hugelino* a second time but uses an exemplar very close to the one earlier used by Cambridge Gg (if not actually the same). It continues its close association with Gg through the *Nun's Priest's Tale*, the *Manciple's Tale*, and the *Parson's Tale*. It thus confirms the survival of Gg-derived exemplars, already seen in our discussion of Ph[1].

Corrections and supervision were at best fitful in Ha[3]. An overall control must have been exercised, or we would presumably not have the tales in the $\underline{b}$ ordering. An effort to order the anthology as a whole shows itself in the red roman-numeral foliation; the numbers, introduced by blue paraphs, serve as running heads and dominate each recto from their position at the top of the second column. The first folio of the *Canterbury Tales* is numbered XX x III + IX (69), a number that fits the present arrangement, if one allows for the four quires lost in the first "book"; these headings continue to be accurate throughout the *Canterbury Tales*.[4] On the other hand the signatures present in the *Canterbury Tales* give evidence of two previous arrangements of the "books" that make up the anthology (M–R I: 208).

The recreational nature of the exercise is perhaps best exemplified by what happens in the *Parson's Tale*. In contrast to the prose of the *Melibeus*, bright with numerous flourished initials, sometimes as many as eight to the page, the *Parson's Tale* after its first initial makes do with occasional paraphs. After four pages, at the foot of a recto, in the midst of a sentence, it simply comes to an end. The verso of the leaf and both sides of the next leaf are lined and a stub between these two was once also a lined leaf. This sudden dropping of what had perhaps become in the *Parson's Tale* a chore reflects the casual way in which the pieces were collected for the anthology. Of Chaucer's other narrative poems two, *Parlement of Foules* and the *Anelida*, are lacking a few lines at the end; the other, *The Complaint of Mars*, breaks off in mid-stanza, short 122 lines. Could this also have been a sign of a scribe-patron's flagging interest? A column of space for continued copying plus two stubs that would complete the quire of eight suggest awareness of the poem's incompleteness.

No single man's taste dominates in Ha[3]. Nor is any system imposed. Rather the manuscript implies a holiday from the institutional copying that was the norm in the scriptorium of St Mary de Pratis.

A manuscript that looks unfinished and that shows signs of uncertainty throughout is Fitzwilliam McClean 181 (Fi). The $\underline{d}$ ordering of tales is broken only by the positioning of the *Franklin's Tale* between the *Merchant's Tale* and the *Wife of Bath's Prologue*. Not only are approximately 2000 lines omitted but

---

[4] The implication in M–R (I: 209f) that the folio numbers after f.49 have not been corrected and are therefore inaccurate is not correct. A whole quire, number 6 in Book III (folios cv through cxii), has been lost. The quire included the last 300 lines of *MeT*, *WBPT*, and the first 112 lines of *FrPT*.

quire irregularities and blank space as if for additional text abound. This unfinished state is reflected in the blanks at the beginning of tales and prologues for multi-lined initials and in what look like numerous ignored signals for paraphs but may in fact be the scribe's way of making paraphs. The unfinished look is the more surprising since we know an early, probably the original owner of the manuscript, Thomas Kent, a wealthy collector of books, who apparently gave this manuscript to his wife before his death early in 1469 (M–R I: 166f).

Associations of quire irregularities with problems of text involve the following: 17, a quire of seven, with the extra first leaf containing only the final 14 lines of the *Franklin's Tale* (one and a half blank pages); 18–20, eights, containing with ii through vii of 17 the D fragment, the last two and a half pages blank; 27 and 28 in different ink, a seven (6 + 1) and a six containing the spurious *Shipman's Prologue*, *Shipman's Tale*, *Prioress' Prologue* (part of it on the last added leaf of 27), *Prioress Tale*, link, *Thopas*, and *Thopas-Melibeus* link (crowded on 220ab, with the last four lines omitted); 29–31, two eights and a six that contain the *Melibeus* with the last page and a half blank; and 32, a single leaf containing the ensuing *Monk's Prologue* with many lines left out including the last 22. The final five quires, 36–40, contain the *Parson's Tale* and the *Retraction*. A number of discrete sections were thus created by the scribe, suggesting difficulty in obtaining exemplars and uncertainty as to their length.

Other evidence of difficulty combines with the quire irregularities to lead to some interesting conclusions. For instance, the *Merchant-Franklin* link on folio 118a, a 16-line adaptation of the d family's *Clerk-Franklin* link, is crowded into a 14-line space with its *explicit* in the left margin. When we remember the added leaf (129) at the beginning of quire 17 containing the last 14 lines of the *Franklin's Tale* and no further text, we are led to conclude that the scribe had trouble finding copytext for the links of the *Franklin's Tale* and even possibly for the end of the tale itself (Fi shifts affiliation for the final 114 lines).

Another evidence of difficulty, the blank half page between the end of the *Monk's Tale* and the *Nun's Priest's Prologue*, associates itself with the quire make-up for the whole B² fragment (Qq 27–35) to suggest the order in which the tales were copied. The *Monk's Prologue* on its single leaf (quire 32) must have been copied after the *Monk's Tale* was started and before the preceding *Melibeus* (29–31) with the two and a half blank pages at the end was finished. Otherwise there would have been no need for the anomaly of a one-leaf quire. Similarly the *Melibeus* on its independent quires must have been at least started before the copying of the first three tales of B² in their different ink on irregular quires of seven and six. The implied order for the obtaining of exemplars in the B² fragment of Fi is thus: the *Monk's Tale*, the *Nun's Priest's Tale*; (*Monk-Nun's Priest* link); the *Monk's Prologue*; the *Melibeus*; the *Shipman-Prioress-Thopas* link sequence (whether the *Monk-Nun's Priest* link preceded the *Monk's Prologue* and the *Melibeus* is uncertain).

The numbering of three of the tales creates a further problem. The *Reeve's Tale* (always in the rubrics called the Carpenter's) is properly numbered three. But the *Summoner's Tale*, actually number 11, in the manuscript is labeled nine, and the *Franklin's Tale* number seven is labeled 12. Manly-Rickertt (M–R I: 166) point out that the assigned numbers would be correct for the c ordering, and that perhaps such an ordering was at one time planned for Fi. Present quire arrangements though flexible would not permit an orginal placing of the *Merchant's Tale* and the *Franklin's Tale* after the *Clerk's Tale*, the order they have in c; more likely, as in the case of Mm and Ph³, the numbers were copied from the exemplars, without thought as to their significance.[5]

As we might expect from the irregularities already noted, the textual tradition of Fi is constantly shifting. For instance in the *Man of Law's Tale* it shows surprisingly with Ellesmere, but the headlink is associated with the ancestor of the exemplars used in three d manuscripts (Dl, Ha², and Sl¹), and the so-called *Squire's Prologue* (the *Man of Law's* endlink) is associated with a set of near-contemporary and contemporary texts (Mc, Ra², Py, and Ry¹). The association with Ra² continues in the *Squire's Tale*, and in the *Merchant's Tale* brings Fi into agreement with Hengwrt, but the marginalia from Hg, so exactly copied in Ht–Ra², do not appear in Fi, indicating perhaps that the exemplars though similar were not the same. A close relationship with the contemporary manuscript Nothumberland (Nl) begins in a segment of the *Squire's Tale* (F 129–349, where Nl breaks off), is especially strong in the *Franklin's Tale* where the two manuscripts are independently derived, and is picked up again in the *Summoner's Tale*, the *Clerk's Tale*, the *Second Nun's Tale* to 140, and the *Physician's Tale*. The two manuscripts are together in omitting F 1423–56 (the end of Dorigan's complaint), but Fi does not share most of the further omissions in Nl at the end of the *Franklin's Tale*. Fitful association with Ra², with the d manuscripts already mentioned, and with the general d* tradition confirms that Fi was copied from a series of individual exemplars, not always available when needed. The text is unusually corrupt with many lines missing, including all but the first two lines of the *Manciple's Prologue* (followed by six unusually inept lines of introduction for the tale).

Relatively unadorned, Fi has most of its *explicits* and *incipits* in red as well as the commentary (*Man of Law's Tale*, mainly) within the text. The running titles in the *Prologue* which consist of the names of the pilgrims are also in red, but for the tales the running heads appear on the rectos only in the ink of the text. There is some red touching of initial letters, some use of display script, and some elongation of ascenders in first lines. Fi uses what in most manuscripts serve as indicators for paraphs as paraphs. Always rubricated, they mark off stanzas in the *Man of Law's Tale*, but in the *Clerk's Tale* the format changes to space for illuminated initials at the beginning of each stanza. The leaving of spaces for additional text and the comparative regularity of tale order indicates a measure of control on the part of scribe or supervisor. The writing of the single scribe, however, is an uneven cursive, and the format is improvised.

Another unfinished manuscript, Harley 7335 (Ha⁵), has a much better text than Fi, but has lost a lot of its paper leaves including two complete quires at the beginning and an even larger number at the end. Both text and ordering come from Additional 35286 (Ad³). But the text breaks off at C 676, where the Pardoner's revelers are learning about the "privee theef" called Death. It thus can follow the ordering of Ad³ in only two of its departures from the a tradition: the *Cook's Prologue* and *Tale* do not appear at the end of Fragment A and the

---

[5]   See Chapter IV, fn.11 (pp. 31f), for numbering of tales in other manuscripts.

Second Nun's Prologue and *Tale* follow immediately on Fragment D. Nothing in Ad³ suggests that the changes, which in addition put the *Cook's Prologue* and *Tale* and the *Canon's Yeoman's Prologue* and *Tale* after the *Manciple's Prologue* and *Tale*, were anything but intentional.

Ha⁵ has a single red initial, a two-line capital I, probably a late addition, on folio 45a at the beginning of the *Man of Law's Tale*. This is the only use of color, but space has been left throughout for illuminated initials, two or three lines high, and for *explicits* and *incipits* of prologues and tales. No running heads appear, and almost no articulation of the text. Horizontal bars in a line of space occur between rime royal stanzas in the *Man of Law's Tale* and in the *Second Nun's Prologue* and *Tale*. In the *Clerk's Prologue* the couplets have bars where other manuscripts have the "Pausacio" divisions, but in the tale the single line of space between stanzas gradually diminishes until folio 103a, where only the bar separates the stanzas.

A few of the spaces left for initials occur within the tales; they mark the parts of the *Squire's Tale* and the *Clerk's Tale*; occasionally they indicate an intelligent response to the text, as for instance after the Pardoner's interruption of the Wife of Bath (63a), at the point where the Friar addresses his audience on the pains of hell (80a), and at the first mention of the falcon in the *Squire's Tale* (135b). Those in charge were apparently still in hopes of locating a conclusion for the *Squire's Tale*; they left blank for it a page and two leaves, later excised, at the end of the quire.

The most interesting aspect of the manuscript is its relationship with Ad³ with which it forms a constant group. Though Ha⁵ gets both ordering and most of its text from the earlier manuscript, Ad³ was clearly not the copytext used. Its many corrections do not appear in the later manuscript, nor does its almost complete set of Ellesmere marginalia. This last point is significant because Ha⁵ does carry the *Man of Law's Tale* commentary and some of the other marginalia developed in Hengwrt. If the additional marginalia developed by El had been available, Ha⁵ would no doubt have had them as well. Because of the numerous corrections in the earlier manuscript, the exact place where a shift of affiliation occurred and even whether a shift occurred is in some doubt. The text in question comes at the end of the *Merchant's Tale* (most certainly in the final 100 lines, but possibly in the final 728), in the *Squire-Franklin* link, and in the *Franklin's Tale*. One certainty: the spurious link connecting the *Franklin's Tale* with the *Physician's Tale* in Ha⁵ (derived from đ's *Canon's Yeoman-Physician* link) has nothing to do with the Ad³ tradition. The presence of this link strengthens the case for a separation in the *Squire-Franklin* link and in the *Franklin's Tale*. In the *Franklin's Tale* Ha⁵ has an exemplar independent of other manuscripts (except for the final 114 lines, where slight connections with the Fi-Nl text are established, M–R II: 312f; VI, 660–71).⁶ The influence of this independent exemplar accounts perhaps for a slight change in format in Ha⁵: With the *Franklin's Tale* spaces for illuminated initials, mostly one-line but

---

⁶ A number of the eleven variants, listed by M–R (II: 312f) as shared by Ha⁵ and Fi–Nl, are not exact and could be *acco*. The statement that Ha⁵ is much later than /Fi–Nl is misleading. We can't know when the exemplars used by the three manuscripts were written. The manuscripts themselves are roughly contemporary.

occasionally larger, become numerous; this change continues even when the text returns in Fragment C to the Ad^3 tradition.

The Ad^3 influence must have been transmitted through another manuscript copied from Ad^3 exemplars. This manuscript would of course not have the corrections so prominent in Ad^3. It was probably copied before the Ellesmere marginalia were acquired. That these were present in the exemplars from which Ad^3 was copied is the simplest explanation for the fact noted by Manly-Rickertt (M–R I: 44) that text and adjacent marginalia were clearly written in the same shade of ink. Loss of text in the *Merchant's Tale* and the *Franklin's Tale* on the part of the transmitting manuscript would best account for the shifts in textual tradition in Ha^5. The only alternative explanation, transmission by a set of exemplars copied from those used for Ad^3 and kept together for some forty years, is a less likely possibility.

We now come to three irregular manuscripts. Each of them has a special interest in its own right. Selden Arch. B 14 presents us with a series of contrasts. A colorful and handsome manuscript with no gaps and no sign of major uncertainties, it orders the tales in a unique way. The only manuscript to bring the B^1 and B^2 fragments together, using the *Man of Law's* endlink as a *Shipman's Prologue*, it places them in an order that retains the geographical anomaly of mentioning Rochester after Siddingbourn. Though it has many small omissions, single words and unfinished lines, Selden gives evidence of having the most carefully prepared copytext of any *Canterbury Tales* manuscript.

Going back in most of its text to the ancestors of the $\underline{d}$ tradition, there is evidence throughout not just of the variants and shifts to be expected of late exemplars, but of access on the part of the editors to manuscripts of all types (M–R I: 496). The contamination of the copytext that resulted testifies to the care exercised on it by those in charge. Many of the "corrections" were apparently made from the early $\underline{c}$ text, Lansdowne, perhaps a model in its "completeness" for the later editors to emulate. These later editors give an example of their ingenuity in the way they handled the problem of the *Squire's Tale*. They took over most of the unique Lansdowne effort to account for its incompleteness, where the Squire out of concern for the other pilgrims puts off to his next turn the conclusion of his tale. They left out the last four lines, where the Wife of Bath is introduced, making brilliant use instead of the two lines in part III of the *Squire's Tale*. The end of the *Squire-Man of Law* link in Selden reads as follows:

> and the day passith certeynly
> therfore oste taketh now good hede
> who shal nexte telle and late him spede
> Appollo whirlith up his chare so highe
> Til that the god Mercurious hous the slighe.

By incorporating the last two lines, with their reference to Apollo the sun moving swiftly up in the sky, the editors stressed the Squire's concern for the passage of time and gave reason for the Host to look up and measure the sun's actual height for the first lines of the *Man of Law's Introduction*.

This linkage by local reference gives a clue to some of the decisions on ordering made by the Selden editors. The Clerk's song to the Wife of Bath and the Host's reference to his own wife apparently justified putting the *Clerk's Tale* before the *Wife of Bath's Prologue*. The genuine *Merchant-Squire* link brought the *Merchant's Tale* into association with the highly original *Squire-Man of Law-Shipman* linkage, giving a great nine-tale sequence as a kind of center-piece to the order: E^b–Fa–B^1–B^2. The spurious *Canon's Yeoman-Physician* link made a four-tale sequence, G–C, to match the two opening four-tale sequences, A and E^a–D. Only the *Franklin's Tale* remained a comparatively unlinked tale before the finale of *Manciple-Parson-Retraction*: A, E^a–D, E^b–F^a–B^1–B^2, G–C, F^b, H–I–R. At the beginning of each of the sequences except possibly the third (the *Merchant's Prologue*) was a comparatively strong introduction to absorb the reader's interest and minimize the lack of connection with what had preceded.

The format to which this highly original ordering was subjected shows thorough advance planning. A highly articulated and colorful manuscript with no signs of uncertainty and no quire irregularities resulted. The opening full vinet was designed to accommodate the four-line rubricated *incipit*, somewhat wordy but showing a knowledge of the *Prologue*. Every tale but the first then has its own prologue, with both prologue and tale set off in its demi-vinet and introduced by a rubricated *explicit-incipit*. Two-page running heads in red and frequent indexing marginalia also in red have alternating gold and blue paraphs flourished in a different color. The initial capital is gold in a five-line champ; the later ones are for the most part three-line, exceptions being a four-line A (171a) at the beginning of the *Melibeus* and the eleven-line I (195a) that variably indents the opening lines of the *Monk's Tale*; within the tales two-line and one-line capitals are used for emphasis; each of these receives its paraph always flourished often to the margin and sometimes ending in a pattern or drawing. Capital letters in the text are sparingly used, normally for proper names, not for the initial letters of lines; paraphs occasionally lend emphasis to these small letters.

Rarely the format breaks down. On 77a paraphs are missed, as one is again at the beginning of a stanza of the *Prioress's Tale* (165b). On 134b two marginal paraphs appear with no text appended. The missing paraph on 165b has the excuse of introducing a two-word line, an example of the scribe's reluctance to guess at what he couldn't read, found confusing, or, as in the case of the numbering of wives in the *Wife of Bath's Prologue* (89b), found conflicting readings for (Cf. the blank for the name of Melibeus's daughter on 171a). The interruptions of Chaucer by the Host and of the Monk by the Knight are not called prologues in the headings nor do they receive demi-vinets. However, the *explicit* before the *Nun's Priest's Tale* recognizes the previous 13 lines as his "prolog".

Marginalia denominate the hymn to the Virgin by the Prioress as a second prologue and the duping of the priest by a wicked canon as a second *Canon's Yeoman's Tale*, indicating some attention to the text but as in most manuscripts a lack of clear distinction between link and prologue and prologue and tale. On the other hand the rubric introducing the *Retraction* (309b) first brings the *Canterbury Tales* to an end: "Here enden the tales / of Caunterbury And next thautor taketh leve."

Those responsible for the Selden manuscript apparently had access to Lansdowne with its c ordering and probably to the a ordering as well.[7] Yet they chose to devise their own independent arrangement of the *Canterbury Tales*. The copytext they developed included exemplars of all the tales. Only the final page with a few lines of the *Retraction* is missing.

Northumberland 455 (Nl) is a complete contrast with Selden. No preparation of the copytext preceded its writing; the exemplars used were frequently deficient; the scribe added by his carelessness to the debasing of the text. Described as unbound by Urry in 1712, many of the quires have suffered loss of leaves. The manuscript is modestly decorated with red and blue capitals set off by blue and red pen trim, with *incipits* and *explicits* in rubric, and with red and blue paraphs. For the first part of the *Canterbury Tales* Northumberland had the model of the b ordering. Whether this model was a manuscript used as a copytext or a collection of exemplars arranged as in the b constant group, the model, damaged at best, apparently gave out with the *Second Nun's Tale*: A B[1] F[a]–E[b] D E[a]–F[b] G[a]; for the ordering of tales thereafter is chaotic: B[2b] C[a] B[2ac] C[b] G[b] Beryn D[2159–2294] B[2def] H–I.

Even at the beginning the materials available to those responsible for the manuscript were defective. For Northumberland almost certainly lacked a *Cook's Tale*; it did not have the *Man of Law's* endlink or the final half (323 lines) of the *Squire's Tale*; and the exemplar for the *Summoner's Tale* left out the final episode with its lesson in "arsmetrik" (2159–2294). The shortened *Merchant's* endlink (six lines) and *Squire's* headlink (F 1–8 turned into a seven-line stanza) used to connect the *Clerk's* and *Franklin's Tales*, as in five of the seven d manuscript families, came to Northumberland in a uniquely lame form.

After its departure from the b ordering the manuscript continues to be defective. It lacks both links for the *PrT*, the *Ph–Pd* link, and the *McP*. Those responsible managed to obtain the conclusion of the *SuT*, labeling it with the *incipit*, "Here endith the tale of the Sompnour within the boke Wryten". The implication that the ending for the *SuT* came from a book, in contrast to the text for the short version used earlier, perhaps tips the balance in favor of exemplars rather than a manuscript as copytext even for the beginning of Northumberland. In any event the scribe copied D 2159–2294 in a way that made the insertion of the lines near the rest of the tale impossible. An inept effort to insert them was nonetheless attempted at some time before the final foliation was made. For the leaf containing on its recto the final lines of the conclusion was excised from its position as the first in quire 32 and inserted in quire 16 where it was numbered 114. This not only made the conclusion copied in after the *Tale of Beryn* incomplete but created the unsatisfactory early sequence, D 2039–2124, 2262–94, 2125–58 for the leaves numbered 113, 114, and 115. At some time the excised leaf was restored to its original position in quire 32.

The placing of *Beryn*, with its account of what happened in Canterbury, to follow after the *Canon's Yeoman's Prologue*, with its reference to Boughton under Blee just five miles away, might indicate some further attention to the

7   Se has an a text for *McPT*. It also has the a link for the *Me–Sq* sequence. M–R report some contamination from Gg, which has an a ordering.

ordering of the tales. The effort was fitful at best.[8] For the *Th–Mel* link introduces without the gap of a single line the *PdP* (instead of Chaucer's second tale), making an adjustment too difficult to effect when the proper tale turned up. After the *Second Nun's Tale* the scribe seems to have copied exemplars with only occasional concern for the ordering. The chief example of this concern would be his saving for the end the Manciple and the Parson.

The textual affiliations, to the extent they can be determined, confirm these observations. A connection with ancestors of the b tradition at beginning (A B^1) and end (H I) shows itself. This connection becomes specific with Ht and Ra^2 at the end of the *KnT* and in the *ReT*, accounting perhaps for the absence of the *CkPT* (Ht and Ra^2 displace the Cook's sequence including *Gam* to different positions after B^1). Also important is Nl's intermittent relationship with Fi and the d tradition from the *SqT* through the beginning of the *SNT* (G 140). This does not include the *MeT* where Ra^2–Fi join Hg, but it does include the *Wife of Bath's Tale*, the short *SuT*, and the *ClT*. The relationship is especially strong in the *FkT*, where according to Manly-Rickert (M–R I: 163, II: 309) the two manuscripts are independently derived from O. After the *SNT* Nl's textual affiliations are constantly shifting, with fragments G, B^2, and C broken up and the ordering dictated apparently by the availability of exemplars.

The manuscript's chief distinction is providing us with the only text we have of the *Prologue* to the *Tale of Beryn*. Here a poet with no ear for Chaucer's verse but a true appreciation of his vision of the pilgrims, imagined what happened when the group arrived in Canterbury. The result is a twenty-page description of their putting up at their inn, the Checker of the Hope, "at mydmorowe" and of the events that happen between then and their departure the next morning. The action includes their visit to the cathedral, a fabliau misadventure involving the Pardoner, and the Merchant's volunteering to tell the *Tale of Beryn* as the first tale of the homeward journey.

No contemporary left a record of response to the *Canterbury Tales* so rich in its implications. It shows that for the author of *Beryn* (probably a monk of Canterbury, M–R I: 392) and for those responsible for the Northumberland manuscript pilgrimages were not one-way journeys and the *PsP* with its reference to a "thropes ende" was not describing the entry of the pilgrims into Canterbury. It shows an absorption into the frame story and a familiarity with the pilgrims on the part of a reader who later turned poet.

Christ Church CLII (Ch), despite its irregularities, is quite different from either Northumberland or Selden. Behind its copytext is a set of undamaged exemplars, many of them independent, the others related to such early manu-

---

[8]   M–R (I: 390) speak of "inserting the quires containing *Beryn*". But *Beryn* begins on the final leaf of quire 24, *CYPT* having ended on the verso of the preceding leaf (33 lines). *Beryn* ends on the recto of the penultimate leaf of quire 31. M–R (I: 391) also speak of the insertion of D 2159–2294, "written later". The conclusion of *SuT* begins on the verso of the leaf *Beryn* ends on, continues on the last leaf of quire 31, and concludes on the recto of leaf i, quire 32. *Mel* then starts on the second leaf, the verso of the first having been left blank (later excised and moved temporarily to the position in quire 16 near the end of *SuT*). The quire arrangements indicate the text was written consecutively.

scripts as Additional 35286 (Ad³), Hengwrt, Ellesmere and Cambridge Gg. The probability is that these exemplars were kept together over a period of at least thirty years, before they were copied out in a clear cursive hand by an amateur scribe connected with Winchester College. This scribe signed his name Thomas Vause on folio 72 and prefaced his manuscript:

> Grayce and good manners maketh mann.

A text results that stands out among its contemporaries not for its appearance but for its comparative freedom from error and editing.

A paper text in quires of 20 in the handwriting for the most part of a single scribe, Christ Church shows little advance planning. It contains, in addition to the *Canterbury Tales*, a copy of Occleve's *Ploughman's Tale* in a different hand (inserted in the *Tales* after the unfinished *Squire's Tale*); Lydgate's *Churl and Bird* in a third and later hand; and Lydgate's *Siege of Thebes* in the original hand. A Table of Contents in the hand for the most part of the second scribe appears on the verso of the first leaf. It has the *Ploughman's Tale* crowded in, clearly a late addition. Still later is the "Tale of the churle and his bryd" in the third hand, the same that wrote the tale.

The format of the manuscript reveals the lack of planning. Lines to the page vary from 35 to 46 for the *Canterbury Tales* section; for Lydgate's *Siege of Thebes* the upper limit increases to 58.[9] *Incipits* and *explicits* are normally in rubric with a suitable gap in the text, but the red initial capitals with no pen trim or further decoration are from two to five lines, and sometimes the text has no gap between segments with the *incipit* and a *narrat* in the margin (the *Reeve* 52a) or a gap of a single line with just the *narrat* (the *Cook* 57b). Cross outs for mistakes are in red with the correction in a heavier black ink, often in a different handwriting. Latin within the text is underlined in red, as are many of the memorable lines, but the Latin marginalia, in the *Clerk's Tale* for instance, are in the ink of the text, very finely written, especially on the rectos where the outer margin (the one used) has more space. The portraits in the *Prologue* are normally set off by a big red initial with the name of the pilgrim in the left margin. But the Franklin's portrait starts without any notice, and the Miller miscalled Manciple in the left margin has his name written correctly in the right. Indexing marginalia occur but there are no running heads.

Two other things happened that suggest a non-professional origin for the manuscript: The red ink used for the headings and initials makes offsets of unusual prominence on practically every facing page. The original binding apparently had the sheets in two of the quires misplaced. The elaborate directions for reading the text correctly by turning backward or forward a number of leaves to a given "signe" remain as a prominent feature of the manuscript, though a subsequent binding corrected the mistakes.

The irregularity of the ordering is deceptive in one respect: A (X) D E^a C B^2 H F^b B^1 E^b–F^a (PlT) G I. Only two of the tales are separated from their fragments, the *Clerk's* and the *Franklin's*. Only one of these, the *Franklin's*

---

[9] M–R (I: 85) give lines to the page for the *Canterbury Tales* as 38–45. There are 46 on 110a; 35 on 63b; 36 on 63a.

lacks its link. Every other genuine link except the *Man of Law's* endlink (probably cancelled) is present, including the Host stanza (at the end of the *Clerk's
Tale*), the *Merchant's* headlink, and the *Nun's Priest's* endlink. Christ Church
also has all five of the added passages of the *Wife of Bath's Prologue*, but none
of the confusion on the numbering of wives in D 451 f, 480, 503, and 525,
associated with the a and b traditions. The original copying included only
genuine text and left space at the end of the two unfinished tales, (the *Cook's*
and the *Squire's*) for conclusions should they turn up. It is this space that later
got filled with the *Gamelyn* (the last three leaves of quire 3, plus the only
irregular quire in the manuscript, a quire of ten, with a watermark different
from all the rest) and Occleve's *Ploughman's Tale* (in the handwriting used
earlier for some of the corrections and the table of contents, filling all but the
last page of the last four leaves of quire 12).

How did such a collection of exemplars, affiliated with only the best of the
early manuscripts come about? We can only give a tentative answer to this
question. The exemplars were perhaps gathered together in the 1420s, either to
provide copytext for a manuscript that has not survived and has no extant
descendants, or to serve as reading matter in their own right. They were then
kept together as the a exemplars were. They acquired, if they did not already
contain, the marginalia developed for Hengwrt and used in Cambridge Dd. But
they did not have any of the ones added in Ellesmere and used also in Ad³. The
presence of the sequence E^b–F^a, as well as the textual affiliations and the
absence of spurious links, suggests that the original order for the fragments was
a rather than b, c, or d. Whatever the original order, it did not survive over the
years. Thomas Vause, when he came to copy his collection, could place adequately only the first and last fragments.

In support of this highly speculative account is the survival, similarly intact,
of sets of early exemplars used in Ph¹ and Ht. There is furthermore the unlikelihood of two phenomena at either end of the time span. In the earlier period
such a complete collection of Canterbury materials could hardly have been
made without awareness of the way other manuscripts had organized the tales.
In the later period a collection with textual affiliations constantly shifting could
not have been made without acquiring exemplars of more recent origin. The
fine quality of the text, the stability of most of the fragments, and the irregularity of their arrangement give Christ Church a very special place in the textual
tradition of the *Canterbury Tales*.

In our discussion of the manuscripts of the sixties two very closely related
ones remain – Phillips 8136 (Ph²) and Bodley 414 (Bo¹). The latter may indeed
not belong in this decade (M–R I: 58 give it the estimated date 1450–1480), but
its association with Ph² makes consideration of the two together essential. They
have in common not only ordering but copytext and elements of format as well.
In both ordering and copytext they shift after the D fragment, or possibly after
the *Clerk's Tale*, from an a model to a d with the result that two of the tales, the
Merchant's and the *Squire's* do not appear.

These are not the only omissions the two manuscripts share. They also lack
the *Cook's Prologue* and *Tale*, part of the introductory material for the *Man of
Law*, the *Wife of Bath* stanza and the *Clerk's* song in honor of the Wife of Bath,
the *Franklin's* headlink, more than half (the final half) of *Melibeus*, and the

possibly cancelled *Man of Law's* and *Nun's Priest's* endlinks. They both contain the two spurious links developed by the d editors to connect the G, C, and B^2 fragments.

The two manuscripts also share certain elements of format. They both employ red underlining and a heavier and bigger script for one or two words at the beginning of prologues and tales. Ph^2 has multi-line initial capitals in red; Bo^1 leaves space for them. Combinations of these forms of emphasis with red paraphs set off important passages in both manuscripts. Touching of initials in red and red margins for writing space also occur in both. Neither manuscript employs running heads or *explicits*, and both tend to use one-line titles in red rather than *incipits*.

With their agreement in so many respects their differences are hard to explain. Ph^2 for no apparent reason leaves out the *Reeve's Prologue*. No shift occurs in textual affiliation over this part of the A fragment. The B^1 fragment is even more puzzling. The textual affiliation for most of the fragment is with the later manuscripts Egerton 2864 (En^3) and Additional 5140 (Ad^1), both of which have all the text. Ph^2 lacks the introduction up to the beginning of the poverty prologue, which it picks up from the Ellesmere group. It then has a series of omissions, mostly of rhetorical material, always in complete stanzas – lines 288–315, 421–27, 771–84, 932–45, and 1086–92, ten stanzas in all. Bo^1 has lines 1–56 and 97, 98 of the *Introduction*, but lacks the entire *Prologue*, 99–133. It does have the ten stanzas missing in Ph^2 with no change in textual affiliation and no indication of difficulty. These omissions in Ph^2 therefore seem intentional, especially since they never disturb the narrative sequence. They might be viewed as a scribal response to the rhetorical extravagance of the tale. On the other hand, all the introductory material to the *Man of Law's Tale* was probably missing from the copytext with the two manuscripts picking up separately and from different sources the lines that they have (M–R I: 59, II: 71f). It is difficult to see how those responsible could have failed to pick up more of the missing lines, especially in Bo^1's recovery of only part of the *Introduction*. The failure to share what each got is even more puzzling. On the whole Bo^1 shows signs of more careful production. It gives a neater appearance, and in the *Parson's Tale* especially it sets off the divisions with space for multi-lined capitals, entirely missing in Ph^2. The system breaks down, however, for the *Retraction*, which begins in mid-line with a red paraph as its only mark of emphasis.

In any event neither manuscript was copied from the other, and the copytext must have been assembled from two distinct and contrasting parts. The portion of the text with the a ordering is especially complicated. The first 320 lines come from the Ellesmere tradition; from A 320 to about 1639 the affiliation is with Physicians 388 (Py) and Hengwrt; the rest of the *Knight's Tale* is with the b* tradition; halfway through the *Miller's Tale* Bo^1 picks up Ra^2–Nl and some associated manuscripts, with which it continues to the end of the A fragment (no *Cook's Tale*); B^1 comes from the same sources as En^3 Ee, the *Wife of Bath* from Gg–Si, the *Friar* and *Summoner* from Hg–El, and the *Clerk's Tale* from Hk–Ra^2 and associated manuscripts.

The portion of the Bo^1 copytext ordered on the d model is more nearly regular textually. Most of it is affiliated with the d* tradition, specifically with

Dl–Ha^2–Fi, but the closeness of the affiliation is variable as well as the number of other manuscripts involved. In *Mel* the group is in close association with El–Sl^3; in the *McP* Bo^1 leaves $\underline{d}$* for what Manly-Rickert (M–R II: 445) call a good but unknown source; and in the *PsT* its association is again with Py.

The material in the $\underline{a}$ portion of the text, perhaps a collection of exemplars, must not have extended beyond the *Clerk's Tale* when it came into the hands of those responsible for the two manuscripts; it had presumably been patched over the years as leaves and quires deteriorated or disappeared. The $\underline{d}$ portion on the other hand must have had nothing earlier than the D fragment, but it was in better condition; it showed less evidence in its textual relationships of having been patched. The operation was therefore quite different from that which produced the Glasgow *Canterbury Tales*. The father-and-son pair who co-operated on Gl had two complete manuscripts available, from one of which they were able to copy the two tales they had inadvertently omitted.

Except for the shared elements of format, there is little sign in Ph^2 or Bo^1 of supervision or attention to detail. The only evidence for an awareness of short-comings comes in the *Introduction* and *Prologue* to the *Man of Law's Tale*, where each of the two manuscripts picks up a different part of the text and neither got lines 56–96. Apparently no mending of the exemplar for this part of the copytext took place, or the two manuscripts would have shared the lines each obtained. An even greater lack of attention must have obtained with the *Mel*, which remained less than half complete without sign that either scribe noticed.

Ph^2 has the distinction of being the only *Canterbury Tales* manuscript in its original binding. The binding is really a kind of wrapping secured against accidental opening, a thorough protection against damage from all sides. By its nature it suggests what non-binding exposed manuscripts to.

The manuscripts of the sixties show a variety of patterns – two huge anthologies, Ph^1 and Ha^3; a number of manuscripts belonging to constant groups, Ne the first complete $\underline{b}$ text that survives, Ph^1 derived exclusively in what we have of it from Gg exemplars, Ha^5 from the Ad^3 exemplars, the curious constant group $\underline{Bo}^1$ that has a text derived in part from manuscripts with the $\underline{a}$ ordering and in part from manuscripts with the $\underline{d}$; finally the three strikingly irregular manuscripts each with its own special interest, Se that has a carefully planned and highly original ordering, Nl that has the unique copy of the tale of *Beryn*, and Ch that has a collection of exemplars dervied from early and excellent texts.

IX

After 1470

With 1470 we are approaching the end of the manuscript period. Caxton's first edition (Cx^1) appeared in about 1478. If printing created a new market, it seems also to have coopted the old. Some ten manuscripts can be assigned to the last thirty years of the century. A surprisingly plain set, seven are entirely on paper, and one has a 2:1 ratio of paper to vellum.

Curiously most of the ten belong to constant groups. Each of the four main groups has at least one member; c̲ is represented by Sloane 1686 (Sl^2), a̲ by Manchester 113 (Ma), d̲ by Laud 739 (Ld^2), and b̲ by the copytext from which Caxton took his first edition and from which later Trinity College Cambridge R.3.15 (Tc^2) got most of its text, In addition a new constant group En^3, Egerton 2864 (En^3) and Additional 5140 (Ad^1), was created. This group used exemplars for ten of the tales and a prologue from Holkham 667 (Hk), one of the irregular manuscripts of the 1440s, and arranged them along with a random collection of others in the a̲ ordering.

Two other manuscripts have regular orderings and derive most of their text from single sources. Barlow 20 (Bw) is prevailingly a d̲* manuscript. Royal College of Physicians 388 (Py) has a b̲ ordering but derives most of its text from descendants of Hengwrt exemplars. This comparative regularity of the post-1470 manuscripts is broken only by two: Glasgow Hunterian U.1.1 (Gl), as we have seen, inherits the irregularities of two earlier manuscripts, Cambridge Mm and a twin of Ra^3. Trinity College Oxford Arch.49 (To) has its own unique disorder both in the way the tales are arranged and in textual tradition.

We should begin by considering the representatives of the constant groups. The greatest length of time between the production of most of the copytext and the manuscript itself occurs between c̲ and Sloane 1686 (Sl^2). The estimated date in Manly-Rickert for Sl^2 is 1480–90. The copytext, either a manuscript or a collection of tales and fragments made from the c̲ exemplars before their break-up and the use of more than half of them in the d̲ constant group, must date from the first quarter, probably the second decade, of the century. Over the sixty years some of the text was lost. The *Canon's Yeoman's Prologue* and *Tale* are missing from Sl^2. In addition the manuscript departs from the c̲ tradition in the *Second Nun's Tale* and the *Physician's Tale*, using an exemplar from a different textual tradition for each. The three tales, contiguous, were presumably missing in the copytext; they make up a sequence of 1779 lines, perhaps three quires (M–R I: 512), but more likely the exemplars for three tales; they constitute along with the absence of the *Parson's Prologue* and *Tale* the only departures from the c tradition.

Sl^2 comes to what looks like a fully intentional end with the *Manciple's Tale*. Not only is there a colophon on the blank half page at the end of the tale (in the same ink as the text), there are also, written just below, the words *Deo gracias*, with the same red pen trim as decorates multi-lined initials in the text. The final quire is missing both its first and last leaves. What happened after the *SNT* is perhaps instructive. There space was originally left for additional text, 19 lines on 216b plus an additional leaf (the third of quire 28); this blank leaf was later excised but the rim is still visible. Similarly the extra final leaf of the last quire, 38, was cut out; its excision left the first leaf of the last quire vulnerable and accounts for its loss.

The only other irregularity in quiring has no textual significance; it comes in quire 32, an original quire of four leaves, beginning in mid-*Thopas* and ending in mid-*Melibeus* (with catchwords intact and even signatures). The unusual two and a half page space which as we have seen was originally left at the end of the *SNT* (with no *explicit* and the only *incipit* a truncated running head for the *PhT*, "a Tale of the") is thus unique in the manuscript. Something in the exemplar (the same as Mc's) must have suggested to the scribe the missing material. He was able to obtain exemplars for two of the missing tales in the sequence but not for the middle one. Apparently even at the end of the manuscript period the *CYPT* were difficult to come by. That one cannot say the same for the *PsPT* gives an added and perhaps intentional finality to the colophon and motto at the end of the *McT*.

Though Sl^2 is the plainest of the three c manuscripts, it does have multi-lined blue capitals with elaborate red pen trim at the beginning of prologues and tales, the washing in red of many line initials and of the first letters of proper names, much red underlining especially of the irregular running heads, and within the text of the *Man of Law's Tale* the Latin commentary in red. Many of the running heads, in display script, have a detached first letter, much smaller, a sign for something even more elaborate but never performed. These characteristics, clearly decorative in intent, make unlikely the Manly-Rickert suggestion that Sl^2 was produced as a shop copy (M–R I: 513).

Manly-Rickert also suggest that Sl^2 was made in the same shop as the three elongated minuscule manuscripts, Ra^3, Tc^1, and Ds. They give as evidence the use by Sl^2 of text for the *PhT* most closely related to Tc^1's, and two elements of format: similarity of page headings to Ra^3's and the use of capitals for the first line of the *Knight's Tale*. However the resemblance of the page headings (very irregular in Sl^2) is not very close, and the capitals of the first line (never repeated in the manuscript) are not at all like the elongated minuscules developed for the other manuscripts. A distant imitation of features seen by the scribe, whose cursive hand bears no resemblance to the others (described by Manly-Rickert as formal scrivener's hands, I: 117, 463, and 522), would better account for what we find in Sloane 1686.

Sl[2] is one of the smallest of the *Canterbury Tales* manuscripts.[1] The format is not regular. It has 28 to 32 lines on each page (with spaced rime royal stanzas not the reason for the lower number). The initials at the beginnings of tales and prologues vary in a spasmodic way from two to five lines. The running heads are especially irregular, usually covering the spread of the b and a pages but sometimes missing from one or both (entirely lacking throughout the *Melibeus*). The display script used for them varies in its elaboration sometimes on successive pages (see 232b, 233a, and the next two spreads). But the scribe indicates sometimes his awareness of what he is writing. He does not label the interruption of the *Th* as a prologue, and he does notice that both the link and the prologue before the *PdT* are introductory, calling the second in both the *incipit* and the running head "Another Prolog". He makes frequent corrections in both the ink of the text and in the red of the underlining and pen trim. There is no sign of a supervisor. The omission of the *PsPT* gives the impression of a scribe pleasing himself, rather than one working under shop discipline. He was perhaps his own patron.

This was probably the case with the example of the a constant group, Manchester 113 (Ma), written by a scribe who called himself Johannes Brode Junior. Ma, as we saw earlier, is a plain paper manuscript, with no decoration at all except for some paraphs and a four-line blue and red capital on the first page. It was clearly written from the same set of exemplars throughout as Cardigan. It has no irregularities of textual tradition, of ordering, or of quiring. The absence of supervision, the paucity of corrections, the unusual number of leaves in a quire (24), the uncommon handwriting, the uneven lineation, the sparse decoration, and the probable identity of scribe and owner lead Manly-Rickert to the conclusion that Ma was an amateur production (M–R I: 351).

Manly-Rickert find in the dialect nothing against an East Midland origin for the manuscript (they mention specifically Norfolk, M–R I: 350). Dan Mosser, however, using the methods and resources of the new dialectology (including *A Linguistic Atlas of Late Medieval English*) finds in both Cardigan and Manchester evidence of a Warwickshire provenance for the scribes with an underlying layer in the copytext of East Anglian.[2] The history of the a constant group with the three manuscripts of its older arm *Dd* showing Norfolk and Essex linguistic profiles tends to confirm Mosser's conclusions.

The representative of the next constant group Laud 739 (Ld[2]) received consideration in the chapter on the d manuscripts (see above, pp. 39f). One of the two vellum manuscripts in this late period, it used Ry[2] as copytext for all but two sections of the *Canterbury Tales*, the first 531 lines in the *General Prologue* and a passage of 1165 lines from E 298 to F 944. The fact that these two passages in Ld[2] are not from the same textual tradition makes even more baffling the decision not to copy at least the second one from Ry[2], which the scribe clearly had access to at the time he made the shift.

---

[1]   Among the collections, Sl[2] 10.75" x 7.5", compares with To 10.5" x 8.25", Ht 10.25" x 7.5", Ad[2] 10.5" x 7", Fi 9.5" x 6.75", Ra[1] 10.5" x 7.5". See Chapter VIII, fn. 2 (p. 69), for dimensions of some of the larger manuscripts.
[2]   Mosser, "The Scribe of Chaucer Manuscripts." See also his work in progress, *The Alpha Text of the "Canterbury Tales."*

Though there is no evidence of supervision, there are many corrections, not only by the scribe but in a hand very little later from Caxton's first edition (M–R I: 315). Elizabethan hands have added running heads and marginalia as well as a leaf containing the Friar-Summoner exchange at the end of the *Wife of Bath's Prologue*, missing originally in both Ry^2 and Ld^2. The provision of spaces for multi-lined capitals at the beginning of prologues and tales and the total absence of color in the manuscript suggests the kind of bespoke trade outlined by Doyle and Parkes in "The Production of Copies".[3] In this case the patrons, perhaps the Johnson family of Spaulding (M–R I: 318f), decided not to hire an illuminator for the decoration of the manuscript.

That they did make corrections from a Caxton and added marginalia and headings shows their dissatisfaction with the scribe's rather mindless work (noted earlier in his copying sequentially the misplaced sheets in Ry^2 without regard for instructions). For instance, in the *Prologue*, they indexed the Yeoman's and the Plowman's portraits with marginal names, the scribe having neglected to set them off with the usual space for an initial capital and with the pilgrim's name beside the portrait. At this point their zeal appears to have flagged, for the last five portraits are not set off at all (the scribe's last effort was to leave space for a capital in the second, not the first, line of the Parson's portrait). The lack of system in format is the more remarkable since the scribe was copying from a well ordered manuscript.

The representative of the b constant group, Trinity College Cambridge R.3.15 (Tc^2), is the most irregular of the four; it used the same copytext as was earlier used by Caxton for his first printed edition. By the time the manuscript was copied, however, a number of things had happened: The *Clerk's Tale* had lost two thirds of its text, approximately E 375 on. In addition the links and the Breton lay prologue of the *Franklin's Tale*, the *Canon's Yeoman's Prologue* and *Tale*, and a large segment of text from line 243 of the *Physician's Tale* through the rest of fragment C and continuing into B^2 through the first three tales had either disappeared or in the case of the *Pardoner's Prologue* and *Tale* lost their place in the sequence. Those responsible had some success in repairing the damage. But they were unable to come by exemplars containing the Franklin's links and prologue, the *Canon's Yeoman's Prologue* and *Tale*, the Pardoner's headlink, the *Prioress's Tale*, or *Sir Thopas* and its links; they also had some difficulty with the ordering.

The result was a departure from the b textual tradition and the b sequence in a number of places. A hint of difficulty occurs at the end of the *SuT* where a quire with two extra leaves bears at the foot of the last page the words "hic grisild". The ensuing irregularities are best indicated graphically:

---

[3] See also Edwards and Pearsall, "The Manuscripts," pp. 257–78.

Text	S_uT	C_iT	C_iT	P_dPT	H_{ost} Stanza	F_kT	SNPT P_hT	P_hT	S_hT	S_h End-link	M_{el}
	(E1-374)	(375-1212) No WB Stanza E1195-1200 at end.	(398-968) No head-links no gap		(E1212b-1212g) called FkP	(F729-1624) No link. Gap at end of tale.	(G1-559) No gap; no link at end.	(C1-242) CW for b text	(243-286) Text different from Cw	$(B^2$ 1191-1624)	(B1625-1634) Gap at end; no Cw	$(B^2$2157-3073)
Affiliation	$b(Cx^1)$	b	Ra^2 etc.	b	b	b	b	b	Ind	Ind	Ind	b
Quiring	13^{14} vi-xiv	14^{12} i-vi	$14^{12}15^{12}$ vi-xii, i-ix	$15^{12}16^{12}$ ix-xii, i-v	16^{12} v-vi	$16^{12}17^{7}$ vi-xii, i-vii, (viii-xii excised)	18^{12} i-ix	18^{12} ix-xii	19^{3} i	$19^{3}20^{5}$ i-iii, i-v	20^{5} v	$21^{12}23^{12}$ i-xii, i-xii, i-ii
Foliation	148^{a}-156^{b}	157^{a}-162^{a}	162^{a}-177^{a}	177^{a}-185^{b}	185^{b}-186^{a}	186^{a}-200^{b} (no 198)	201^{a}-209^{a}	209^{a}-212^{b}	213^{a}-213^{b}	213^{b}-220^{a}	220^{b}	221^{a}-246^{a}

The rather complex picture of the difficulties encountered leads to some interesting conclusions. There seems to be no reason for the quire of fourteen at the end of the D fragment unless the *CIT* had already been started. The loss of text in both the *CIT* and the *PhT* accounts for the confusion about the tales that followed these two in the b ordering, the *FkT* and the *PdT*. The sequence Pardoner, Host Stanza (labeled *Franklin's Prologue*), Franklin, Second Nun, Physician, with the text b (Cx^1) except for the last 43 lines, with almost no linking passages, and with the loss of three complete tales, suggests that the copytext used for Cx^1 and Tc^2 was a collection of exemplars many of which especially in the central section were single tales. The recovery of text for two thirds of the *CIT*, for the last 43 lines of the *PhT*, and for the *ShT* shows that some effort was made to repair the surprising amount of damage. Suggestions of access to complete manuscripts (M–R II: 318) like the Ellesmere cannot be sustained. Tc^2 must have gotten the El marginalia for the *WBPT* and the *SuT* (it misses all but the first for Dorigen's complaint in the *Franklin's Tale*) from exemplars of single tales. Contact with a complete manuscript would have made possible the recovery of the missing tales, two of which (*PrT* and *Th*) could have been inserted without disturbing the quire arrangements. The use of the same copytext as Caxton makes the apparent isolation of those responsible for Tc^2 an anomaly. It also breaks the chain development that sets off the b constant group from the others.

Tc^2, a paper manuscript, has moderate arrangements for decoration. Two-lined capitals in red with brown trim normally mark the beginnings of prologues and tales, with enlarged initials sometimes extending into the space for the red *explicits* and *incipits*. Divisions of tales and even important passages receive similar recognition. Marginalia are in red and red underlining frequently sets off proper names or Latin or even images in the text. One or two ascenders of the first lines on a page frequently extend into patterns. There are, however, no running heads, and as in the other b manuscripts no recognition of stanzas.

Tc^2 has some of the other characteristics associated with the b tradition. It

identifies the first husband as a reveler at D 453 but avoids the other renumbe-
rings associated with the a tradition. It includes the pornographic lines in the
pear tree section of the *Merchant's Tale* but misses them in the *Shipman's Tale*,
where it is using a non-b exemplar. Like the other b manuscripts it brings the
Parson's Tale to an end before the *Retraction*, this time in the most elaborate
display script the scribe has used: Explicit Tractatus Galfridi Chauces de
pe/nitencia ut dicitur pro fabula Rectoris.

The creation of the new constant group En^3, consisting of the two manuscripts Egerton 2864 (En^3) and Additional 5140 (Ad^1), was perhaps the most
remarkable development in these final years of *Canterbury Tales* manuscript
history. The survival of copytext for ten tales and a prologue, used some forty
years before in the production of the highly irregular manuscript Holkham 667
(Hk), provided some of the incentive for the enterprise. The filling out of the
text from miscellaneous exemplars brought the editor in contact with the
Cardigan tradition. This must have occurred fairly late, for the *PsT* is the only
full tale with its text from Cn. The influence of Cn, however, was considerable.
It provided En^3 with a number of the links and the a ordering. It transmitted
some of the Ellesmere glosses, suggested a search for more, and inspired not
only the expansion of extant marginalia but the creation of many original ones.
It was finally available to those responsible for the later of the two manuscripts,
Ad^1, when they had to replace 220 lines of text in the *Knight's Tale*.

The following graphs will help to keep clear the complex relationship
between the four manuscripts:

Graphs of Relationship for Hk-En^3

$G^a = G^{1-119}$ *En^3 gets NPendlink, $D^{2159-2294}$ (end of SuT), Cl-Me link, Me-Sq link, Sq-Fk link from Cn*

Ad^1 also gets A 1661-1880, 220 lines from the end of Part II of KnT, from Cn

Underlining indicates text from Hk exemplars.

...derlining indicates text used by En^3. The B^2 fragment lacked text through loss of leaves in Shipman's Tale (306 of 434 lines), in all but 11 lines of Thopas, in the link with Me-
...us, and in Melibeus (509 of 922 lines).

...exemplars not used by En^3: A^{cd} F^b B^1 D^{ab} E^a D^c

Study of the graphs will lead to a number of conclusions: the Hk text came to
the En^3 editor through its exemplars. Access to the manuscript itself would not
have resulted in a such a random selection, and the variety of sources drawn on
for the rest of the text leaves no doubt as to which came first. Moreover the Hk
copytext was in the form of single tales and one small sequence (the first four
tales of B^2). A further conclusion can be drawn from the 220 lines of the *KnT* in

Ad[1] derived from Cn rather than Hk. Ad[1] must have used the same copytext as En[3], not the manuscript itself. If the latter had been the case, there would have been no need to shift exemplars in mid-tale.

Four features of the new collection confirm this reconstruction of its history. (1) Hk never had more than the *Prologue* of the *Second Nun's Tale* (G 1–119). The scribe left a page and a half blank at the end of a quire for the continuation which he never obtained. The exemplar for this segment survived and became part of the En[3] copytext. It is followed by the tale with a text from the cd* tradition and the rest of the G fragment from Hk. (2) The only part of Hk's D fragment to survive was the *Summoner's Tale*, but in Hk it was lacking D 2159–2294. En[3] picked up the ending from Cn. (3) The sequence E[b]–F[a] also formed part of the En[3] copytext. The exemplars for the two tales came from Hk, but the ordering and the linking passages were from Cn. (4) Finally, and perhaps most decisively, En[3] got from Cn its version of the *Nun's Priest's* endlink with six spurious lines at the end appearing only in Cn–En[3]. These six lines connect the endlink with the Hk-derived *Second Nun's Prologue*. The *Tale* with a text from the cd* tradition had presumably earlier filled the gap in the Hk-derived exemplars for fragment G, as described in (1) above. This sequence from the *Nun's Priest's* endlink through the *Canon's Yeoman's Tale* epitomizes the stages in the En[3] editor's gathering of the text.

The pervasiveness of Cn's influence, once the editor had come under it, can be seen at two further points in the copytext. He got his version of the *Wife of Bath's Prologue* from an independent exemplar. Later he went over the Cn version carefully, comparing it with the one he already had, to spot the revision in the numbering of husbands Cn had inherited from Dd (D 452,3, 480, 503, 525). He changed the numbering to agree with Cn.[4] He also took the suggestion from Cn to add the words "sine prologus" to the *incipit* for the *Physician's Tale*.

The question naturally arises: did more of Hk's copytext survive than has come down to us in the mutilated manuscript. The only possible instances are at the beginning where Hk lacks the first 1064 lines through loss of leaves and in its final B[2] fragment. There similar damage has taken 306 lines from the middle of the *ShT* (B 1305–1610), all but the first eleven lines of the *Th*, the Host's interruption and the beginning of the *Mel* (B 2157–2256a), and everything after B 2669a, including the final 409 lines of the *Mel*, the *MkT*, and the *NPT*. The textual affiliations give us no reason to doubt that En[3] had complete Hk exemplars for the *KnT*, the *ShT*, and the *Mel*; no new connections occur in En[3] for the passages missing in the mutilated Hk. The affiliation of En[3] with Ry[1] in the *Th* might throw some doubt on the contiguous opening section of the *Mel* (B 2157–2256). On the other hand the evidence is strong that the Hk copytext was made up of single tales even where the tales were linked to one another. The *KnT* survived but the *MiT* and the *ReT* did not; the *SuT* survived, but the

---

4   En[3] actually has "thridde" in line D 452 (with Ii); firste in 453, which starts with a two-line capital M. Lines 480 and 503 also have multi-lined initial capitals, but not 525. The series comes to an end in En[3] at 587 with a marginal "quintus maritus" and a two-line space with a capital W. Ad[1] has "firste" in both 452 and 453, indicating that the En[3] copytext had the a reading in both lines.

preceding *FrT* did not. The possibility exists, to judge from the almost independent nature of the En^3 copytext for these sections, that the *General Prologue*, the *Monk's Tale* (but not the Prologue with text from Ry^2), and the *Nun's Priest's Tale* derive from Holkham exemplars (M–R II: 84, 86, 404f, and 420f).

The careful preparation of the En^3 copytext included the development of a set of commentary marginalia. The editor picked up many of the ones that had appeared in Ellesmere. Where these included Biblical references, he frequently added to them references of his own. The idea of including marginalia probably came to him from Cn. The following graph will prove helpful:

$M_{of}L$	$W_{of}BP$	S_uT	C_iT	M_eT	F_kT	P_dT	M_cT
9	36	5	26	11	25	11	0
(8)	(0) + 2	(0)	(17)	(3)	(0)	(2)	(6)
9	12 + 27	0	13	3	4	5	6 + 1
					Ad^1 has 1	Ad^1 has 4	

= Ellesmere   ◯ = *Cn*. The last number is En^3 (with Ad^1 if different, below.)

The relationship of the En^3 marginal glosses with Cn's is evident from what happened in the *CIT*, the *MeT* and the *McT*. We must remember that Cn was in existence for many years before En^3 was thought of. Cn carried 17 of Ellesmere's 26 marginalia in the *Clerk's Tale*; En^3 had all but four of those 17 and no others. The two manuscripts have the same three of Ellesmere's 11 in the *Merchant's Tale*. In the *Manciple's Tale* Cn apparently composed six of his own. All six appear in En^3, three of them in slightly different form, plus a new and original one. Cn and En^3 shared another original one in the *WBT*. Two things are clear. Cn's glossing influenced the En^3 editor. The latter had an independent mind. He left out some of Cn's marginalia; he altered others; he composed some of his own.

This last activity is apparent in the *WBP*. He adapts (and adds to) 12 of the 36 in Ellesmere, which he must have searched out independently of Cn, for none of them appear there. He then added some 27 of his own. In the *WBT* he composed four more. In the *FrT* he expanded the Biblical reference to Psalms in Ellesmere (for line 1657) and added a reference to I Peter. He must also have found an independent source for the marginal glosses in the *MLT*; for he carried all nine of them while Cn had only eight.

The marginalia probably rule out a direct access to Ellesmere. True he was independent in what he took from Cn. But he would hardly have passed up all five of the marginal glosses for the *SuT* in Ellesmere, not to mention all of the ones on Dorigen's complaint and majority of those in the *PdT* and the *MeT*.

A more difficult question is the nature of his access to Cn. Was it to the manuscripts or to the exemplars? The evidence of variants in the sections of the En^3 copytext taken from Cn leans slightly in the direction of the exemplars. For instance, in the *Nun's Priest's Epilogue* (22 lines counting in the six spurious ones) seven of the variants in the manuscript did not get copied into En^3 or Ad^1, presumably because they were not in the copytext.[5] In the *Parson's Prologue* (74 lines) one Cn variant made its way into En[3] versus 14 that did not.[6]

The variants common to both manuscripts in the Cn tradition and therefore present in the exemplar made their way in great numbers into En[3]. In the 136 lines at the end of the *SuT* 36 are present; in the 220 lines of the *KnT* (A 1661–1880) the number in Ad[1] is 80. The ratio of Cn variants not copied to those that appear (by acco?) is still impressive: The numbers are 7:3 in the *SuT* and 15:5 in the *KnT*.[7] The near certainty that Ma (dated 1483–1485) was copied from this same Cn copytext rather than the manuscript shows that the materials were still together during this period and in the proper ordering.

The editor of En[3] was clearly a learned man, capable of recognizing Biblical echoes. He also showed considerable patience in the way he prepared his copytext and some critical sensibility in imposing on it the a ordering. That this was not an obvious choice is apparent from the printed texts that were beginning to appear. No hint of commercialism affects his procedure. He was in all probability working on his own behalf, as he collected his materials and prepared them thoroughly for copying.

The manuscript that resulted, written on paper, has a minimum of decoration and a relaxed, unsystematic format. The most striking feature does not obtrude itself on the reader – the irregular quire arrangement. Most of the quires are made up of leaves rather than sheets and the number of folios to the quire varies from seven to eighteen (the last quire has only two). Only twice do successive quires have the same number of leaves. These irregularities have nothing to do with the text. Though the scribe chose sometimes to begin tales (or prologues) at the top of a page (14a, 111b, 193a, 225a, 234a), this never happens on the first page of a quire.

The only catchword appears on 74b, folio v in a quire of 14. Another irregularity is the reversal of leaves 50 and 51 with the scribe's numbering indicating that the order was originally correct. Thus the present quiring does not reflect the state of the manuscript in the fifteenth century. The reversal of leaves must have occurred in the next hundred years, for a note in a sixteenth century hand on 49b instructs the reader to skip a leaf to a sign at the top of 51a. That no loss of text ensued from such a history, that we have in En[3] one of the very few undamaged manuscripts of the *Canterbury Tales*, testifies to the care

---

[5] The variants in Cardigan, not in Ma, not in En[3], occur in lines B 4643, 4644, 4646, 4651, 4652, and in the second and fourth of the six spurious lines. The *NP* endlink appears only in a, Ch, En[3], Ry[1]; the six spurious lines only in Cn, En[3]. See M–R VII: 614f.

[6] The variants in Cardigan, not in Ma, not in En[3], occur in line I 6, 15, 23, 26, 28, 32, 34, 39, 43 and 44 transposed, 48, 50(2), 66. The one in Cn also in En[3] is at line 19, shared with b, c, and 25 other manuscripts. See M–R VIII: 177–183.

[7] In *SuT*, the 36 variants shared by Cn and En[3] are D 2159, 61, 63, 72, 74, 76, 77, 80, 85 (2), 86, 91, 92, 96, 97; 2204, 14, 18, 22, 25, 28, 36, 38, 45, 49, 50, 54, 58, 62, 72, 79(2), 81, 90, 91, 92. The seven lines where the Cn variant is not in En[3] are D 2178, 81; 2219, 26, 53, 71, 83. The three, where the Cn variant is in En[3] are D 2160, 2217, 2261. See M–R VI: 227–240. For the *KnT*, see M–R V: 159–180. In these 220 lines Ad[1] has 32 variants not from Cn or Cn.

given it by its editor-scribe-owner and those who subsequently refrained from scribbling their names on its pages.

The scribe made provision for a six-line capital at the beginning of the *Canterbury Tales* and for smaller ones (one- to three-line) at the beginnings of prologues and tales, at divisions and important passages within tales. Occasionally (83b, 145a,b, 155a), he wrote in the ink of the text capitals that don't quite fill the space. Otherwise the manuscript is unadorned, no color, no patterned ascenders, no display script. Each recto has in its top right corner the folio number in Roman numerals and just below it a running head. The commentary marginalia appear in a smaller script, somewhat crowded on the verso, extending sometimes (82a, 89b, 96b) below the text.

The initial heading reads "Incipit liber Galstid Chaucer de gestis peregrinorum versus Cantuariam." Thereafter headings appear in Latin and English with a natural ease that implies bilingualism. Some show a knowledge of what he was copying. After calling the *Man of Law's Tale* the "tale of Alle" in the *incipit* for the prologue and introducing the poverty prologue as the start of the tale, he wrote above the real beginning (B 134) "Heer bigynneth the substaunce of the tale". Similarly after labeling the *Sq–Fk* link a prologue and the "olde gentil Britouns" passage the "tale of the Frankeleyn", he wrote the following heading for the story itself: "he begynneth the tale of the Rokkes of Brytayne". The *Pardoner's* headlink is called "Prohemium" (171a, 171b); "Incipit Narracio" heads the tale (173b).

Manly-Rickert (M–R I: 144) detect a probable second hand taking over at I 515 on folio 274a in the *Parson's Tale*. They describe both hands as "small, neat, well-formed". The distinction in the lettering, in the forms of d, v, w, and g, is not entirely consistent. It is accompanied by difference in the color of ink. There is also a slight change in format. The numbering of folios stops after 262, 12 leaves earlier than the postulated shift in scribes (occasional mistakes show that the running heads were done in batches as a separate chore). The change must have been unanticipated, occurring as it did in mid-page and mid-section. Dan Mosser ascribes the differences to an interval of time. Other duties or illness might have called the scribe away from his work on the *Canterbury Tales*.[8]

When a second scribe took over, or when the original one returned, he not only finished the *Parson's Tale*, but he went on to copy what he called (292b) "the Laste tale of Cauntirbury / talis tolde homward and maad bi Dan / John Lidgate Monk of Bury." A more drastic change occurs at this juncture than earlier, but paradoxically it tends to confirm that no change had actually occurred. The lines per page suddenly increase from a range of 34 to 38 to a range of 45 to 47.[9] The handwriting is correspondingly much smaller. It is in fact the same earlier employed on the numerous marginalia in the *Wife of Bath's Prologue*. The quires continue to be irregular, consisting of leaves rather than sheets and numbering successively 16, 10, 9, 13, 10, and 2 leaves. The text

8 Personal communication from Dan Mosser.
9 The range for the *Canterbury Tales* generally, as M–R I: 143 states, extends to 40 (258b), even to 40 lines plus an *explicit* (233b). The change for the *Siege of Thebes* to the bigger range of 45 to 47 is immediate and permanent.

continues to be neat, with sparse but adequate indexing and almost no adornment. The headings continue to be in English and Latin. If there were indeed
two scribes, they bear a remarkable resemblance to one another in handwriting,
in taste, in technique of bookmaking.

The *Siege of Thebes* brings the two manuscripts of En^3 into an interesting
relationship with British library Additional 18632 and provides an additional
link with the Cn tradition. Cn, En^3, and Ad^1 used the same exemplar for the *ST*
as Additional 18632.[10] The likelihood is that the BL manuscript was the first to
be copied, that the exemplar came to the En^3 editor with the Cn materials and
that it remained with the En^3 copytext from the time the first manuscript was
produced to the end of the century, when in all probability Ad^1 came into being.

The copytext for En^3 survived almost intact. The only segment of text that
needed replacement when Ad^1 was copied was a 220-line section of the
Knight's Tale (A 1661–1880). Curiously, the men in charge were still able to use
the Cn tradition in replacing what had originally been part of Hk's copytext.
The only other difference from the En^3 text involves a 65-line gap (4094–4158)
almost at the end of the *Siege of Thebes*. This gap occurs between iii and iv in
the final quire (an 8; the norm is 12). That it occurred between leaves in Ad^1
implies a mistake in copying rather than a loss in exemplar.

Ad^1 has a much more colorful appearance than En^3. The only one of these
final ten manuscripts to have a full vinet on the first page, it continues with
multi-lined blue initials flourished in red for prologues and tales. Divisions and
important passages within tales also have the blue initial letters with red pen
trim. The manuscript features generous gaps for *explicits* and *incipits* in large
display script. Its running heads are often underlined in red (simply, or with an
attached vertical line at the beginning). The same applies to the indexing
marginalia and to the Latin commentary, this last in very small writing (in the
longer ones with a brace up the left side). Occasionally the red underlining
shifts to blue.

The manuscript has quires of 12 with the inner and outer sheets of each quire
vellum, the other four paper. Loss of text has been confined to two paper leaves,
iii and iv of the second quire, which carried away 131 lines of the *KnT* (A
969–1099). Two other missing paper leaves, one each in quires 25 and 26 had
no effect on the text; they must have been excised before the copying. Three
watermarks follow one another with no irregularities and confirm that the
copying took place sequentially. The third is dated in Briquet 1488, an indication of the lateness of the manuscript.

This time there is no question about the handwriting. A second scribe took
over on 227a at the beginning of the *Sh–Pr* link. His hand is slightly smaller
and better controlled. The change is especially noticeable in two elements of
style. The first scribe used elongated ascenders on the first line of almost every
page. usually not satisfied with one or two, he often got up to eight, nine, or ten.
On 31a and 181a he has 12; on 12a and 52a, 11. These abruptly cease with the
shift. The display script for the second scribe is heavier and far less flamboyant,

---

[10] See Robert Earl Lovell's University of Texas dissertation, "John Lydgate's *Siege of
Thebes*."

without the elaborate pattern the first scribe occasionally developed at the upper and lower extremities of his initial letters (55b, 108a, 182a, 205b).

Both scribes use Latin for their headings, though the first occasionally lapses inadvertently into French (de le Reve 55b; de le Frankeleyn 181b, 182a). The second, who is perhaps the better Latinist, calls the *NP* in the *explicit* for his tale "Sacerdotis monialium" and the *CY* in the *incipit* for his prologue "famuli Canonici". He also makes a distinction three times that he must have picked up from something in the copytext, since the En^3 scribe as we have seen makes the same point in English – that the *PsT* is only the final *CT* composed by Chaucer. The last tale is the one composed by Dan John Lydgate, Monk of Bury: "Explicit prohemium Rectoris Incipit narracio eiusdem et est ultima de hiis quas Chauncer composuit".

A curious inconsistency in a manuscript that otherwise gives evidence of professionalism is the wide range in the number of lines per page. The manuscript starts out as Manly-Rickert indicate (M–R I: 29) with 34 to 37 lines. But the norm soon drops to around 30. The spaced rime royal stanzas are always four to the page, the equivalent of 31. Toward the end of the first scribe's stint (at about folio 175) the norm drops even lower to the mid-twenties. The second scribe, starting in on his first two pages with the *SNP* has three rime royal stanzas. But he reverts to the four-stanza norm on the next page and keeps the number of lines per page above 30 for the rest of the manuscript. This irregularity on the part of the first scribe reflects the lack of shop discipline also represented in the variety of underlining (even to its absence) and the laconic nature of the running heads (Prolog of Bathe, with the Prolog often abbreviated and Bath without the e). Clearly the En^3 copytext owes its preservation not to a professional scrivener but to a private owner, who made it available for copying either to scribes, or more likely to a patron.

The shield that appears at the bottom of the vinet on the first page suggests who that patron might have been. The arms are those of an archbishop of Canterbury with no family escutcheon. An eighteenth century note identifies Henry Dene as the owner of the arms. Henry Dene held the see of Canterbury from 1501 to 1503. Ad^1 may well bring the chronological history of *CT* manuscripts to a close.

Barlow 20 (Bw), the second all-vellum manuscript among the final ten, has the ḏ ordering for a copytext remarkably varied in its textual affiliations. More of the exemplars come from the ḏ tradition than any other, but Ln, Ra^2, and Ht sometimes with other manuscripts also appear periodically. Many of the links derive from Ry^2, the closest associate among the seven branches of the ḏ tradition and probably the main influence in the ordering. In the *MLT* Bw has an exemplar seemingly independent (M–R II: 180); in the *FkT* the text is derived from Hengwrt (M–R II: 308), in all probability from the only one of the Hg exemplars to survive from those earlier used by Ht. Exemplifying the complexity is the additional association for more than 300 lines in the *FkT* (F 709–1050) with Ry^2 – an association there is reason to assign as well to the last 900 lines of the *ClT* (from 298 on; M–R II: 248) and to the linking passages that connect the two tales.

Loss of the first gathering carried way 573 lines of the *Prologue*. The rest of fragment A has textual affiliations shifting twice within tales until the final one at the end of the *RvT*: A 574–1249 (436 into the *KnT*) from d̲*; 1250–3615 (429 lines into the *MiT*) from Ad² where present, from *b** to 1740, from *b**c 1740–2609; 3616–4324 (through the *RvT*) from d̲; 4325–4422 (*CkPT*) from Ht; the *Gam* introduced by a two-line link from d̲*. The textual affiliations of the rest of the manuscript are as follows:

Loss of text in Ad² and Ra² may have affected our appreciation of the interrelationships between Bw and not only those two manuscripts but Ht and Hg as well. This is especially true of the early part of the text in Ad², almost totally lost except for *MLT* and parts of fragment A, and of a sequence of two quires in Ra² involving almost certainly the *CkT* and the *FkT*. Ra²'s influence on Bw continues after its close association with Ht comes to an end – in the *ClT* and the *SNT*, in the *Mel* and the *MkT*, the tales in each of these pairs being contiguous in Ra². The complexity of textual relationships in the first fragment suggests that it came to Bw as a single body of text, kept together long enough to have suffered loss and repair more than once. The presence throughout the manuscript of undifferentiated d̲* exemplars reflects the situation described earlier as constituting the constant group. Bw seems to have collected its exemplars from a large group of textually related materials rather than from a single collection.

Considerable preparation must have gone into the copytext. The editor came up with every tale until the last and found all the links, genuine or spurious, connected with the d̲* tradition. The result is a manuscript with no apparent lapses in continuity. The only breaks in linkage occur at the end of *Gam*, after the *SuT*, after the *FkT*, and at the end of the *NPT*. At each of these junctures, except for the one of the *FkT* with the *SN*, extensive headlinks divert the reader's attention from the lack of comment on the preceding tale. In the case of the Second Nun, the rubrics provide the only introduction of her as speaker (164b). Her long *Prologue*, which follows, gives an appearance at least of transition. With its d̲ ordering and its d̲* associations Bw should perhaps be viewed as the eighth and final branch of the constant group. Like the other late single manuscripts, Dl and Ha², Bw tended not to use the same exemplars as other d̲ manuscripts; rather it drew on the common pool of single tales and small groups of tales that went back to the ancestors of the early d̲ collections. Its belatedness accounts for its more extensive departures from the common tradition.

While the evidence indicates a careful preparation of the copytext, the manuscript itself makes an uneven impression. The quiring consisted originally of a completely regular series of 34 eights (the first one only missing). The lines per

page vary from 33 to 38;[11] the handwriting by the single scribe is correspondingly rough, even erratic. For the beginnings of tales the gold capitals with red,
blue, and white trim are extensively flourished into the margin with intricately
curved stems rich in flowers; but for the prologues they are much plainer. Their
irregularities in size seem to have no rationale. The "Knight's Prologue" (A
859–892) has a three-line capital; the "Tale" (A 893) has a two. The *MiP* and
MiT have four- and five-line capitals respectively; the *WB*'s four- and two-. A
similar appearance of improvisation marks the headings and the running heads.
The headings, all but one in English and almost all rubricated, have gaps of one
(204a), two (51b), and three (45a) lines to accommodate them. Occasionally
the space is left blank, as for the *SuP* (127b) and the *ClPT* (136a, 136b). For the
WBT (116b) there is neither gap nor rubric, just the two-line flourished capital.
For the *MeP* (89b) the scribe found the one-line gap he had left not big enough;
he started his *explicit* in the right margin beyond the last line of the *SqT*. For the
MkT the words Tale and Prologue are reversed. The running heads are if
anything more erratic. They start out in rubric at the top of every page. The first
variation occurs when on 57a, the beginning of a new quire, "The Coke"
changes to "Gamelyn". Then on 73a, the beginning of another quire, we get
instead of "The Man of Law" simply "The Man". The next two pages spell
out the new plan: "The Man" on versos, "Of Law" on rectos. But the second
verso fails to carry "The Man"; the third reverts to the original plan (along
with the adjacent recto); and the rest of the versos are like the second blank in
face of their rectos' "Of Law". The *SqT* (another new quire) initiates having
the running heads only on the rectos. A large number of offsets indicates that
the running heads are done as a separate chore. It's hard therefore to under-
stand why the rectos beginning with 106a confine themselves to "Of Bathe".
But the same thing happens with "of Oxenford", except that the second recto
has "The Clerke" (137a, again i of a quire) and the tenth verso (145b) also has
"The Clerke", the only one to make the two-page spread complete. With 175a,
one leaf before the end of a quire, we get the final running head for the whole
manuscript (264 leaves).

The treatment of the marginalia and of stanzaic verse is similarly erratic. Bw
carries six of the nine Latin commentary glosses for the *MLT*. They appear in
rubric in the outer margin. These are the last ones in the manuscript. The *MLT*
has what look like signs for paraphs in the left margin for the beginnings of
each stanza. Gradually even this differentiation of stanzaic verse gives out. We
can see this happening in the *ClT*. When we get to the *MkT*, there is not only no
recognition of the stanzas; the tragedies are treated as if they constituted a
single story; no marginal indexing, no rubrics, no special capitals appear.

---

[11] M–R (I:55) list the range as 34–38, but 245a, 248b, 255b, 262a, 263b all have 33
lines. The folio numbers and the later ones in the text referring to folios in Barlow are
the actual numbers, as given at the bottom of rectos in the M–R microfilm of Bw. In the
original foliation, there are three 20s, two 135s, and two 180s. The final leaf is
mislabeled 259. It should be with the misnumbering 260 (actually 264; M–R I:55 have
the foliation wrong. On I:57 they say "H ends on 259a, middle of page, with 3 pages of
quire blank." The *McT* ends on the recto of the final leaf in quire 34. The catchword for
the quire is on folio 256b.)

The termination of the running heads, of marginalia indexing or commentary as well, means that the end of the manuscript has far less rubrication. Long stretches have no color at all. This impression of unevenness, this carelessness of format, suggests an absence of shop discipline. The scribe was probably hired for the occasion by those who had already prepared the copytext.

What happened at the end has further implications. The *Maniciple's Tale* has its *explicit* on the recto of folio 264, some nine lines from the bottom of the page. The verso, originally a blank page, has been filled with scribbles. Either the scribe tired of his work, or the *PsPT* and the *Retraction* were purposely omitted. A final anomaly has the patron or possibly a scrivener hiring an illuminator. In contrast to the scribe, the illuminator did a thorough and careful job. He did golden initials decorated with sprays for the beginning of every tale, even the Wife of Bath's for which there is not even a rubric. He did plainer gold initials for every prologue, again even the Wife's for which the scribe left a four-line indentation. He missed not a single one of the spaces the scribe left within tales to set off a division or an important passage. This careful and intelligent finishing of the manuscript did not extend to adding the final tale. It is hard to believe that those who collected every tale and picked up almost every link, spurious or genuine, had no knowledge of the *Parson's Tale* or the *Retraction*.

Like many of the late manuscripts, Royal College of Physicians 388 (Py) has some striking relationship with other manuscripts.[12] One of these involves the scribe, whose hand has been detected in a number of other secular manuscripts, including the second half of Ry[1]. He also worked on Harley 2251, though not on the first half which included among a number of poems on the Virgin Mary the *Prioress's Tale*. Both he and his fellow scribe inherited comments from Shirley, which they inserted in the manuscript. Harley 2251, however, gives no evidence of supervision or shop discipline, a condition which it shares with both Ry[1] and Py.[13]

Py gives the impression of being all by one man. The first page has the most elaborate decoration in the manuscript, but nothing requiring the special talents of an illuminator. A four-line blue initial with red pen trim starts the poem. Above the first line a straight segmented bar, alternately red and blue, joins a similar bar on the left of the text that extends to the last line on the page, an approximation of a demi-vinet. The initial letter of each line after the first is washed in red, and proper names have red underlining that develops in the case of the Ram (line 8) into a cradle-like extension on either side of the word.

Blue and red continue to be the colors used throughout the manuscript. Blue paraphs combine with the red cradle-like underlining, extended often along part of the top, to set off the names of the pilgrims, (marginal index for the portraits of the *Prologue*). Paraphs and underlining that sometimes becomes a box mark the headings and even the catchwords. Two-line capitals in blue without red pen trim become the norm for the beginnings of prologues and tales. Occasionally the blue initial is followed by a red capital (one-line) for the second letter. The scribe leaves a generous space for the *explicits* and *incipits*. But there are

---

[12] Py used to be Royal College of Physicians 13.
[13] See Chapter VIII, fn. 1 (p. 68), for further information on the Py scribe, John Multon.

no running heads and after the *General Prologue* few indexing marginalia. Many of the tales have cursory headings, as if the scribe were not concerned with the specifics of pilgrims or the tales they told.

Evidence of haste on the part of the scribe comes early in the skipping of a page (11b). Similar inattention results in the mindless copying of misplaced text that gives six breaks in continuity in the *WBP* and similar breaks in the *Mel*.[14] It also results, as we shall see, in some crossing out of links and the one irregular quire in the manuscript.

Though the quiring is for the most part regular and the watermarks in this paper manuscript come in perfect sequence, the number of leaves in a quire, 20, is unusual (exceeded in *Canterbury Tales* manuscripts only by Manchester and Cambridge Dd, both produced by amateurs for their own use). It is perhaps significant that one of the other manuscripts the scribe worked on, Harley 2251, is also in twenties.

Py has a b ordering of the tales, though occasionally the scribe seems unaware as to what should come next. Py's great distinction comes from its textual affiliations. The majority of its exemplars derive from Hengwrt through a varying number of intermediaries; in C, where the text seems independent, some influence from Hg is discernible; what probably happened is an increase in the number of intermediaries. At beginning and end, for the *General Prologue* and the *Parson's Tale*, Py has a close association with Bo¹. For text never present in Hg, Py turns exclusively to Ry¹ for exemplars. This means that the *ML* endlink, the *CYPT*, the *Cl–Me* link, and the spurious *CY–Ph* link derive in Py from Ry¹. These are the only elements of text in Py that were not present in Hg. In the *WBP*, the *SuT*, the first two tales of the B² fragment, the *ShT* and the *PrT*, and in the *McP*, Py's text, full of variants, is independent. The following chart will include order, textual affiliations, and the places where the manuscript betrays uncertainty:

$$\overline{Bo|}\ \ \overline{Hg}\ \ \overline{Hg}\ \ \overline{Ry^1}\ \ \overline{Hg}\ \ \overline{Hg}\ \ \overline{Hg}\ \ \ \overline{Ind\ Hg\ Ind\ Hg\ Hg}\ \ \ \ \overline{Hg^1}\ \overline{Ry^1}\overline{Ry^1}\ \overline{Hg}\ \overline{Ry^1}\ \ \ \ \ \overline{Ind}\ \ \overline{Hg}\ \ \ \overline{Ind}\ \overline{Hg}\ \overline{Bo|}$$

$$A^{a}\ bcde\ \ B^1\ -\ F^a\ -\ E^b\ D^{a\ bc\ d}\ E^a\ F^b\ G^{a\ bc}\ -\ C\ -\ B^{2\ ab\ cdef}\ H^{a\ b}\ \ I$$

s   x   x   b
                                                  16

s = summoner in B 1179   x = text crossed out   b = blank space   16 = quire of 16

Text from Ry¹ often signals uncertainty. Though the *Man of Law's* endlink is called "Prologus Armigeri", B 1179 reads "Sompnour". At the end of the *Canon's Yeoman's Tale* on 226b (vii of quire 12) we get an *explicit*, then "Incipit prologus Mancipii" and H 1–3 crossed out. At the top of 227a we get

---

[14] The *Wife's Prologue* reads as follows in Py: D 1–156, 429–50, 397–428, 451–478, 223–396, 157–222, 479–856. The first section is followed by the fifth of 22 lines, the fourth of 32, the sixth of 28, the third of 174, the second of 66, and the seventh of 378. The length and ordering of these sections, as M–R point out (I: 443) seems to have no rationale behind it. The range of lines per page in Bw is 26–32 (not 27–32, M–R I: 439; 246a, 247a and b, for instance, have 26).

the spurious *Canon's Yeoman-Physician* link (from Ry[1]) and the *Physician's Tale*. Apparently the scribe continued to copy the *Manciple's Prologue* for the next three or four pages before he discovered his mistake. He then removed the sheets he had written on, the eighth and ninth of the quire, making quire 12 a 16. The *Manciple* would indeed follow the *Canon's Yeoman* in the a ordering. The Ry[1] copytext for the *Canon's Yeoman's Tale* derived from the a tradition; it perhaps carried an indication that the *Manciple's Prologue* should follow. In any event the Py scribe was not copying from a single manuscript but rather from a set of exemplars.

A similar mishap occurs at the end of the *Pardoner's Tale*. At the top of 244b the heading "Incipit prologus Mercatoris" introduces the *Sq–Fk* link, already used to link the *SqT* and *MeT* (both times Franklin is changed to Merchant in F 675, 696, and 699). The whole page is stroked out. Then, without any heading, 245a has the Ry[1]-derived *Cl-Me* link in a different ink. This runs over four lines on the verso (245b), ends with "Explicit prologus Incipit fabula", and leaves the rest of the page blank. The *ShT* (with its first words "A marchant"), again with no heading, starts at the top of 246a in the same ink used before folio 245. Having left a blank leaf for a link after he had crossed out the repeated lines, the scribe went on with his copying. Later he found what he considered an appropriate *MeP* for the tale whose *explicit* reads "fabula nautis". He copied it using a different ink, but it didn't fill the space he had left for it. His fixation that the *Shipman's Tale* was a *Merchant's Tale* prevailed over the fact that he already had a *Merchant's Tale* introduced by the very lines he had crossed out.

The evidence from the scribe's behavior that he was copying from exemplars rather than a single text receives confirmation from the nature of the Hg materials he was using for most of his manuscript. Py never changes its association with Hg in the middle of a tale. But in almost every tale the association with Hg involves a discrete history, from the *Nun's Priest's Tale* where Py shares almost all the Hg variants and is the only manuscript linked closely with it, to the *Pardoner's Tale*, where the seven shared out of the sixteen in Hg suggest to Manly-Rickert the possibility of contamination rather than a common ancestor (M–R I: 441; II: 335). Py never has the kind of direct access to Hg exemplars, indicated in the case of Ht. But its relationship with Hg is more extensive, if variable, than that of any other manuscript.

The possibility that this extensive textual affiliation resulted from a casual gathering of exemplars is so remote as to be ruled out except as a last resort. The London connections of Py could be helpful. For what is suggested is a pool of Hg-derived exemplars circulating in a close group of readers and being copied as the need arose (replacement or more copies) at an uneven rate. From this pool those responsible (scribe? patron? scrivener?) drew the copytext for Py, acquiring a few exemplars of independent derivation and arranging the materials in a b order.

That still leaves the use of Bo[1]-derived text for the beginning and end to be accounted for. The selective use by the scribe of Ry[1] materials to which he clearly had access makes even less sense on the surface. Could it have been pure coincidence that the Ry[1]-derived text in Py is exclusively text left out of Hengwrt? Of course, once the scribe had used the Ry[1] exemplar for the *CYT* and had realized his mistake in following it with the *McP*, he might well have remembered the spurious link to the *PhT* he had himself copied in Ry[1] and sought it out. A third of the four borrowed elements, the *Cl–Me* link, played no part in the scribe's original intentions. Only his obstinacy in seeing the *Shipman's Tale* as a *Merchant's Tale* led to the late inclusion of the *Merchant's* headlink he had already used. The choice of the Ry[1] text for the *Man of Law's* endlink, given its absence in the Hg-derived exemplar and its importance in the ordering, has only a tolerable element of coincidence.

Two points need to be stressed. (1) Py had access only to exemplars at several removes from Hengwrt, not to the manuscript itself or its exemplars. The contrast with Ht makes this clear, not only from the text but from the commentary marginalia as well. The two of these last in the *Knight's Tale*, the two out of nine in the *Man of Law's*, the three out of eleven in the *Pardoner's*, all of them in the Py text with red underlining, show the interest that with access to Hg would have resulted in the inclusion of a greater number. (2) The eighteen tales in Py derived from Hg through a varying succession of intermediaries imply the existence of many copies of these tales in the three quarters of a century between the production of the two manuscripts.

The first of the two irregular manuscripts in the final ten, Glasgow Hunterian U.1.1 (Gl), has figured twice before in the history of the *Canterbury Tales* manuscripts, compounding as it does the irregularities of two earlier manuscripts. It starts out using Cambridge Mm, one of the Petworth family in the $\underline{d}$ constant group, as its copytext: A X B^{2abc} B^1 F^a E^b D 1–192. At the point where the Wife of Bath starts describing life with her three old husbands the manuscript shifts to a twin of Ra^3: D 193–2294 G^a C^b H B^{2cdf} C^a B^{2ab} F^b I R. Later the two missing tales were added using Mm again as copytext: E^a G^b.

Responsible for this disorder and bent as we shall see on claiming credit for it were two prominent citizens of Norwich, Geoffrey and Thomas Spirleng, father and son. Professional scriveners, they show little aptitude for literary work, and their hands have not been detected in other poetic manuscripts. They brought their work to an end in January 1476.

A paper manuscript in double columns, Gl has an air throughout of improvisation. Lines to the column range from 43 to 55. *Explicits* and *incipits*, always in English and rubricated, appear sometimes in generous gaps, sometimes crowded, and sometimes in the margin (29a). Occasionally there is no notice at all of the juncture (the Host's interruption of *Thopas*, 65a). Runnings heads, also rubricated, involve a variety of styles and even handwritings (note the shift in script on 75a). We even get the Knight as a running head for the *Prologue* (2b, 3a), an *incipit* for the *Franklin's Tale* above the column that has the first three lines of the *Prologue* at the foot of the page (81a), and "The Shipmannes or the Maryner" as the second running head for the *Shipman's Tale* above the first column of 78a. A certain exuberance finds expression through all of this, especially in the patterned ascenders for the first line of 74b and the patterned descenders for the last line of 58a.

Three different ways of distinguishing stanzaic verse occur – simple red dots in the margin on the level of first lines (most of the time), what look like signs for paraphs but in rubric (*MkT* 29b–31a, 33b), and actual paraphs (red, 57a on the first page of the *SNT*). Some running heads, many headings, and the sparse indexing marginalia have underlining in red, most of the time with curved ascenders at either end.

Loss of the first two leaves has carried away the first page, but the first two initials, one three-line and the other two, have blue letters with patterned red pen trim extending below and above for most of the column (3b, 4a). The rubricated quotation from Statius and the heading for the *KnT* show off a heavy display script that does not appear again until the end. All the initials after the first two are an undecorated red. In the *PsT* we begin to have passages of five or six words in red and an increase in the number of underlinings. The *Retraction* has the first five words, most of the titles, and the whole of the sentence on the good works in red. There is nothing in the way of color in the manuscript that the Spirlengs could not have done for themselves.

The two men apparently took turns copying without worrying about stints. They frequently stopped in mid-tale, the one picking up where the other had left off. Their enthusiasm did not include critical reading of what they were copying in advance. But the father as supervisor filling in the rubrics must have given the manuscript itself a careful reading, for he made a number of corrections in the same red ink. When he added a passage omitted by his son on folio 101a (near the end of the *Parson's Tale*), he copied it from Cambridge Mm, not Ra³, every one of Mm's variants being present.[15] His "corrections" even involve incorrect readings from Mm (I 593, 865). Obviously Mm was still available though superseded long since as copytext.

Geoffrey Spirleng must have recognized while he was making the corrections (though he left no sign of it in the manuscript) that he and his son had repeated two of the tales, the *ShT* and the *PrT*. Some time elapsed before they figured out that they had in their enthusiasm for Ra³ left out two of the tales.

A number of things, including the corrections, happened first. (1) Using the same heavy display script he had used for the Statius at the head of the *KnT*, Geoffrey wrote "Qui cum patre", then after an interval of some ten lines (in the same script) a colophon, a request in Latin for the reader's prayers, that includes his name, his claims to status in Norwich, his son's name, the month they finished copying "this" book, and their respective ages at the time, 50 and 16. (2) While making his corrections in red ink, he came upon the blank space, almost half a column, between *Mel* and the *NPT* (the two tales follow one another without link in Ra³); he patched together two lame couplets:

> Whanne ended was the tale of Melebe and prudence
> Oure hoste swore by goddes dere pacience
> I had lever than a barel of ale
> That Goodelief my wife herde this tale

---

[15] The omission by Thomas was due to eyeskip from Seint Augustyne, I 985, to Seint Augustyne in 987. The eight variants in Mm, shared in the passage added at the foot of folio 101a by Geoffrey include "worthy" for "digne" and the omission of "of hevene" in the phrase "God of hevene." It took close reading indeed for Geoffrey to spot this omission, and the shorter omission in I 667, folio 95b. There, the first word not omitted, "ofte" in Ra³, is corrected at the end of the omitted passage to "oute", as in Mm.

He then wrote the couplets in big red letters and followed them with a well-spaced *incipit* for the "preestes tale", inadvertently stressing the lack of continuity (especially for any one who remembered the introduction to the misplaced *MkT* that followed the first *PrT*, the sixth tale in the manuscript). (3) He tidied up the end of the *Canterbury Tales* by excising the final blank leaf (viii in quire 14, making it the only irregular quire in the manuscript as it then existed). (4) He copied out on quires of two and three leaves using paper with the same watermark as for the last seven leaves of the *Canterbury Tales* the *Purgatory of St Patrick*, according to the display script of the *incipit*, a "mirabilis tractatus" for expelling heretical depravity.

When he became aware of the omission, Geoffrey took two quires of eight and five to copy out from the still available Cambridge Mm the *Clerk's Prologue* and *Tale* and the *Canon's Yeoman's Prologue* and *Tale*.[16] He used paper with a watermark different from any of the three previously employed. He then tried to make sure that no one would think the *Canterbury Tales* had ended with the *Retraction*. he crossed out the colophon explaining in ordinary red script that "This writyng is drawen" because the "book of Canterbury is nat yet ended" and the same words are written in [miscounting] the twelfth leaf following "by cause that ii tales arn yet folwyng immadiatly". He added to the "Qui cum patre" a reminder in slanted display script that the two tales "folwen immediatli in the next leef". And he did indeed repeat the colophon with its request for prayers in the same heavy display script, the only contemporary writing on the verso of the thirteenth leaf following. The two tales as the notes tell us precede the *Purgatory of St Patrick*.

We know more about Gl than any other collected manuscript. We know who wrote it. We know when and where it was written. We know the status and age of the two scribes. We have the actual copytext for the first part of the manuscript, for the corrections, and for the last two tales. From the time it remained in the Spirlengs' possession, from the absence of any other early claims to ownership, and from the inappropriateness of the colophon in a manuscript prepared for any one else, we can infer that Gl was made for the scribes' own use and probably did not leave the family until after Thomas's death in 1514.[17]

Trinity College Oxford Arch. 49 (To) was, like Gl, Sl[2], and Ma, probably written by a scribe for his own use. The John Leche who as vicar of Ludlow exchanged parishes in the 1480s with the vicar of Saffron Waldon in Essex has the best claim to the writing of the manuscript (M–R I: 540–44). He would have been originally from Nantwich, Cheshire, where many of those lived whose names appear in the pages of To, members of the Leche family as well as

---

[16] The norm for Gl is quires of eight. The loss of leaves involves i, ii, and vii in quire 1 (the first leaf and the second sheet); iii–vi in quire 4 (the two middle sheets); in quire 6, ii, iii lost, vi (the gemel of iii) labeled 14 because for a time bound as first leaf in 3 (the folios in 6 are now numbered as follows: 35, 36, 37, 14, 38, 39, with the missing ii and iii originally between 35 and 36); viii in 14 cut out (blank after *Retraction* and colophon on vii); vi in 16 cut away (*CYPT* ends on v recto, with colophon on verso); 17[2] and 18[3], the last two quires contain *The Purgatory of St Patrick*.

[17] Kate Harris, "The role of owners," p. 169, speaks of "manuscripts copied by scribes for their own use" and gives as the first of her examples Gl.

some of their neighbors. Leche himself lived to a ripe old age, died at Saffron Walden in 1521, left money to the local grammar school, and had four of his books given to Trinity College by its founder Sir Thomas Pope less than a century after one of the four (To) was written and less than fifty years after the death of its probable scribe.

The irregularity of To's ordering results to some extent from the availability of exemplars. The clearest instance occurs in the B² fragment. Here the *Pardoner* and the *Man of Law* intervene between the first two tales, the *Shipman's* and the *Prioress's*, and the last four, the *Thopas*, the *Melibeus*, the *Monk's*, and the *Nun's Priest's*. The scribe twice indicates his discomfort with the series. After the *PrT* he started writing the *Pd*'s headlink. He got no farther than two lines. Recognizing the inappropriateness of the Host's comments on the *Physician's Tale*, he crossed out the two lines, wrote vacat in the left margin, and proceeded with "Prologus Pardoner". Similarly on three lines at the end of the *Man of Law's Tale* he has first "Explicit", then "Allocutio hospitis ad Chauceris" cancelled, finally the second line repeated, this time indented, with a paraph, and underlined. If he had had the exemplars for all these tales at the beginning, he would surely have seen the reference to the Prioress's "miracle" of the Virgin in the first line of the *Thopas Prologue* and connected the two parts of Fragment B².

The overall order of To strengthens the case: A X D E–Fᵃ Cᵃ Fᵇ B²ᵃᵇ Cᵇ B¹ B²ᶜᵈᵉᶠ G Hᵇ I R. The presence of *Gamelyn*, the absence of the *Manciple's Prologue*, and the misplacement of three tales, the two parts of the C fragment and the *Man of Law*, disrupt what would otherwise be an a-Ellesmere ordering. We shall see later connections in the text with the Cn and Ps traditions, perhaps accounting for the influence of a.[18] The presence of *Gamelyn* may stem from an even stronger d* set of textual affiliations.

The quiring in the manuscript is most irregular. The scribe starts out with a norm of eight leaves to the quire, shifts at what is now the eleventh to a norm of ten, has a run after the fourteenth of 11, 18, 12, and 9. Except at the beginning and end, where we have gatherings of three and two leaves respectively, and in the one of 18, the irregularities have nothing to do with text; they never permit flexibility in the placing of tales. What all of this adds up to is that Leche despite occasional signs of uneasiness does not show much interest in the ordering of his materials.

The one exception occurs at the very beginning, where he seems not to have had exemplars for the *General Prologue* until he was well into his enterprise. The first two quires tell the story. The second, a regular eight leaves, contains A 179–831, 653 lines of the *Prologue* with text missing at both ends. Each page of the quire contains at least 40 lines with the first (4a) having 43 and the last two

---

[18] In the To ordering, I have emphasized the a influence by listing E–Fᵃ. The linking of *CtT* and *MeT* is not in the a manner, but it is reasonably firm. The Clerk's song has the "archewyves" stanza at the end (no Host stanza). Lines F 1–8 with merchant for Squire in line 1 are then followed by the Merchant's headlink (E 1213–1244), *MeT*, the Me–Sq links (F 1–8 repeated, but with Squire in line 1) and *SqT*. The sequence is only slightly disturbed by the difficulty in fitting in the last 747 lines of *MeT* (not present in the original exemplar), to be described later.

(11a, b) 44 and 43, a crowding of text unparalleled in the manuscript but not so crowded that space could not have been found for the 27 missing lines at the end of the *Prologue* (A 832–58) if they had been in the exemplar (there are six pages in the sequence with 40 and six with 41 lines).[19] The next quire with the *KnT* starting at the top of the first page (37 lines) provides a real contrast; the fifteen pages following have a maximum of 34 lines. Clearly the scribe was spacing the *Prologue* text to fit the eight leaves of his second quire, after he had written the tales of Fragment A. The paper in the second gathering has a watermark not to be found elsewhere in the manuscript.

The makeup of the first quire shows that A 1–178 were probably the last lines of the *Prologue* to be written. The scribe left the first recto of his three leaves blank, an unwise procedure if he had got hold of this part, a mere fragment, of the *Prologue* first. As it was he miscalculated and left himself only 29 lines for his last page (3b).[20] That he did not fill the clear gap of four lines strengthens the likelihood that the lines after A 178 were already copied. The watermarks are again significant, matching the ones to be found on the final 228 leaves of the manuscript but not on the 43 that immediately follow. As we shall see later, the textual affiliations change with the segments of Fragment A.

The omission of the last lines of the *Prologue* is characteristic. More serious disruption occurs at the end of the *WBP* when Leche copied D 672–748 after 818. No doubt present in his exemplar, the resulting sequence, 671, 749–818, 672–748, 819–28, destroys the continuity of the narrative three times. As in the *General Prologue*, Leche gave no sign he was aware of the problem.

What happened in the E-F[a] fragment is more complex. There the insertion of F 1–8 (with *Squire* in line 1 changed to *Merchant*) between the "archewyves" stanza of the *Clerk's* song and the *Merchant's Prologue* does little harm, since the echo in line 1 of the *Prologue* is already distanced. The failure to recognize 446 lines of the *MeT* (to E 1690) as a mere fraction of the whole and to make some provision for a continuation is another matter. When the rest of the tale turned up, he started copying at the end of a leaf with E 1672. This time he failed to space his text and left himself with a blank page at the end of the ten leaves which he then inserted between iv and v of quire 16. Thus the *MeT* comes to a satisfactory close, but is followed by the only blank page in the manuscript (139b), a repetition of 1672–90 (on 140a), and the "Prologus Armigeri", which includes as a single linking passage E 2419–40 and F 1–8 (again; this time with *Squire* in line 1). The awkwardness of this transition suggests that it may have preceded the smoother work on the *General Prologue*.[21]

The textual affiliations of To are sometimes hard to determine. Portions of the manuscript have large numbers of unique variants and an absence of any

---

[19] The 653 lines of the *Prologue* (A 179–831) have some irregularities: A 187 is omitted; 653, 727, and a sequence 751 (with a mistake), 754–56, are crossed out and repeated in their proper places or correct in wording.
[20] Again some irregularities: A 176 is copied twice, and A 36 and 80 are omitted.
[21] Irregularities in the 747 lines for the end of *MeT*: omission of lines 1816, 1821, 1927, 1928, 1948, 1972, 2230, 2340, 2356, and 2357; line 2013 out of place, crossed out; extra lines after 1817, 2060, 1722; line 1815 miswritten.

consistent relationship with extant manuscripts. Fourteen of the tales derive from the d* tradition but avoid a close connection with any of its seven branches. The only exception occurs in the first 178 lines of the *Prologue* (possibly the last to be picked up in the whole manuscript, M–R II: 92f), where To clearly derives from Lc–Ha^2. In the rest of the *Prologue* To is independent, its more than 200 variants (70 of them unique) showing no pattern of association with any manuscript. This independence continues in the first two tales, but in the *KnT* the influence of Cn is discernible, in the *MiT* that of El. The *ReT* derives from El–Gg–Ps; the *CkT*, like the later (and displaced) *MLT*, from Ra^3–Tc^1–Ln.

The Ps connection of the *Reeve's Tale* recurs at the end of the *Summoner's Tale*, in the two tales of Fragment G, and in a number of the links, those in E–F^a and those before the *Thopas* and the *Monk's Tale* in B^2. There are also three more tales in which the text seems to be independent – the *Shipman's Tale*, the *Thopas*, and the *Melibeus*. To seems to have gotten most of its copytext from exemplars not related to other collections. Its closest relationships come from single tales or isolated segments, links, and prologues.

Textual affiliations thus tend to confirm what we can see in the ordering, that the manuscript depends for its copytext on exemplars of single tales and very small groups. The only intact fragments are D, G, and I (with a single tale). Of the other two single-tale fragments, the *Manciple's Tale* in H lacks its *Prologue* and the *Man of Law's* in B^1 not only appears in the midst of another fragment but lacks the endlink its textual affiliations would lead one to expect.

To is a plain paper manuscript, written in a fluent cursive with few of the first letters of lines capitalized. The most consistent element of the format is the use of abbreviated running heads, usually single words like "Bathe", "Phesik", "Grisilde", "Chauntecler", and "Chauceris", which begin after the *Prologue* and are normally set off by a red paraph that develops into a cradle-like box, open for most of the top. Only at the end do we get "Fabula Rectoris". Headings for the prologues and tales are similarly sparse, sometimes omitted (92a), sometimes in a simple "Explicit" (170b), set off when present in a similar paraph-cradle. Two- and three-line capitals in a faded red or blue for the first letters of most prologues and tales constitute the only other adornment. Little preparation or forethought and little expense went into the production of To.

In the last thirty years of the century the manuscript tradition of the *Canterbury Tales* dwindled to a close. None of the final ten manuscripts has distinguished decoration. None shows signs of shop discipline. Some of them use extant copytext, either actual manuscripts (Ld^2, Gl) or collections of exemplars made for previous manuscripts (Ma, Tc^2). Perhaps the most surprising development was the creation of a new constant group (En^3), using a collection of exemplars for half of the text that originated in the 1440s with Hk and piecing together the rest from a variety of sources. As in every period a great number of manuscripts with single tales or small groups of tales are available for use as exemplars. Bw and Py drew on different pools of related manuscript materials, Bw on the d tradition, Py on a set of exemplars derived through a varied number of intermediaries from Hg. In each case those responsible were able to complete their collections from other traditions.

X

Single Tales and Small Groups

I

The existence of a large number of small manuscripts containing single tales or small groups of tales lies behind the theory presented in this book about the *Canterbury Tales* manuscripts as a whole. Some of these fragmentary manuscripts preceded any of the collected texts and served as exemplars for the earliest collections. No doubt those responsible for Hengwrt, Harley 7334, and the collection from which Corpus 198 was copied had a number of the tales in their own possession and knew where they could find others. But the evidence would seem to show that at the time the earliest "complete" manuscripts were made no central depository existed to which editors could turn for missing tales and links, or for authoritative word as to ordering.

When we look for examples of these small manuscripts, we find very few, especially in the earliest period. Most of the early small manuscripts are collections of one, two, or three stray leaves accidentally preserved, that may indeed have been parts of collected manuscripts. From manuscripts like Merthyr, Plimpton, or Cambridge Kk.1.3, we can draw no firm conclusions. The same holds for the single leaf, Harley 5908 (Hl⁴), and for the double leaf, the Devonshire Fragment (Ds²). The complete absence of signatures prevents conjecture as to the extent of their original content. Additional 10340 (Ad⁴), a real sport, has the Parson's portrait written from memory on a flyleaf of a very early Chaucer *Boethius*.

Of the two exceptions the earliest and the most important is Longleat 29 (Ll²), dated by Manly-Rickert (M–R I: 345) in the decade of the twenties, contemporary therefore with Cambridge Gg, Pw, and the vellum part of He. Like the later Ha³ the product of a number of scribes, it is an uneven collection of religious works in four books with one hand picking up where another leaves off. Its origin in a monastic establishment near Canterbury can be deduced from names in the manuscript; the progress of its ownership can be traced with reasonable assurance from the Goldwell family near Canterbury to its current owner, the Marquess of Bath at Longleat.

Much the longest item in much the longest of the four books is the *Parson's Tale*, called "Penitencie" throughout, with no reference to Chaucer or the *Canterbury Tales*, but using as copytext a twin of the Ellesmere exemplar. This second book consists of 14 quires of eight, but the *PsT*, which takes just 48 leaves starts on vii of quire 8 and ends on vi of quire 14. A certain amount of planning went into the book, for the scribe, who had started his work on ii of quire 7, in the middle of Hilton's *De Vita Activa et Contemplativa*, brought the *PsT* to an end with "deo gracias" as colophon some 61 folios later. He then left the last two leaves blank. The first of these leaves was at some point excised. The final one remained to give protection to the end of the "book".

The monks were at some pains to give their manuscript color. The principal divisions and subdivisions of the treatise have six-to-nine-line capitals, blue with red pen trim, to set them off. Red paraphs at the beginning of sentences and to introduce indexing marginalia and running heads are also the rule. But the system is by no means rigid. Occasionally we get red initials with black pen trim, usually for less important two-line capitals. We also get blue paraphs. The biggest initial of all, a ten-line blue with red trim, introduces the section on the seven deadly sins. The running heads, drastically abbreviated, sometimes get omitted entirely. But at the end the two-page spread revives – "Tercia pars" on the verso, "Penetencie" on rectos.

The most important aspect of Ll^2 is the textual relationship with Ellesmere. For it shows that even for a section of the *Canterbury Tales* with relatively few independent textual traditions, exemplars were beginning to circulate in the 1420s quite apart from any association with the larger work. The one copied by Ll^2 was pristine; not only was it lacking the *Prologue* and the *Retraction*; it did not carry the editorial changes so marked a feature of the Ellesmere manuscript. There were other copies as well, witness the independence from Ellesmere of every other early manuscript, even the ones associated with it in Group II, the second of the two independent traditions for *PsT* (M–R II: 464), i.e. Gg and a̲. All the other early manuscripts, Hg, Ha^4, and Cp–La–Pw, were associated in Group I, the other tradition.

Stonyhurst B XXIII (St), some twenty-five years later and by a single scribe, has the *Melibeus* as the third longest in an anthology of four religious and didactic pieces. No suggestion of its *Canterbury Tales* connections appears in the manuscript. In fact the end of the tale has five large omissions plus some shorter ones that add up to 466 of the final 558 lines. These omissions include the visit Prudence makes to Melibeus's enemies and her dissuasion of his impulse to penalize them cruelly when they throw themselves on his mercy. The result is a heavier didacticism and some incoherency.

St has close textual affiliations with three roughly contemporary manuscripts, Mc, Ra^1, and Tc^1. The text of all three derives from the ancestor of the c̲d̲ line. The relationship is an important one. Mc (1440–50) picked up its text from a variety of sources. The mutilated Ra^1 inherited the Mc exemplars intact. The Tc^1 scribe, who started with Ra^3–Ln exemplars, was able to use five from Mc in the late stages of his manuscript, one of which was then used by St. As we shall see later, the exemplar for the *Prioress's Tale*, apparently not available when Tc^1 was made, still existed apart from its fellows and became the copytext for Hl^1 (dated 1470–90 by Manly-Rickert).

Manly-Rickert surmise for St an amateur scribe copying out texts chosen for a patron (M–R I: 520). The narrow double-column format with very few words to a line suggests a lack of professional training. The manuscript starts out with a demi-vinet in gold, blue, and red, but the *Mel* has for adornment only a six-line opening initial and two three-line ones at arbitrarily chosen passages on facing pages, both of which begin with "First" (B 2306 and 2363).

II

After 1450 there is a notable increase in the number of tales appearing separately or in small groups. Only a single example of stray leaves occurs – Douce d.4 (Do). Dated 1450–70, it carries 71 lines of the *General Prologue*, A 298–368, on a single leaf. Like the other earlier ones Do gives no clue as to contents or ordering. It probably owes its survival, like Merthyr, to having been used in the binding of another book. In a clear book hand the manuscript has a stark appearance, no color, no running heads. One portrait, the Man of Law's, monopolizes the indexing marginalia: "Sergeaunt" appears three times at intervals of a few lines, but nothing distinguishes the portraits of the Franklin or the Guildsmen. The text, unmistakably Gg, must have been copied from the same exemplar, (or possibly even from Gg itself, though it does not seem influenced by Gg's East Anglian dialect).

Two of the manuscripts belong to the decade of the fifties, and five more were probably written before 1470. One of the early ones, Arundel 140 (Ar), contains only *Melibeus*, mutilated at the end and lacking also two late folios. Distinct in format and handwriting from the five earlier pieces in the manuscript, *Mel* must have once been circulating independently; it presumably owes its survival to being included in the volume. It has the heading "Chaucer" and "Melibee" at the top of the first page, space for a two-line capital A at the beginning of the text, and some indexing names in the margins. Otherwise it is a plain and undistinguished work, its handwriting a rough cursive.

The textual affiliations of Ar are interesting. It has more than 130 unique variants. Its closest association is with Ad^3, but intervening between their common ancestor and the much corrected but still corrupt Ar (M–R II: 387f) must be a number of intermediaries. The genetic relationship with Gg–Ph^1–$\underline{b^*}$ is even more distant. Furthermore the corrections in Ar are from no other extant manuscript. What we have in Ar is a text that goes back through intermediaries to an ancestor of Ad^3 and then to an ancestor of the very early Gg without association with any other known manuscript or textual affiliation. That the relationships of the affiliated manuscripts hold only for *Mel* shows the extent to which the tale circulated individually, apart from the collections.

The other fifties manuscript, Naples XIII.B.29 (Np), contains *Griselda* as the final item in a collection that devotes the first 20 leaves to medical prescriptions and then turns to five romances.[1] Np starts the *Clerk's Tale* on line E 92 at the top of the first page of a new quire with no heading. This means that the

---

[1] For an interesting bit of detection that uncovered the name of an early Italian owner of the manuscript, the philospher Tommaso Campanella, see M–R I: 379f.

exemplar must have lacked the 56 lines of the prologue and the first five stanzas of the tale as well. It had perhaps lost its first leaf. It included everything at the end, Wife of Bath stanza, Clerk's song (labeled Cantus), and the Host stanza. The absence of a title reflects perhaps awareness on the part of the scribe that there were lines missing at the start. For though he gives no title to this poem, he does to others – "Of Seint Alex of Rome," p. 80; "Sir Isombrase," p. 114. He is interested enough in headings to leave space for *explicit* and *incipit* in an elaborate script for each division of the *Grisilde*. The quiring is also suggestive. The preceding romance, *Sir Isumbras*, is a mere fragment; the scribe left three blank pages for further text. He then began the *Clerk's Tale* on the first page of a new quire. The second of its quires is a two, the only irregular one in the manuscript at the time it was written – a sign that the scribe intended the *Clerk's Tale* to bring his work to a close.

The question inevitably occurs: why did the scribe end his collection of romances with material associated with the Wife of Bath and the Host? Why did he not put his "Explicit Finus at the end of Petrarch's moral (E 1162)? Fortunately the scribe, who gives us his name, More, and the date, 1457, gives also an oblique answer to our questions. He probably did not know the *Canterbury Tales*. If he had, he could presumably have remedied the lost leaf at the beginning of his exemplar and copied out the beginning of the tale. However, he caught sufficiently the "slant" nature of the concluding materials, especially the ludic quality of the Clerk's song to add the envoy of a Lydgate poem, an amusing double quatrain addressed to women, as an epilogue to his collection. He advises them to prepare themselves against men's assaults by arming themselves with "A myghti schilde of doblenesse".

The appearance of Np is dominated by the separation from the main text of the initial letters for each line. The position for these letters is set by the double ruling of the margins, which on the left has two lines $\frac{5}{8}''$ apart. The three exceptions to this rule therefore stand out and substitute as it were for the lack of title and running heads. *Grisilde*, when it occurs as the first word of a line, E 274, 344, and 537, is written right across the space (curiously this does not occur later at lines 1029 and 1030).

As in Ar, Np's textual affiliations are almost nonexistent. It has 96 unique variants. After putting to the test Koch's classification of Np with Gg, Manly-Rickert come to the conclusion that Np "is not closely related to any manuscript or group" (M–R II: 254f). It thus testifies further to the existence of independent copies of tales, circulating in this case with a full panoply of *Canterbury Tales* elements.

III

We now come to two manuscripts already discussed because of their close relationship textually with earlier ones – Harley 1239 (Ha[1]), which inherited the exemplars for five of the tales from Ps, and Longleat 257 (Ll[1]), which has two tales derived without intermediary from the d manuscript, En[2]. Both are dated by Manly-Rickert 1450–1470. Ha[1] is important, as we noted earlier, because the exemplars from which its five tales were copied must have been circulated as a small group from the time they were used by Ps for at least ten and possibly as many as thirty years before being copied out in his peculiarly shaped book by the hermit of Greenwich.

Perhaps chosen by Jean D'Angoulême as tales he particularly admired – *Knight's Tale*, *Man of Law's Tale*, *Wife of Bath's Tale*, *Clerk's Tale*, and *Franklin's Tale* – they passed out of his control before his return to France in 1445. The use of exemplars as copytext rather than Ps itself is confirmed by the substitution in Ha^1 of six spurious lines for a passage present in Ps, F 709–89 (the beginning of *FkT*, where the exemplar had apparently lost a leaf after being copied by Ps).

Ll^1 presents a striking contrast with Ha^1. The volume contains two books, lavishly decorated, each by a different scribe and with a different format. The first is the one that concerns us – a collection of four narratives, the *Siege of Thebes*, the *Knight's Tale*, the *Clerk's Tale*, and the prose *Ipomedon*. The book was clearly intended for the highest level of society and has on folio 98b (in the middle of *Ipomedon*) an authentic signature of Richard III, while he was still Duke of Gloucester.

A more important area of contrast is the probable use of En^2 itself (rather than its exemplars) as copytext (M–R II: 63f). It is in fact extremely unlikely that those responsible for assembling the text would have found for the two tales exemplars from the same much earlier manuscript unless they had been kept together, something we have no reason to assume. This argument, the textual considerations presented by Manly-Rickert, and the light thrown by Benskin on the habits of the kind of scribe engaged in both En^2 and Ll^1 overweigh the evidence for the use of exemplars as copytext.[2]

Some of the features of Ll^1's decoration are worth noting. The first page is a full vinet enclosing a 12-line initial and a title in the right margin, "The Prolog of / The Sege of/Thebes", with initial letters for each line of the title in blue, the others in red. The *Arcite and Palamon* has a 10-line capital, yellow, blue, red, and green, with flourishes that enclose three sides of the text and include the two-line capital for "This Duk" (A 893). It has a marginal title, "Arcite and / Palamon", similar to the one for the *Siege*. The running heads also have the same blue and red color scheme. The first letter on most pages is elaborately patterned; in the *Grisilde*, where alternating red and blue initial letters set off the stanzas, this makes for a syncopated effect. Bright and a little vulgar, the manuscript gives an overall effect of opulence.

The last three manuscripts probably written before 1470 have each a single tale. Harley 2251 (Hl^2) includes the *Prioress's Tale* in a great collection of 133

---

[2] Benskin, "Translation and *Mischsprachen*," would put the Ll^1 scribe on the translation end of the spectrum, one who imposes his own dialect on the text he is copying. The evidence for the use of the En^2 exemplars rather than the manuscript itself would include the dialect features in Ll^1 quite different from those in En^2 and the absence of reference to the *Canterbury Tales* except for the Wife of Bath stanza. The headings and *explicits* call the tales "Arcite and Palamon" and "Grisilde." The Clerk's song has the heading "Lenvoie Chaucer." Finally, the omission of the *ClP* (present in En^2) contrasts with the inclusion of the *Prologue* to the *Siege of Thebes* with its reference to the *Canterbury Tales*.

religious and secular poems. Some planning went into the work of the two scribes, for the *PrT* appears in the midst of a series of poems on the Virgin. Nothing identifies it as by Chaucer or as a part of the *Canterbury Tales*. A flourished two-line initial, red with some blue, distinguishes the opening prayer, and red paraphs set off the stanzas, but there are no running heads, no *incipit* at the beginning, and only a marginal Amen at the end. The next line has the flourished initial of another poem. The textual affiliations are with the ancestor of the d* line but show no close connection with any manuscript.

Harley 1704 (Hl[1]) also includes the *Prioress's Tale*, the fourth of eight items in the second of its four "books". The first book is the only other one written in the fifteenth century. It contains the "Leges Edwardi" on 12 vellum folios and has nothing to do with the rest of the manuscript. The second book contains religious pieces in verse and prose on 63 paper folios (watermark near a Briquet dated 1462–69), torn, dirty, and mutilated at beginning and end. The eight items of this second book change in handwriting and format after the second, a prose life of Adam, which had to have its four central leaves replaced in the sixteenth century. But the book itself was never divided; the second paper quire includes parts of items 2 and 6, and all of those in between.

The *PrT* carries the title *Alma redemptoris mater* in a red display script. The exemplar must have been badly damaged at the start, for the opening prayer (the prologue) starts out with two lines of pastiche, based on the first three lines, then skips to the third stanza. The opening three-line capital O is in heavy undecorated rubric, and a slight red tints the first letters of lines. But there is no recognition of stanzas, there are no running heads, there is only the red underlining of Alma redemptoris mater, wherever it appears in the text. At the end of the Hugh of Lincoln stanza "Amen" serves as colophon, followed on the next line by a rubricated title, "Alas that ever love was Synne", lined out in rubric, and in its turn followed by another title, "In thy most helth wisely be ware", and the first quatrain of the poem, "As I fared in a frith".

The text comes from the exemplar earlier used for Mc and Ra[1], an exemplar that had separated itself from the set before Tc[1] was made. Tc[1], one of the elongated minuscule manuscripts, used En[1] as copytext for its last four tales, including *PrT*, after using Mc exemplars for the five tales immediately preceding the last four. One of those five was also used for the Stonyhurst *Mel*, as we saw earlier in this chapter. The time element here is worth emphasizing. The Mc exemplars were copied so accurately by Ra[1] that Manly-Rickert concluded Ra[1] could have been copied directly from Mc (M–R I: 451). Shortly after Ra[1] was copied the set must have broken up into small groups, perhaps even individual tales. For Tc[1] used only five of the exemplars in a quite different ordering from the one used by both Mc and Ra[1]. St then used the one for *Mel* also employed by Tc[1]. All of this must have happened close to the year 1450. Later the Ds scribe copied his whole text directly from En[1], and later still the Hl[1] scribe used the Mc exemplar for the *PrT*.[3]

The last of the manuscripts of single tales probably written before 1470 is

---

[3] See Chapter VI, fn. 4 (p. 50). An Mc exemplar for the *SNPT* was also used by Sl[2] to replace text lost from its c-derived exemplar (M–R II: 428). Sl[2] never did obtain *CYPT*, though the editor was apparently aware that something was missing between *SNPT* and

Phillipps 8299 (Ph[4]), now in the Huntington as HM140. It contains two booklets quite different in format and contents. The first booklet has the *Clerk's Tale* as the second in a collection of eight poems by Chaucer and Lydgate. The anthology opens with the longest of the poems, Lydgate's *St Alban and St Amphibal*. Two other Chaucer poems appear, the balade *Truth* (without envoy and not distinguished in any way from *ClT* which it follows) and Anelida's complaint from *Anelida and Arcite* (item number 5).

A plain manuscript with the only decoration of *ClT* the heavy red three-line initial and the tinting of line-initials in red, the booklet consists of 91 folios with the inner and outer sheets vellum, the rest paper, in quires normally of 16 (a lost inner vellum folio carried away E 189–260). The *ClT* has no title, no running heads, no marking of stanzas, and no divisions of the tale. It starts at line 57 (no *Prologue*), leaves out the two stanzas after the Petrarch moral (E 1163–1176) that direct the Clerk's song to the Wife of Bath, has lines in the song out of order, and copies the 21 lines of the balade as if they were part of the tale (no title, no gap, no initial capital). The final page (83a) has as its only writing the last eleven lines of *Truth* and an elaborate underlined *Explicit* taking up five lines.

The text is corrupt: 100 unique variants, and a number of transposed and omitted lines. Ph[4] derives, probably independently, from an ancestor of the early manuscript Ad[3] and the later Ra[3]–Tc[1] (M–R II: 253). Its skipping of the two stanzas before the Clerk's song, present in all the related texts, could hardly be unintentional – an additional sign that the exemplar and some of its immediate ancestors (perhaps all) were circulating independently of the *Canterbury Tales*.

IV

The last thirty years of the century saw the introduction of printing and the effectual end of the *Canterbury Tales* in manuscript. The number of fragmentary texts (nine) is for the first time almost the equal of the collected ones (ten). Of the nine only three were of single tales. All three were paper manuscripts, presenting us with a real contrast in their textual affiliations.

Sloane 1009 (Sl[3]) presents a miscellany of nine pieces, that were originally in separate booklets, with a text of the *Melibeus* the sixth in the collection. The volume includes a second miscellany from the late seventeenth century. Manly-Rickert see items 2–5 from the first group as belonging together and 1 and 6 as perhaps forming another booklet, based on an original use of rubrication in the two pieces (the handwriting, but not the ink in 1, 2, and 6 is also similar). However, the first folio of *Mel* is badly torn and the text breaks off in mid-sentence some 43 lines (prose) from the end. It looks as if it did not originally have the protection of inclusion in a volume. The rubrics in question involve what is perhaps punctuation at the end of paragraphs, a filling in with red at the end of lines. Different actually from the practice in item 1 are the three-line red

PhT (also non-ϲ affiliated with Ad[2]–Ht–Ln–Tc[1]). He left a half page plus a leaf (later excised) blank at the end of *SNT*.

initial and the red marginalia. The *Mel* in Sl³ has no title, no running heads, and no identification with Chaucer or the *Canterbury Tales*.

Sl³'s textual affiliation gives it unique distinction among the manuscripts of the last thirty years. It used an exemplar derived from the immediate ancestor of the Ellesmere copytext. The evidence presented by Manly-Rickert (M–R II: 381f) makes this clear. Sl³ does not copy the Ellesmere editing (El has 19 unique variants). But it is alone with El 29 times and with the Bo¹ group and El in the early part of the tale (to B 2650) more than 40. What this means is that an exemplar contemporary with Ellesmere and derived without intermediary from its ancestor survived independently for more than half a century (presumably without the protection of other tales), while a similar exemplar used by Ha² and later by Bo¹ lost almost half its text in a much shorter time. Sl³'s exemplar did suffer some damage over the years as indicated by the missing text near the beginning of *Mel*. The thirty lines present at the beginning (81 lines in Riverside) show that the 39 missing (2186–2224; 124 in Riverside) represent three folios in the copytext.

The second manuscript with a single tale is Cambridge Ee.2.15 (Ee), which has a badly battered *Constance* as the first item in an anthology of six pieces including a part of Gower's *Confessio* and two poems by Lydgate. The volume has a fragment of Mirk's *Festial* at the beginning (16 folios), written earlier and unrelated to the anthology. The anthology itself is probably a collection of separate books, the Chaucer, the Gower, the Lydgate, and the final two pieces (M–R I: 127f). This would account for the condition of the *Man of Law's Tale*, which has a badly torn first page, other pages where the text has been lost to wear and tear, two gaps of four leaves and one leaf (B 463–686 and 743–798), and a mutilation at the end that carried away the final four stanzas.

Ee suffers from an elaborate and sometimes irrelevant decoration. On the first page the heavy initial I (red, green, yellow, and brown) contains two salamanders biting each other that make the left part of the I an f; also a fish with the letters "er" next to it; also a hanging shield enclosing a paraph that is emblematically a fish with er below in what could well be the tail of another fish. The initial extends the length of the text indenting variably the lines of all three stanzas. It was thus part of the plan from the beginning, a "Costauns" for a patron named Fisher – a sign of the "bespoke" trade even for single tales.

The norm for Ee is four clearly spaced stanzas to the page. The lines on all but the second page have extensions in rubric to the writing margin. Costauns as running head, rubricated and often much patterned, appears on rectos to the right of the first stanza. Elaborate patterns often develop from ascenders of first lines on the page and from descenders of last lines. Crude multi-lined initials occur at the beginning of part two (B 386) and at line 904, four stanzas beyond the beginning of part three. On 19b and on 23a totally irrelevant figures are drawn in the colors used by the illuminator. Probably unbound for some time despite the lavish decoration, the manuscript shows by its condition how tenuous was its survival.

The textual affiliations of Ee confirm its independence. It derives from the ancestor of the two late constant groups, Bo¹ and En³, a tradition that has close association only with El, judged by Manly-Rickert to be the result of contamination or accidental coincidence (M–R II: 183–87). The *Man of Law's Tale* is the only one in which the two late constant groups are related. The exemplar in each case, as well as for Ee, was presumably a single one.

The last of the single-tale manuscripts is Trinity College Cambridge R.3.19 (Tc³), a collection of 14 booklets, each with its own set of folio numbers, one of which contains a conflation of the *Monk's Tale* with part of Lydgate's *Fall of Princes*. A curious piece of work that was probably copied in part from Caxton's first edition, the text does not mention Chaucer, the Monk, or the *Canterbury Tales* but calls itself at the top of the second page "The translation from / Bochas by / John Lydgate". It starts off with the Monk's discussion of tragedy, the definition of tragedy at the beginning of *MkT*, and the Lucifer stanza, all labeled a Prohemium (folio 170b). It continues with Lydgate material for eight leaves, returns to Chaucer's tragedies (Samson to Cresus, 179a–188a), then after an *Explicit* ends up with more of Lydgate's *Fall of Princes* to folio 202. The manuscript has rubric titles for each of the tragedies and space for two-lined initials.

The assimilation of Chaucer's work by Lydgate indicates the extent to which the latter had made the fall of princes his own private domain. A number of Chaucer's other works, including the *Legend of Good Women* and the *Parlement of Foules*, appear in the other "books" of Tc³. Chaucer is even mentioned by name.

The six manuscripts still to be discussed all contain more than a single one of the tales. What was probably the earliest is also the one to have the largest number of tales – Sion College (Si), now in the library of Takamiya in Tokyo. Si contains the *Clerk's Tale* and the D fragment. It has two other important distinctions: (1) It was never part of a bigger book; it was neither the fragment of an anthology nor the mutilated remnant of a "complete" *Canterbury Tales*. (2) It is the only one of the final nine to be entirely on vellum, a circumstance that perhaps accounts for its survival.

The manuscript came into being in quite a different way from Ha¹, the collection of five *Canterbury Tales* copied by the Hermit of Greenwich from a set of Paris exemplars. These five reflected the taste of some one with access to the Ps copytext, perhaps even Jean d'Angoulême himself. They remained together over a number of years before becoming copytext for the hermit. With Si the evidence strongly indicates that the manuscript evolved into its present form as it was being written, and that the scribe, probably his own patron, was at least reading his copy carefully enough to make critical judgments on what he had written.

The man responsible for Si was clearly interested in the *Canterbury Tales*, not just in a collection of stories. He included the *Clerk's* headlink, omitted not only in Ha¹, but in all the manuscripts with one or two tales as well (Ll¹, Ph⁴, Np, and as we shall see Ra⁴). Originally he may have intended the *explicit* on 29a, the only one in the manuscript, to bring Si to a close. When he chose to continue, it was with the dramatic D fragment rather than another single tale. He showed his delight in the connection between the Clerk's song and the beginning of the *Wife of Bath's Prologue* by enclosing the *explicit* in a box linked by a diagonal set of lines from the word "wayle" at the end of the song to the first word of the *Prologue*, "Experience". But when he had finished copying the *Summoner's Tale*, he understood what he had been reading sufficiently to realize the D fragment should precede *ClT*. He therefore wrote out the first line of the *Clerk's Prologue* again and, under it, "ut sup" in letters three times the normal size.

The handwriting is a heavy cursive, with lines per page adding up to 21 for rime royal, 24 for couplets. The only heading is the opening *incipit*; the only flourished initial is the first; the only gap in the writing is bridged by the partially cancelled *explicit*. Two-, three-, and four-line initials mark the beginnings of prologues and tales. The quiring in eights is regular; the signatures reveal that there was no loss of text at the beginning. Two blank leaves show that the end is undamaged as well. The absence of color, the small size, the excerpting from the *Canterbury Tales* of a good sample reflect an economy in both writing and reading.

Textual affiliations differ for the two parts of the work. The *ClT* derives from the exemplar for one of the earliest manuscripts, Ha[4]. The breaking up of the *Prologue* into stanza-like parts (without the word "Pausacio" as in El and Cp) was not part of the Ha[4] tradition. It could have resulted from contamination in an intermediary. More likely, in view of what happened in the D fragment, it stemmed from the influence on the scribe of another manuscript. The text for the D fragment derives from another early manuscript Gg, but two of the four added passages present in Si (D 575–84 is not) and the misnumbering of husbands at D 452f, 480, 503, and 525 could not have come from Gg. The influence of the a tradition is the only way to account for both phenomena.[4] The contemporary Ry[1], which also has the added passages and the misnumbering, got some of its text from En[1] exemplars. The influence of Cn exemplars was also active in the period, especially in the copytext of the last constant group En[3] and in mending that copytext for Ad[1], probably written at the end of the century. The important thing is the activity of the Si scribe in consulting other manuscripts than the one he was using as copytext; in this he was emulating the early scribe-editor who assembled the exemplars for Dd, the first a manuscript.

The remaining five manuscripts contain each a pair of *Canterbury Tales* in either an anthology or a miscellany. The first, Rawlinson C.86 (Ra[4]), has the *Clerk's Tale* (called *Grysill*) as the thirty-first and the *Prioress's Tale* as the thirty-third in a volume containing 35 items. Originally four or five separate booklets, only the first (30 folios) is on vellum. The booklet with the two tales (folios 141–77) is still a miscellany; for instance the item between the two consists of Latin verses lamenting the death of Edward IV. This is not a later inserted piece, for it occupies the recto of the leaf on the verso of which the *PrT* begins. That the booklet was once separate is confirmed by the probable loss of leaves at the end. The *PrT* breaks off in mid-stanza (B 1822) at the foot of the thirty-seventh folio.

The separation of the two tales, the omission of the *ClP*, the failure to have any reference to Chaucer or the larger work suggest that the two were picked up separately from single exemplars. The textual affiliations, while similar, are

---

[4] Sion has the added passage D 44a–f present only in a–b, Ch, Ii, Ry[1], Se, and Si. Of Ch, Ii, Ry[1], and Se each is deficient in at least one of the misnumberings of husbands. Sion must therefore have gotten the added passages and the misnumbeings from an a or a b manuscript.

clearly distinct. The text in the *ClT* derives from a common ancestor with the late manuscripts, Fi and Nl. It is followed by three spurious lines, a badly corrupted version of a couplet present in Nl. The text for the *PrT* on the other hand uses the actual Fi exemplar (M–R II: 354). This must itself have suffered some damage. For while the *ClT* has a title, "Grysill", and has "Finis Gryseld" at the end, the *PrT* is never named. The scribe would surely have given it a title if he had had one in the exemplar.

Carelessly written as well as casually planned, Ra[4] has no decoration. It lacks running heads and any recognition of stanzas. Even the Clerk's song and the Prioress's opening prayer have nothing to distinguish them from the rest of the text.

The next two manuscripts share two tales but in reverse order. Both are amateur anthologies, almost certainly written out by clerics for their own use. Harley 2382 (Hl[3]) has the *PrPT* and the *SNPT* as the fifth and sixth in a volume that now contains eleven religious pieces. The details of quiring, watermarks, and paper size show us the scribe putting together in a single volume what he originally regarded as a number of separate booklets and inserting two pieces before the *PrT* in order to make his volume open with the sequence: Lydgate's *Life of the Virgin*, *The Assumption of Our Lady*, the "Oracio ad Sanctam Mariam", and Lydgate's *Testament*.[5] Clearly the manuscript was a labor of love, evolving as the scribe worked on it.

He took the trouble also to decorate his work with red paraphs, red underlining for headings, red multi-lined initials, and a red tinting on important initial letters (titles, the first letters of each stanza, and the final *explicit*). He called the two stories "Fabula monialis de Scta Maria" and "Vita Scte Cecilie".

Textual affiliations tell us that though they may have come to him together, the two exemplars were not derived from the same tradition. His text for *PrT* was independent of all other extant manuscripts (M–R II: 359), while the exemplar for the *SNT* derived from the second large group, which included Hg, a, Gg, and Ch (M–R II: 430f). He had good exemplars but his copying left something to be desired.

Hl[3] was the third smallest in size of page of all the *Canterbury Tales* manuscripts; Chetham 6709 (Ct) is the smallest. Another anthology of religious writings, Chetham has the *Life of St Cecilia* (*SNT*) and *Miracle of the Virgin*

---

[5] The evidence for this sequence of events is as follows: The scribe left blank spaces at the end of item two, at the end of the *SNT*, and at the end of what is now the eighth piece. For a time he regarded items 1 and 2, 5 and 6, 7 and 8 as separate booklets. What are now the last three works he started copying on five originally blank pages and completed a quire of nine, using paper of a slightly smaller size. He then came upon two pieces he wanted to insert ahead of *PrT*. He started on a page he originally left blank, continued on an inserted quire of the smaller paper (a ten), filled the inserted quire, and still had to run over on the blank pages left at the end of items 6 and 11.

His quires were formed by folding the sheets twice (in quarto). The inserted quire of ten and the final quire of nine must have been formed as follows: Originally the final quire was a ten with one of the sheets cut in half. The half sheet left over he used in the inserted quire of ten. When he had finished copying the *Testament* (the second of the inserted pieces), he still had a blank leaf at the end of the final quire. He excised it, making the quire a nine.

(*PrT*) as the second and third of its collection, preceded only by a table of contents and a life of the Virgin. Every one of Ct's works is narrative, and all but two, (*PrT* and another miracle) are saints' lives. The scribe identifies himself as a Canon named William Cotson and gives us the date, March, 1490.

His manuscript is a combination of vellum and paper, eight paper sheets enclosed between two sheets of vellum for quires of 20. He was thus able to fit his two tales into a single quire (with a blank leaf to spare). The running heads on each of the rectos, "Quaterno nono" followed by the word folio and the number of the leaf, suggest that this quire was once treated by the scribe as a separate booklet.

The decoration is limited to what the scribe can do for himself: rubricated three-line initials for prologues and tales and a curious set of red marks running through the first letters of each line and a parallel series to the right of the text that often catches a letter in the longer lines. The text of both tales was copied from Caxton's second edition (1484).[6] The scribe did a good job of assimilating what he called in his *incipits* "Vita Ste Cecilie" and "Miraculum Ste Marie Virginis". No sign of their belonging to another work intrudes.

Pepys 2006 (Pp) presents us with two anthologies, probably not bound together until the seventeenth century.[7] The first contains works by Chaucer, Lydgate, and others (pp. 1–224). Of concern to us is the second, which puts together the *Melibeus*, the *Parson's Prologue* and *Tale*, and the *Retraction* with a short collection of nine Chaucer lyrics at the end (pp. 225–391).

The man responsible knew the *Canterbury Tales*: he preceded the *PsT* with its prologue, referred in the *explicit* of the *Mel* to "Chauceres owne tale of Thopas and/of Melibee and Prudence his Wyfe", and in the titles of the two tales always included the pilgrims' names. His choice of the two long prose pieces gives a character to his anthology abruptly altered by the short poems that follow. The possible presence of the *Thopas* would have moderated slightly this contrast, but the quiring and the *incipits* (one each for the *Mel* and the *PsP*; none for the *PsT*) make this unlikely.

The two scribes who worked on the *Canterbury Tales* section did very uneven stints. the first wrote 122 pages; the second took over in midphrase for the last 32 pages of the *PsT* and the 14 pages of lyrics. The change in scribes could hardly have been planned.

The decoration of Pp is irregular, almost experimental. The three-lined multicolored flourished initial for the *PsP* is much more elaborate than the two-line red initial for the *Mel*. Rubricated *incipits* and *explicits* in display script with elaborate flourishes are the norm, but the *incipit* for the *Retraction* is in the ink of the text. Red source notes within the text are at times numerous, at times not (p. 233). The *Mel* contains some Latin indexing and even occasional translation into Latin of the text, all in the red display script, but very unevenly distributed; the same applies to titles of subdivisions in the *PsT*. The first lines

---

6 Neither Chetham nor Cx[2] are included in the M–R Corpus of Variants.

7 *Manuscript Pepys 2006: A Facsimile*; Magdalene College / Cambridge / "Introduction" by A. S. G. Edwards / Published for / A Variorum Edition of the Works of Geoffrey Chaucer by / Pilgrim Books, Norman, Oklahoma, / and D.S. Brewer, Cambridge, England / appeared in 1985.

of pages have flourished and patterned ascenders washed in yellow (sometimes in red as well) with increasing frequency (pp. 264,5; 271,2). Towards the end of *PsT* the number diminishes. Experiment with elaborate patterning of top-line initials extends for eleven pages (pp. 265–75).

The textual affiliations of the two tales have a great deal in common. It is possible they were copied from a "complete" *Canterbury Tales*; if so, it is from a manuscript that has not survived. They could also have used two separate exemplars or ones that had come to the Pp editor already coupled. Both tales include in their textual derivation Ch, a, and Ln. Ln leaves the group at line I 386; then Ch and Pp leave a and its associates for the completely separate Hg group at about I 958, "Secunda pars Penitencie", (133 lines from the end). Pp and Ch may have shared a common ancestor for both tales. The textual affiliations would seem to rule out the conjecture by A.S.G. Edwards that the Pp texts were "copied from a printed source, whether Caxton or Caxton derived".[8]

Huntington HM 144 (Hn) is a collection of sixteen items in eight books, religious or highly moral in character. The sixth book contains the *Melibeus*, called "Proverbis", and the *Monk's Tale*, called "The Falle of Princis". Written by a single scribe, perhaps for his own use, possibly for a religious house of which he was a member, the manuscript ends five of its books with blank leaves, and indicates by quire irregularity as well that each of the books was regarded as separate while they were being written (M–R I: 289ff).

Daniel Mosser in "Manly and Rickert's Collation" has corrected Manly-Rickert's reconstruction of how Hn was put together, showing that the tales could not have been written in reverse order.[9] What the scribe designates as "Proverbis" and the "Falle of Princis" lack not only linking passages but ties to Chaucer and his collection of stories. A blank page, quite possibly three blank pages originally separated the tales, made them appear distinct.[10] Later the scribe saw a thematic connection between them, if there was a blank leaf excised it, and admonished readers in a special colophon at the end of *Mel* to remember the "noble proverbis, that rebukyth covetise and vengeaunce takyng

---

[8] Edwards's conjecture, xxviii and xxix of his Introduction to the Facsimile, may have been intended to apply only to the lyrics at the end, not to the *Mel* and *PsT*. If so, the point is not made clear (See N.F. Blake, "Manuscript to Print," p. 420).

[9] The sixth book of Hn has two quires of 16 and 17. M–R (I:292) envisaged the *MkT* as being written out first on a quire of 12, then the *Mel* as being started on a quire of 16 with the rest of the tale being put on the first three leaves of the four sheets in which the *MkT* quire of twelve was enfolded. The fourth sheet was then removed as unnecessary and another leaf at the end of *MkT* was excised. Two things are wrong with this reconstruction: (1) The third leaf with the end of *Mel* has as its gemel the last leaf of *MkT* (it cannot be a leaf added for the copying of *Mel* since its gemel is not one of the two blanks at the end); (2) the leaf with no gemel is not one of the first three in the second quire; rather it is xiv (in the quire of 17).

[10] An extra leaf (xiv in the quire of 17) could have been added, as Mosser proposes, because of a copying mistake (the skipping of a leaf in the exemplar by the scribe). Or a sheet could originally have been included to provide another two blank pages after *Mel* in a quire of 18 (there is already one blank page – and two blank leaves at the end of *MkT*).

in truste of Fortune, whiche hath causyd many a noble prince to fall, as we may rede of hem here foluyng."

He also took pains to prepare his copytext, liberally cutting passages from the *Mel* and adding Latin translations for some of the pithier sentences (these are never the same as the ones in Pp). He left a small space between stanzas in the *MkT*; he used a big and elaborate display script for running heads, most of the proper names, key sentences and everything in Latin within the prose, the marginal titles of the tragedies, and the admonition connecting the two tales quoted above. This use of display script constitutes the main visual feature of the manuscript.

The textual affiliations are especially significant. Hn–Ld^1–Ha^4 form a close group in both tales. When we remember that Ha^4 was one of the earliest manuscripts and that Ld^1 derived its text for the B^2 fragment H and I (the final eight tales) from Ha^4, the use of two of the same exemplars (or immediate derivatives) in Hn without any sign of a connection with the *Canterbury Tales* shows the vicissitudes the text of the tales was subject to – first the gathering of a set of exemplars for one of the earliest collected manuscripts; the use of eight of these that must have survived in a group for another "complete" *Canterbury Tales* some thirty years later; finally, after an even longer interval a scribe-editor's fresh appreciation of two of the tales, perhaps still circulating together, but no longer recognized as part of the bigger work.

Two general observations can bring this chapter to an end. Few manuscripts with single tales or small groups from the early years of the century remain even if we count in some of the four fragments that could have been parts of collected texts. If we leave those out of consideration, only two survive from the first fifty years, seven from the next two decades, and nine from the final thirty years of the century. The pattern is different from that presented by the collected texts. The difference can probably be accounted for by the sheer bulk of a collection of the tales and by the greater likelihood of a binding. In fact those small manuscripts that do survive owe their continued existence to inclusion in a bound volume, whether that occurred immediately or only after a period of circulation. The conclusion that many more once existed receives support from the findings of John Thompson and Julia Boffey with respect to the unbound pamphlets and booklets used as copytext for anthologies and miscellanies.[11]

A further observation concerns the variety of ways in which the manuscripts with single tales or small groups came into being. Some were copied from "complete" texts, two of them printed (Tc^3 and Ct). The majority, however, derive from tales circulating independently or in small groups, copied by an amateur for his own use or chosen by scribe or patron for their appropriateness in an anthology. Some of these have two tales, each with a different textual tradition (Hl^3 and Ra^4). Some derive their texts from the set of exemplars used in an earlier collected manuscript but (1) do not copy the editing in those manuscripts (Ll^2 and Sl^3), or (2) use the exemplar after the set has broken up (Hn, St, and Hl^1). Four do not have close textual associations with any extant

---

[11] "Anthologies," pp. 280ff.

manuscript but go back through intermediaries to the earliest copies or to the ancestors of tales in the constant groups (Ar, Np, Hl^2, and Ee). Finally we have the two manuscripts with more than two tales (Si and Ha^1), the first copied from a single tale and a small group, the second from a set of five Ps exemplars, culled out and kept together over a number of years.[12]

[12] Silvia, "Some Fifteenth Century Manuscripts," divides the anthologies by subject matter (p. 157) – "courtly": *KnT, MLT, ClT*; "moral": *PrT, SNT, MkT, Mel, PsT, Ret*; he discusses three in some detail, Ph^4, Hn, and Ra^4, emphasizing their context.

XI

Conclusion

A surprising set of patterns emerges from the history of the *Canterbury Tales* manuscripts, a history that began with Chaucer's death in 1400 and ended approximately one hundred years later with the cooption of the market by printing. On the one hand we have the symmetry of a slow beginning and a slow ending for the collections, with about ten in the first thirty years and the same number in the years after 1470. On the other hand there is the steady increase in the number of manuscripts with single tales or small groups. The first forty years see an orderly development with two arrangements of the tales becoming standard. Then suddenly in mid-century experiment revives; a number of manuscripts appear with eccentric or random orderings, a state of affairs that continues until the dwindling output of the final years.

It is worth noting, however, that in the first forty years none of the manuscripts with the d ordering and only three with the a reproduce the "standard" arrangements exactly. For the a ordering we have Ellesmere (or Cambridge Dd if as seems unlikely it was later), Cambridge Gg, and Egerton 2726. In the cases of Bodley 686, Paris, and Additional 35286 (Ad^3) we have intentional rearrangements of the a ordering. Bo^2 presents us with a striking contrast: the most elaborate of the spurious conclusions for the Cook's Tale coupled with no conclusion at all for the *Canterbury Tales* (only two of the last seven tales, one of them attributed to Lydgate). Ps shows the patron not only choosing to break off and perhaps omit tales but explaining his choices with critical comment.

The collected manuscripts fall naturally into two categories, the constant groups and those that result from an independent gathering of exemplars. Of the first six, only Corpus and Lansdowne fall into the first category. Cambridge Dd exemplifies the anomaly that the first manuscript of a constant group will usually result from an independent gathering. In the case of the d family the categories blur, for it inherits two thirds of its text from another constant group.

Of the principal constant groups each has its distinction. The a family has its origin in an amateur's effort to collect, edit, arrange, and write out a text for his own use and the retention of a second set of exemplars and copies as another collection. The name of this amateur was Wytton. He was perhaps the Richard Wytton, who served as Master of Mickle Hall Oxford from 1426 to 1430. This early association of the academy with the *Canterbury Tales*, if it occurred, was probably responsible for the most influential of the orderings, an ordering also adopted by the most beautiful of the manuscripts Ellesmere.

The a family shows little sign of commercialism in its long history (three quarters of a century, c. 1410 to c. 1485). The last of its five surviving members, Manchester English 113, also has an amateur as scribe, possibly the Johannes Brode, who wrote his name as a fifteenth century owner. The Cardigan exemplars used by Ma had an influence on other late manuscripts including the constant group En^3.

From the c group, the smallest but for manuscripts in some way the most influential, we have what is probably an early (rather than the first) member Corpus, another early but much edited member in Lansdowne, and evidence in the late Sloane 1686 (Sl^2) for another early member. More than half the c exemplars then became the basis for the d family with an arrangement for the whole collection derived from c with the shift of a single tale.

The d family is the most numerous and the most amorphous. Its seven branches share a textual tradition rather than a set of exemplars. The earliest extant manuscript Petworth reflects the earliest state of the d text but was clearly not the first copy of its own set of exemplars. The six other branches derive from later arrangements of the cd materials with some sharing of exemplars between the branches but without the clear derivation from a single set that one might expect. All these manuscripts but the late and much edited Harley 1758 (Ha^2) lack significant elements of the collection (prologues or tales), and were therefore not only copied from exemplars but also without ready access to a "complete" text. What we experience in d is not so much a constant group as a family of constant groups drawing on a pool of common textual materials, including a set of links (some of them spurious) that help to make the d ordering seem complete.

The latest of the big constant groups b has the distinction of being produced in the main by enchainment rather than by radiation. We have what probably was the first of the b family in Helmingham, the enclosure of an early vellum fragment in a later and much larger paper manuscript, still lacking two tales and the completion of a third. The first complete b text appears in New College D 314, itself a step on the way to the manuscript from which the first printed text was copied and from which (or from its exemplars) the last b manuscript Tc^2 was made.

The smaller constant groups, those with only two manuscripts, shared copy-text rather than being copied from each other. They give insight into the variety of ways the tales circulated in the second half of the century. A manuscript or a set of exemplars derived from the copytext of Ad^3 (1430–50) served twenty years later as the somewhat damaged exemplar of Harley 7335. Bo^1 on the other hand got two fragmentary units, one with the first eight tales in an a ordering, the other with the last fourteen in a d. Since neither was complete, the copytext used by Bodley 414 and Phillips 8136 omitted the *Squire's Tale* and the *Merchant's Tale* with no evidence that any one noticed the deficiency. Again we have the putting together of manuscripts by patrons, editors, and scribes without access to a complete text. The assumption often made that collections of the tales were readily available is not borne out by the evidence.

Ps, Mc, Ra^2, and En^3 show each in its own way that small collections of exemplars were not uncommon. The five romances from Paris Anglais 39, that circulated together and remained behind when the owner returned to France with the parent manuscript, became copytext in the fifties for Ha^1. Mc, itself a manuscript picked up from many different sources, furnished the exemplars for Ra^1; five of these then helped to piece out copytext for Tc^1, and three different single ones provided the text for tales in the anthologies, Stonyhurst and Harley 1704, and for the missing *Second Nun's Tale* in the final member of the c group, Sloane 1686.

Ra^2 is misnamed in two ways: (1) it is only by courtesy a constant group, Ht and Ra^2 sharing exemplars for a mere fraction of the whole; (2) Hatton Donat 1 is almost certainly the earlier of the two manuscripts. Ht apparently obtained small groups of six (or more) tales from the now mutilated Ad^2 and, miracle of miracles, from the earliest manuscript Hengwrt. It also had a small group from the d manuscript Ph^3. Using these exemplars as a nucleus and paying little attention to tale order, the editor put together an eclectic copytext, only the first part of which remained together and available for use by Ra^2.

The last of the constant groups, En^3, inherited a set of exemplars for ten tales and a prologue from the irregular manuscript Hk (1440–50). The editor in his search for the rest of the tales came finally into contact with the Cn tradition; he used Cn exemplars for the *Parson's Prologue* and *Tale* and many of the links; he imposed an a ordering on his copytext pieced out from a variety of sources; he included an exemplar for the *Siege of Thebes* in his collection. It remained together until the end of the century, when Ad^1 was copied from it for the Archbishop of Canterbury.

The "elongated miniscule" *Canterbury Tales* manuscripts, though interrelated textually, are not quite a constant group; they provide evidence for the nature of the book trade in the second half of the fifteenth century: its "bespoke" quality, the variety of ways in which it collected its copytexts, the patterns of interaction between scribes, illuminators, supervisors on the one hand, and patrons and owners of exemplars on the other. Ra^3, the first and biggest of the group, probably once an anthology on the scale of Cambridge Gg but never in contact with a "complete" *Canterbury Tales*, depended for copytext on small collections and single exemplars; a ghost manuscript then used the Ra^3 exemplars and in 1476 served as copytext for 14 tales in Gl; the more modest Tc^1, able to come by only thirteen of the exemplars used by its predecessors, completed its *CT* from single exemplars and a small group (from Mc) until the last four tales, which it was finally able to pick out from the a manuscript En^1; Ds, the most elaborate of the "elongated miniscules", used En^1 for both copytext and order. Really surprising in this segment of manuscript history is the length of time it took an enterprising group of artisans engaged in the book trade and familiar with the works of Gower and Lydgate as well as Chaucer to find a "complete" text of the *Canterbury Tales*.

Manuscripts that result from an independent gathering of exemplars by their nature resist categorizing. Each one tends to have its own special quality. Selden Arch. B 14 for instance carefully works out a new arrangement of the fragments, an arrangement that has no observable influence. Phillipps 6750 gives every sign of having once been a virtual library of reading matter; the fragments of the *Canterbury Tales* that remain base their text on exemplars close to those used by Cambridge Gg; they testify to the survival over a long time of another body of text related to one of the earliest of the manuscripts. Laud 600 (1430–50) used a similar group of exemplars from Harley 7334 for the last eight tales of its collection.

More problematic is Christ Church CLII (1460–70). Irregular in its ordering and with varied textual relationships including a number of tales where it is independent, Ch has a text free of the corruption characteristics of its contemporaries. It must have inherited its set of exemplars from an earlier period. Royal College of Physicians 388 has a set of exemplars dominated by the Hengwrt influence. They derive from Hg however through a varied number of intermediaries with diverse associations for different sections of the work. What is implied is a pool of Hg-related materials circulating freely and over the years being copied and occasionally replaced.

The presence of numerous "booklets" with tales and small groups is everywhere apparent – in the make-up of the earliest manuscripts, which for the most part do not share exemplars; in their descendants and the descendants of their immediate ancestors scattered through the later manuscripts, even the ones in constant groups; in the affiliations of the later manuscripts, especially the ones Manly-Rickert call "picked up", where parts of the text go back, sometimes through intermediaries, or on independent lines, to the earliest copies.

Hengwrt stands as witness to the state of the text in the first years after Chaucer's death. Already the circulation of the fragments and the tales was uneven. The ground was already laid for the varied number of textual traditions for the different tales. The best text generally of any of the manuscripts brought with it no authority as to order and no sense of how much was available.

We have in Hengwrt, in its spacing of text, its different inks, its quiring, a history of what was undoubtedly the first attempt to bring all the tales into one manuscript. A refusal to read that history vitiates many of the theories about the *Canterbury Tales*. The best account of it occurs in the Doyle and Parkes introduction to the *Variorum Chaucer* facsimile.[1]

If their conjecture is correct that what they label Section IV was the first to be started, Hg began as an anthology of tales, *Man of Law's Tale, Squire's Tale, Manciple's Tale, Franklin's Prologue* and *Tale*, space for the *Second Nun's*

---

[1] Ralph Hanna III, "The Hengwrt Manuscript," adds to the Doyle and Parkes analysis some valuable suggestions with respect to Section I, the A fragment. He also considers two possibilities, (1) that Hg was written during Chaucer's lifetime, and (2) that it was written with no access to Chaucer's own copies. A collection would only be made in Chaucer's lifetime if it were known that Chaucer had stopped working on the tales. Such knowledge would involve a kind of access. It is difficult to conceive of a person with such knowledge being unable to get other information those responsible for Hg were clearly seeking, such as whether Chaucer had written more of the *CkT* and what links were available for the stories in Section IV, especially those in the E–F fragment.

Prologue and *Tale*, and the *Clerk's Prologue, Tale,* and *Epilogue*, with gaps between for possible linking passages. Even if, as Manly-Rickert deduce from the signatures, A (Section I) was the first to be written, the succession of single tales would have followed. Only later were C, the two parts of Fragment B², and D obtained. Probably last of all were two out of the three linking passages in the E–F fragment. The *Canon's Yeoman's Prologue* and *Tale* never came to hand.

The copytext for Hg came to the scribe in small segments. There developed as he wrote a partial appreciation for the value of the frame narrative. This is reflected in the effort to create continuity by the change of names in three links (F 675, 696, 699; F 1; I 1), and in my view to bring the *Canterbury Tales* to a "suitable" end by including the treatise on penitence and the seven deadly sins as a "Parson's Tale".

Hg made possible the reading of the *Canterbury Tales* as a single work for the first time. Such reading inspired the early efforts to improve on the ordering and to add to the text. That the other early efforts were based on fresh sets of exemplars with very little overlap testifies to the great number of fragmentary texts, single tales or small groups, then circulating. The description by Julia Boffey and John Thompson of the way anthology poems circulated, especially those of Chaucer, is relevant. Those pieces, used in the second half of the century as copytext for the big collections, "descended originally from independent groups of gatherings (booklets), each containing a single longish work, or a group of lyrics".² This description applies to the way the tales of Canterbury, far from completion and never in Chaucer's lifetime put together as a single text, originally circulated.

The copytexts of later manuscripts testify to the continued circulation in large numbers of these "booklets". More than half the manuscripts in the first fifty years are based on an independent gathering together of exemplars. The proportion diminishes in the second half of the century.³ But To picks up independent texts for the *Prologue* and five of the tales and uses 14 d͟* exemplars with no close associations to any previous extant manuscript. Many of Barlow's d͟* exemplars are similarly unconnected. A third manuscript from the final thirty years, Py, derives most of its text from copies of copies of Hengwrt exemplars. Many of the anthologies derive their texts from single tales not associated with any of the collections.

The chances for survival of these manuscripts, small and unbound, are practically zero. As Kate Harris points out, in commenting on the "fallacious test of surviving books", popular books were sometimes "read to pieces"; small books were only less vulnerable than cheap books; "the substance of a book seems to outweigh its subject matter as a factor affecting its chances of survival in the Middle Ages and, especially, beyond.⁴

The result of this failure to survive has been the undue influence on modern

---

² "Anthologies," p. 280.
³ The manuscripts before 1450 are Hg, Ha⁴, Dd, El, Gg, Bo², Ad³, Ps, He (vellum), Ad², Ln, Ii, Ox, Hk, Mc, and Ld¹. After 1450, there are Ht, Tc¹, Ra³ He (paper), Fi, Ry¹, Ha³, Se, Nl, Ch, En³, Py, and To. Some are more independent than others.
⁴ "The role of owners," pp. 165–167.

readers of the "complete" texts. One of their arrangements of the collection of fragments Chaucer left behind has coopted critical attention from some of the real issues raised by the *Canterbury Tales*. A deeper reading of the manuscript record to which this book will, I hope, contribute may correct this almost universal misreading.

In this century of manuscript history no evidence connects any ordering of the fragments to Chaucer. It is time we gave up the impression of completeness or near-completeness editors like the Hengwrt-Ellesmere supervisor tried to give the *Canterbury Tales*. It is time we went back to the text Chaucer wrote and let it speak to us. There we will find if we look carefully three different beginnings of the storytelling and two projected endings. There we will find the evidence for the different plans on which Chaucer at different times worked. We will perhaps even have the courage to reject, as earlier editors rejected the *Gamelyn*, that final piece of prose which the author himself calls "this litel tretys" from any of the plans Chaucer made for his unfinished masterpiece.[5]

---

[5] Scholars and critics have paid little heed to this possibility despite the strong opinions expressed in Manly-Rickert II: 454–56, 471ff. But see Rossell Hope Robbins, review of Heiner Gillmeister, *Chaucer's Conversion: Allegorical Thought in Medieval Literature* (Frankfurt, 1984), in *SAC* 8 (1986), 191. See also David Lawton, "Chaucer's Two Ways: The Pilgrimage Frame of *The Canterbury Tales*," *SAC* 9 (1987): pp. 3–40. Lawton accepts the possibility (probability?) that the compiler responsible for including the *Parson's Tale* and the *Retraction* in the *Canterbury Tales* was not Chaucer. He sees this compiler as more sensitive to Chaucer's final intentions than would I. The plan in the *General Prologue* for a judgment of the storytelling at the Tabard supersedes in my view the ending projected in the *Parson's Prologue*.

Manuscript Index

Manuscripts may appear several times on a page. The abbreviations within a list specify manuscripts with text influenced by the main manuscript. I am indebted to Dan Mosser and Derek Pearsall for sharing with me their information on the current whereabouts of some of the manuscripts.

Constant Groups

a (Dd–Cn): 15–22, 38, 39, 43, 45, 47, 53,
   65, 82, 84, 98, 114, 115, 117, 120, 121
   Dd (Dd–En^1): 15–20
   Cn (Cn–Ma): 87, 88, 89, 90, 92, 102,
      104, 114, 121, 122
   En^1 (En^1–Ds): 67, 114
b (He–Ne): 44, 48, 57f, 65, 69, 77, 80, 82,
   86, 94, 114 fn4, 121
   Ne (Ne–Cx^1): 58 fn6
   Cx^1 (Cx^1–Tc^2):
c (Cp–La–Sl^2): 9–11, 29f, 31 and fn11, 33–
   36, 41, 42, 43, 45, 48, 82, 121
d (Pw–Lc–Ry^2–En^2–Dl–Ha^2–Sl^1): 11, 28–
   32, 33–44, 45, 47, 48, 63, 70, 72, 73, 76,
   77, 80, 82, 93, 94, 102, 104, 110, 120, 121

Pw (Pw–Ph^3–Mm or Mm): 28–32, 36,
   42, 60
Lc (Lc–Mg): 38, 42
Ry^2 (Ry^2–Ld^2): 39f, 84f
En^2 (En^2–Ll^1): 41, 109
Mm (Mm–Gl): 32, 99–101,
Ad^3 (Ad^3–Ha^5): 45–47, 56, 72–74, 121
Bo^1 (Bo^1–Ph^2): 70, 79–81, 112, 121
En^3 (En^3–Ad^1): 65, 82, 87–90, 92, 104, 112,
   121, 122
Mc (Mc–Ra^1): 45, 50–52, 122
Ps (Ps–Ha^1): 28, 108f, 122
Ra^2 (Ra^2–Ht): 61–64, 122

Manuscript Orderings

Hengwrt (before misbinding)   A D B^1 F^a E^b F^b G^a E^a C B^2 H I
Harley 7334   A X B^1 D E F G C B^2 H I R
c-ordering   A X B^1 F^a D E^a E^b F^b G C B^2 H I R
a-Ellesmere   A B^1 D E–F C B^2 G H I R
d-ordering   A X B^1 F^a E^b D E^a F^b G C B^2 H I R
b-ordering   A B^1 F^a E^b D E^a F^b G C B^2 H I R

Irregular: 45, 49, 50, 54, 61f, 65, 74–79, 81,
99–104
Harley 7334 ordering: 10; with change: 3, 48
c-ordering: 10f, 29f, 33, 43, 44, 71f; re-
jected:76
a-Ellesmere: 9, 11–13, 24 and fn5, 43, 49, 57,
82, 87, 90, 120; with change(s):26f, 27,
45, 47, 72, 79, 120; rejected (?): 76 and

fn7; first 8 tales only: 79, 121; disrupted:
102
d-ordering: 33–44, 67, 93, 121; with
change(s): 28–32, 42, 60, 64, 70, 120,
121; after the D fragment: 79, 121
b-ordering: 42, 44, 47, 57f, 70 (but note
abandoned PsT), 82, 98; with change(s):
48, 54, 57, 76, 85

Other Manuscripts

Chaucer
Troilus and Criseyde
'Cecil' fragment, Hatfield House: 1 fn1
Bodleian Digby 181: 1 fn1
Legend of Good Women
Cambridge Ff.1.6: 5 fn12
Bodleian Rawlinson C.86: 5fn12
Cambridge Gg.4.27: 5 fn12
B.L. Additional 9832: 66

Gower
Confessio Amantis
Trinity Cambridge R.32: 1 fn1, 8 fn2 and 3, 9

Magdalen (Oxford) 213: 54 fn2
Folger (Washington) Vb 29: 54 fn 2
B. L. Harley 7184: 54 fn2
Bodleian Lyell 31 ('Clumber'): 54 fn2
Robert S. Taylor MS of the *Confessio* at
   Princeton: 1 fn1, 8f fn3
Corpus Christi (Oxford) 67: 8 fn3
Plimpton (Columbia) 265: 8 fn3
Christ Church (Oxford) 143: 8 fn3
B. L. Egerton 1991: 8 fn3
Bodley 294: 8 fn3
Bodley 902: 8f fn3

General Index

Anderson, David: 20 fn7, 58 fn5

Baker, Donald: 1 fn3
Beadle, Richard: 25 fn6; see also Parkes and Beadle
Benskin, M.: 1 fn2, 109 and fn2
Benson, Larry D.: 3, 4
Beryn, Tale of: 76f and fn8, 81
Blake, Norman: 2f, 117 fn8
Boffey, Julia and John Thompson: 69 fn3, 118 and fn11, 124 and fn2
book trade: 2, 53, 56f ("elongated miniscules"), 122
book trade, "bespoke" nature of: 56 (Tc¹), 85 (Ld²), 112(Ee), 122 ("elongated miniscules")
book trade, difficulty of access to "complete" collections of *CT*: 63 (Ht), 79–81 (Bo¹), 86 (Tc²), 121 (d), 121f (Bo¹), 122 ("elongated miniscules")
book trade, lack of shop discipline: 66 (Ph¹), 68 (Ry¹), 81 (Bo¹, Ph²), 93 (Ad¹), 96 (Bw), 96 (Py, Ry¹, Hl²), 104
book trade: see also under exemplars and scribes
book trade, shop production of manuscripts: 20 (Ds), 21 (Cn, Ma), 28 fn8 (Ps), 36–38 and fn3, 53, 60 (Ha²), 83 (Sl² shop copy?)
Boyd, Beverly: 1 fn3

Carraunt, William: 41
Caldwell, Robert: 24 fn3
Chalmers, John: xi
Charles d'Orléans: 69
Chaucer, *CT* and individual tales: passim; *Troilus and Criseyde*: 66; *Legend of Good Women*: 5, 66; *Parlement of Foules*: 70; *Anelida*: 70, 111; *Complaint of Mars*: 70; *Truth*: 111; poems: 68; lyrics: 116; spelling: 8 and fn 3
Chaucer, Thomas: 41
Christianson, C. Paul: 53 fn 1, 68 fn1
"complete" collections of CT, difficulty of access to: see book trade
Corsa, Helen: 1 fn3
Crow, Martin: 27f fn8

Davenport, Geoffrey: xi
Dempster, Germaine: 3, 5, 34 and fn2, 36–38
Dene, Henry, Archbishop of Canterbury: 93
Doyle, A. I.: 38, 53; see also Doyle and Parkes

Doyle and Parkes: "The Production" 1 fn1, 8fn2, 38 fn3, 53 fn1, 85; "Paleographical Introduction" 1 fn1, 3 fn7, 8 fn2, 123f

Edwards, A. S. G.: 1 fn1, 38, 116 fn7, 117 and fn8; see also Edwards and Pearsall
Edwards and Pearsall: 38 fn3, 53 fn1, 54 fn2, 85
Ellesmere manuscript, Huntiungton Library facsimile of: 14 fn8
"elongated miniscule" manuscripts: 20 and fn7, 32, 54–57, 83, 122
exemplars, ad hoc set of: 7 (Hg, Ha⁴, El), 11 (Ha⁴), 17 (Dd), 24 and fn5 (Gg), 25 (Bo²), 27f (Ps), 47 (Ln), 74–76 and 122f (Se), 97 and 124 (Py), 101–104 and 124 (To), 123f (Hg), 120 and 124 and fn3 (general)
exemplars, pools of: 42 and 43 fn5 (d), 94 (Bw from d), 98 (Py), 121 (d), 123 (Py)
exemplars, sets of, remaining together over a period of years: 17 (Dd, Cn), 21 (Cn), 24 fn5 (Gg in Ph¹), 48 (Ha⁴ in Ld¹), 61–63 (Hg in Ht), 79 (Ch), 87 (Hk in En³), 122, 123
exemplars, single tales and small groups as: 4f, 9 (Hg), 17 (Dd), 24, 27 (Ps), 28 (Ha¹), 44, 49 (Hk), 50 (Ht, Mc), 50 fn4 (Ra¹), 54 (Ra³), 56f (Tc¹), 72 (Fi), 77 (Nl), 87 (En³), 94 (Bw), 99 (Py), 104 (To), 105, 107 (Ar), 109 (Ha¹), 110 (Hl², Hl¹), 111 (Ph⁴), 114 (Si), 114f (Ra⁴), 118 (Hn), 119 (Si, Ha¹), 122–124

Fisher, patron of Ee: 112
Fisher, John H.: 4
Fusco, Maggie: xi

Gaylord, Alan: 14 fn8
Goldwell family: 105
Gould, Karen: xi
Gower, John: 7 and fn2, 8 and fn3, 53 fn1, 54, 56, 57, 69, 112
Griffiths, Jeremy J.: 1fn1, 2 fn4

Hanna, Ralph III: 123 fn1
Harris , Kate: xi, 101 fn17, 124 and fn4
Hassell, W. C.: xi
Henderson, Cathy: xi
Hill, the Reverend Prebend: xi
Huntington Library: 14 fn 8
Huws, Daniel: xi